Skydiving
for Beginners

A JOURNEY OF RECOVERY AND HOPE

by Jo McFarlane

Dear Lindsay,
thank you for making
this book happen,
and for being the best
friend I have ever had.
Love you so much,

J 🙂 x

Published in 2014 by The Scottish Independent Advocacy Alliance (www.siaa.org.uk) with support from the Scottish Government Health & Social Care Directorate
Copyright © Jo McFarlane.

First Edition

A CIP catalogue record for this title is available from the British Library.

This book is sold at cost price without profit to the author. All proceeds will go towards further re-prints to keep the cost to a minimum.

Website: www.edinburghjo.co.uk

Dedicated to all
who have walked in my shoes
or held my hand on the journey

with special thanks to my 'soul mother'
Jenifer Neilson

Trigger Warning

The following potentially upsetting topics are discussed throughout the book: suicide, self-harm, poverty, abuse, sexual content, threat of violence, mental illness, hospitalisation, drugs, alcohol, religion. If you are of a sensitive disposition or have experienced these issues they might be triggers for your own distress. Do seek support should you need it. The Samaritans, for example, can be contacted at any time on 08457 90 90 90 (UK) or 1850 60 90 90 (ROI).

Contents

Introduction

BY DR ALLAN BEVERIDGE

(CONSULTANT PSYCHIATRIST, QUEEN MARGARET HOSPITAL, DUNFERMLINE &
AUTHOR OF RD LAING: PORTRAIT OF THE PSYCHIATRIST AS A YOUNG MAN)

This is the remarkable story of a remarkable woman.

Jo's account of her early years reminds me of Charles Dickens' portrayal of damaged childhoods: a world where adults are capricious bullies and sadists, and where children have no rights, the victims of the whims of grown-ups. I remember finding this a truly frightening world to read about and Jo's story evokes all of this. Except, of course, Jo is not a fictional character and the reader wonders: how does one recover from such a start in life?

A major part of the book is concerned with Jo's experience of mental illness and psychiatric treatment. Jo does not hide how disturbed she was, how difficult she could be with psychiatric staff or the serious nature of her suicide attempts. She encounters many dedicated and compassionate members of staff and is very grateful to them, but she also meets some who are uncaring, uninterested, judgmental and, on one occasion, sexually abusive.

There is much in Jo's account to make psychiatric staff ponder. For example, at one stage her diagnosis is wrongly changed from Bipolar or Schizoaffective Disorder to Borderline Personality Disorder. As a result she is treated very differently by staff. She is made to feel she is entirely responsible for her actions, that she is somehow a bad and willful person whose attempts at killing herself are 'attention-seeking' and should therefore be ignored. Those who work in psychiatry will be familiar with this situation: well-meaning (and not so well-meaning) staff can find themselves persecuting rather than helping their patients.

Jo has frequent changes of doctors and nurses. While this might meet the institutional needs of the system, it can have catastrophic effects on the patient, especially on someone like Jo where issues of attachment and abandonment have been so important. The real heroes amongst the psychiatric staff are those who were flexible enough to make a long-term commitment to Jo despite her frequent moves of accommodation, for which the system demands a change of psychiatric team. Our new models of service delivery with their multiplicity of teams have led to an appalling discontinuity of care. Jo's story reminds us of something we already knew but seem to have forgotten: the most important ingredient in psychiatric treatment is the personal relationship between patient and therapist.

Jo gives a compelling account of the long-term effects of being sexually abused as a child and the subsequent difficulties in forming intimate relations in adulthood. For the first time I've understood more fully why female victims repeatedly get involved with abusive men. Jo describes passively accepting unwanted sexual contact because she was made to feel this was her role. As she puts it she was 'well-enough versed in my rag-doll compliance to know what was expected'.

Despite the often alarming and distressing nature of Jo's experiences, this is ultimately an uplifting story. This is largely due to Jo's sheer resilience, great good humour and generosity of spirit. In the latter part of the book, we find that Jo becomes an active member of the Patients' Council and fights to better the lot of the mentally ill. She has a spiritual awakening which reveals to her that God is to be found in the love of others; in being receptive to the beauty of the world; and even in the torments of her mental suffering. Or, to put it more simply: in the capacity 'to relish the miracle of being alive'.

Jo discovers she is a talented poet and, amongst her wide range of subject matter, she writes poems about mental illness and psychiatric treatment. These are, by turns, funny, poignant, dark, but always shot through with a deep humanity and concern for others. Jo has now found a purpose to her life and recites her work regularly at mental health and arts conferences throughout Scotland. I think it is fitting to end with one of Jo's poems, 'Once We Were Free'. In this poem, Jo demonstrates that the experience of madness is not all negative; in fact, there are many aspects to celebrate:

When we were mad

When we were mad
we danced ourselves giddy in the lexicon of nonsense.
Time spilled like a river through our consciousness.
The days became flowers; the sunlight was ours.
We might have ripped the moon out of the sky
and swum in its silvery tides. We might have, and we did,
go skinny-hipping with the lack of need for food.

When we were mad
we were mythical beasts in a fairy tale book,
flouting the boundaries of dream and sleep.
We did not care for industry or hard-edged truth,
we paid no heed to the shackles of expectation.
Conformity belonged to mice;
Mortality — the fate of fools.
We spun our web of possibility beyond the universal
laws of gravity and space; debauched ourselves
in unfamiliar landscapes.

When we were mad, little did we know
the snares of sanity were waiting.

Now we sit in glass-eyed tombs
watching the world go mad around us,
and we — afraid of our next breath — open mouths
just to swallow pills, and gape in wonder at the idiots,
the freedom-fighters that we were back then.

Preface

"If at first you don't succeed,
then skydiving is not for you"

Portfolio Ltd London 2004

They say a cat has nine lives. What if I were to tell you I have had 19? That's how many suicide attempts I've survived. From jumping off Salisbury Crags to almost drowning in the sea, I've walked the tightrope of existence all my life. So why is this book called 'Skydiving for Beginners'? It's certainly not an instruction manual, nor a delusional claim to supernatural powers. I'm not a hero as you'll soon find out, but a flawed protagonist in a real tale of survival against the odds.

Skydiving is a risky business. But the kind I'm referring to is metaphorical. It's about "being in the moment", taking a glorious leap into being alive. Some people seem to occupy the present naturally but for me it has taken a lifelong struggle. Well, here I am at last, staking a claim on the here and now and open to life's wonderful possibilities; confident that I can rely on the lessons of my past to act as a parachute to guide me gently towards a safe landing.

All my life when I thought I was plummeting I was actually freefalling towards this discovery. This is the story of how I gradually learned to trust in myself and survive—with some lucky breaks and a lot of help from my friends.

Jo McFarlane

Some names in the book have been changed to protect identities.

"Let today
embrace the past with rememberance
and the future with longing"

from The Prophet by Kahlil Gibran

Picking up my parachute

1971–1983 | EARLY YEARS

I was born the youngest of four in Simpson's Maternity Pavilion, Edinburgh, on 11th October 1971. The only facts I know about my infancy are that I hardly ever cried and I slept with our black cat, Smoky, in my cot. Maybe that's why I've always been lucky.

For the first fifteen years I lived in 37 East London Street, an old ramshackle town house near the city centre that would have been elegant, desirable even, had its inhabitants not been us. I never discovered how my parents found the means to buy our house; both were uneducated and in low-paid jobs for the first few years of their marriage. Thereafter they relied entirely on state welfare. Neither of them came from families with the means to support them financially. My father was a porter and my mother a cleaner. Any savings they might have accrued from the mere two to three years they were employed would hardly have been sufficient to purchase a four bedroom house in the centre of town.

The house may have been theirs but they certainly did not have the means, financial or otherwise, to maintain the property. We lived in virtual squalor with dry rot and gaping holes in the floor. Ours was a dirty, freezing home infested with vermin. My earliest physical sensations were of being cold and hungry—food as well as heating was in short supply. There were cobwebs everywhere, so thick they formed a film on the skirtings and in every corner of the walls. Mice were a daily feature, freely running round the house, even with the TV blaring and the cat (we always had a cat) stretched out beneath the stove. I wonder now were the cats too emaciated to hunt? They were rationed to one tin of cat food a week, left open on the floor for them to dig out with their paws.

There were things so disgusting in that house it makes me squirm to recall them: mouse droppings everywhere, maggots and fleas. A particularly vivid memory is of a frying pan thick with congealed lard and half-dead flies trapped on its surface. The stench was vile even to our well-accustomed noses: stale grease, food cast aside to rot on the floor, cat excrement and unwashed body odour (there was rarely sufficient hot water for a bath) all combined in a malodorous cocktail.

I only attended nursery for a day or two. My parents were told not to bring me back. I was so dirty and flea-ridden that the other children's parents had complained of contamination. I remember my mother told me this one day when I was crying "why can't I go back to nursery?" To hear that I was too dirty to mix with other children made me feel like a leper and the feeling of being toxic and infectious has stayed with me ever since. Thus my early years were spent tethered to my mother's hemline, a contact so intense that it shaped the person I would become.

Mummy and Daddy

My mother had learning difficulties, though I didn't have the frame of reference then to understand it. She could not read or write, could barely add beyond one and one, and lacked the facility to grasp basics which even I—a pre-school child—took for granted. Her vocabulary was restricted to the concrete world, limited all the more because English wasn't her first language. She had received no education growing up in Italy. She met my father shortly after she arrived in Scotland and would have no hope of improving herself because he constantly sought to limit her opportunities. But it was not just a matter of education. It was clear to me at an early age that my mother had a functional impairment.

I grew up thinking of her as a child. I knew no different, only that she lacked the sophistication of other adults and was vulnerable and malleable to my whim.

My mother, in another epoch, would have been called an 'innocent'. She had a heart so pure and free of motive that we siblings took on ourselves the role of parent, each protecting her in their own way. My domain was the emotional. I became her confidante, the conduit for all her trauma and unhappiness. She also saw me as her greatest hope, her symbol of emancipation.

All this weighed on me so heavily that I was a sullen child, and hunched with the cares of an adult long before I went to school. Some of the stories my mother shared with me about her life were so horrific that they resurfaced in my bed-wetting nightmares — full technicolour visions of the scenes she painted so vividly from her deep-seated distress. She would come into my bedroom late at night and wake me up, kneel by the bed and, in a trance-like state, recount details of events that whirled around in my mind like a ghastly blizzard.

There were stories of her childhood growing up on a small family holding in war-ravaged Monte Cassino, infamous among that generation as the site of a pivotal battle. The Nazi-occupied historic monastery and surrounding area were bombed by the allies. It was the greatest concentration of civilian casualties anywhere during the Second World War. My pregnant grandmother was killed by a piece of shrapnel which shot through her abdomen. My mother, who was three at the time, has no memory of that fateful night. I have since learnt from my aunt, who would have been nine, that she was hugging my mother to soothe her from the sound of air raid sirens when a bomb hit. My mother was blasted from her sister's arms across the room. They crouched terrified in the dark for the whole night. That is how long it took for their groaning mother to die her agonizing death. My two uncles were a little older than my aunt. There were no accounts of their, or my grandfather's, whereabouts at the time. Though my mother doesn't remember it, the bomb blast and the loss of her mother must have had a profoundly traumatic effect on such a young child. In addition there was a history of mental illness on my mother's side of the family and she was later to succumb to this.

Some of the stories my mother told me were fantastical. Though I took them to be true I realise now the details were coloured by her confused state and florid imagination. For example, she told me how, at the age of two, she died and was placed in a coffin wearing a beautiful blue dress with white stars. As the coffin was being lowered into the ground they realised she was still alive and battering to get free. Another unlikely story was how, when my mother was a baby, the health visitor deliberately broke all her bones in order to steal her ration card. I did not think to question the details. As a child you accept what you are told.

Then there were more plausible accounts of the distant, sometimes cruel way her stepmother treated her and her older siblings. When my grandmother died, my grandfather (whom I never met) re-married and had five more children clearly favoured by their mother over the original four. My mother used to talk of this and how she missed her own mother—or rather longed for her forgotten presence—with such inconsolable grief that my heart ached for her and I felt it was I who had been orphaned. Years later, in therapy, I was to discover that it wasn't just empathy for my mother which brought tears to my eyes but my own grief for the parent I longed for her to be.

My mother couldn't help but burden me with horror stories. She was like a child possessed, the wreckage of demonic spirits leaking from her every pore. The stories which affected me most, though, were those involving the people who were in my life: my father and paternal grandmother. I learnt before I could articulate the concept of despising, that my father had punched me when I was in my mother's womb. Every beating she described—from the first blows three days into their marriage—was hammered into my psyche. Neither were details spared of the sexual violence and humiliation she endured at his hands. She told me how his brother had raped her in the room next door to mine. When my father found out his response was to shame my mother by dragging her to the police and flaunting her stained underwear to them as evidence of her 'infidelity'. All this I learnt before I could count to ten — before I had the means to disassociate and take refuge in imaginary worlds.

I was shocked that adults could be so inhuman even though being surrounded by such cruelty became second nature to me. I never liked my paternal grandmother. She was cold, formal and distant. But after my mother told me how my grandmother colluded with my father in her abuse after they were first married, I hated her all the more. My mother was a vulnerable soul and it was despicable to me that they should have made her life such hell.

My father was a paradox. On the one hand he was lavish with affection, on the other cruel and tyrannical. His moods, like flames, could blaze at the slightest provocation and burn for hours; at other times they were extinguished in a breath. We were frightened of him, tip-toeing round his temper like rabbits round a sleeping fox. So unpredictable were his rages that the atmosphere was like a bomb ticking towards its inevitable climax. It would be fallacy to say he was a strict disciplinarian since the beatings he inflicted were not so much punishments as random acts of violence. He ruled the house with an invincible will; there was no escaping his domination.

Night times were worst. Every evening he went to the pub and downed the fuel which would ignite his ire. The few hours he was gone were a blessed reprieve and we took full advantage of the respite — but always, like a deluge fast approaching, was the promise of his return and the torrent of abuse that would follow.

My sister remembers how he would go inebriated into her room, turn on the light and yell at her to provoke a response. When she invariably caved in he would take off his belt and beat her, presumably justifying to himself that her precocity in answering him back had caused the punishment. I have no memory of actually being beaten. Perhaps the trauma has blocked it out but I do remember the prelude and the agonizing terror as he glared right through me whilst slowly taking off his belt.

Most nights, thankfully, he was too drunk to exercise this ritual. He would crash out in the armchair (his 'throne' as we used to call it) comatose with beer, twitching and grunting like some gruesome bear. I was often still up when he returned as there were no set bedtimes in our house. I was left to please myself however late the hour, this area of discipline being outwith his chosen jurisdiction.

My father's propensity towards violence no doubt originated in his own unhappy childhood. He was born in 1937, the product of an extra-marital affair which left his mother abandoned by her husband for having cheated on him. My grandmother therefore brought my father up alone, her older children having flown the nest. The two were bound by the scandal of illegitimacy, a social outrage in those days. My father was referred to locally as 'the bastard' and I think he always felt like an aberration. We did not find all this out until a few years ago. The shame had prevented him from telling us.

What we did know of his childhood is that my grandmother was a very strict disciplinarian. He would reminisce with an affectionate glow how his 'Ma' regularly 'leathered' him for various transgressions. He would round off the details with "it never did me any harm" or "it was for my own good" presumably justifying the beatings as a sign of love. Indeed he was fiercely protective, even reverential towards his mother. We were raised with the expectation that we too should revere her as a staunch but benevolent matriarch. She was represented as a sacred icon though the reality was quite the contrary.

All the other stories from his childhood handed down to us were sugar-coated. He would recount his adventures with his friends as they 'got up to no good' whizzing down Smoky Brae on a makeshift go-kart, stealing jam jars (worth a penny) for the picture house or playing soldiers in the 'King's Park' next to the street where he lived. Though we heard these stories so often we could recount them in our sleep, it was a pleasure to see my father light up when he told them. His fondness for anecdote was an endearing aspect of his personality. As we grew older, we squirmed, as all teenagers do, at such adult reminiscence but in our early age of innocence we were agog with delight at hearing these stories—not least because my father was happy and therefore less likely to blow up.

As I mentioned earlier, he could be lavish with affection. I have many memories of sitting on his lap being cooed and cuddled or skipping alongside him on the way to the sweetie shop and of receiving birthday cards with protestations of undying love and kisses dripping down the page. I have no doubt that my father loved us in spite of his propensity to be cruel and tyrannical. Looking back, it is strange that we trusted in his love given the overwhelming evidence to the contrary.

School of hard knocks

Two months before my fifth birthday I started primary school, eager to escape the intensity of my mother's constant presence. It was a Catholic school not far from where we lived—an imposing neo-gothic building with iron bars on windows which looked down into the playground. From the first I hated being at school. Far from being the nurturing environment and antidote to home I imagined, I found the teachers strict and unrelenting.

I was not a popular child, either in the eyes of the teachers or my peers. In the playground I was bullied for being small and quiet. In the classroom I was humiliated for being below their interpretation of what was acceptable academic performance. Most of the other children could read or write a little but, because of my mother's illiteracy and my father's lack of support in our development, I could not. I will never forget being scolded in front of the class because I couldn't spell my name on a piece of artwork—all the more devastating because I so wanted the teacher to like me. She was maternal towards, and popular with, the other children, but for some reason I could not understand she seemed to hate me. I did not then realize the poor state of my hygiene and personal appearance. I perceived her voice changing from its mellifluous tone to a cold, grudging impatience. She would give me cursory acknowledgement when I got something right and severe reprimand when I invariably fell short of expectation. Her treatment of me seemed so contrary to the way she presented to the other children that I have no doubt it coloured their view of me too.

As a consequence, school was a hostile environment and I felt isolated and unhappy. I dreaded getting up in the morning for, although home life was terrible too, I could at least take refuge under the covers. It was also freezing cold in the house which compounded my reluctance to get up. My poor mother had to try every bribe imaginable to cajole me out of bed. I always dragged my heels getting ready. I was sluggish in the mornings anyway because of late nights and nightmares and was invariably late for school. This did not go down well.

At school I was forever being threatened with the belt, but corporal punishment was on the wane in our Region and I think it would have been hard to justify its use on a child who was never outwardly naughty. They seemed, though, to love torturing me with the threat of the belt and I lived in constant fear that they would carry it out.

On the mornings I was late I would have to stand at the back of the class with my head hung in shame while the class recited daily prayers. I was so frightened of what would follow that sometimes I would wet myself and be made to mop it up. The school auxiliary nurse was well used to supplying me with clean knickers. She at least was kind to me.

Lessons were a dreaded chore, particularly Arithmetic for which I had no aptitude. I think I showed some talent for writing stories but this was never nurtured. The class was divided into 'sets' based on academic ability. I was always seated with the bottom group positioned closest to the teacher's desk; we were perceived to be the most unruly and in need of a corrective eye. The attention I received was never positive. I believe this arrangement was designed to shame me as much as anything. Certainly I felt shame at being relegated to the ranks of failure and I could not understand why I was lumped together with the naughty children when I never intentionally misbehaved.

My few happy memories of primary school involved the priests who visited from our local church. They were warm, avuncular characters who would tell us nice stories as we sat cross-legged round them on the floor, glued to their every word. Our teacher would leave us, adding to the treat, and the atmosphere lightened without the threat of reproach hanging over me.

I also enjoyed hymn-singing in the hall but was always wary of the headmistress who accompanied us on the piano. She was somewhat stern and didn't suffer dilly-dallying or the slow turning of pages to which I was prone. On Holy Days of Obligation we would all traipse in orderly queues to Mass. This was a welcome relief from lessons. However, we had to be on our guard as the teachers were extra vigilant; they were punitive over covert giggles and whispering under the benign gaze of the saints.

One of the most exciting events in the life of a Catholic child is the celebration of her First Holy Communion. We spent months preparing. Careful instruction from the priest showed us what it meant to receive the Body of Christ and closer to the day itself there was all sorts of fuss and practice going up to the altar in pairs with our hands joined correctly — palms flat, fingers toward heaven.

When the big day arrived we stood proudly at the back of the church, the girls in white dresses, the boys in white shorts, all waiting to make our entrance to the gasps of "aw" and "ah" from the parishioners. Processing slowly up the aisle trying our best to look holy with demure smiles, we cast glances to the side now and then to take in the awed response. As an adult, watching children's communion processions always moves me to tears — not least, I think, because it is a symbol of the purity and innocence I felt so far from as a little girl.

A multitude of sins

I do not remember at precisely what age I was first sexually exploited but I was very young, most likely pre-school. Sex was a pervasive feature of our family home, much like nausea or the unpleasant smells. The politics of my parents' sex life was played out openly among their children. We knew that he wanted it all the time and that she hated it. This was an enduring source of tension in their marriage and they often embroiled us in the drama. My father, who believed that I possessed a Rasputin-like hold over my mother, would say to me "You should tell your mother to be a proper wife to me" the subtext being inferred. My mother meanwhile would squirm and cringe as she confided in me how he would force himself on her and expect her to do disgusting things. It was always painful for her and she would do anything to avoid it.

One of her avoidance strategies was to have me sleep in their bed between them. I soon became an outlet for his sexual frustration. He would grope and finger me and come to orgasm as he rubbed himself against me. I knew my mother was awake though I tried to delude myself otherwise. If I let myself, I could hear her softly sobbing to the wall. I can hear her even now. She sacrificed me to him as a matter of self-preservation. In all honesty, I think she had not the facility to understand the damaging effect that this would have on me.

When my sister asked her a few years ago "why did you put Joanna in the middle and let him do that to her?" my mother was genuinely baffled by the question. She replied "I had to. If I hadn't he would have done it to me".

How could I blame my mother for what happened? Her own emotionally starved childhood ill-equipped her for parental responsibility, not to mention her obvious learning difficulties and the fact that her life with my father was hell. She did her best in the face of overwhelming odds and with very little outside help. I will always love and respect her for the many sacrifices which she did make.

The other source of sexual exploitation from an early age was with my brother — the first born in our family and older than me by eight years. Although this was also unwanted contact, the relationship between us was complex since my brother was a very disturbed child. He was a teenager by the time he started abusing me. Even at that early age the thought was in my mind that I had to make up for what he lacked emotionally. So I did not fight off his advances, and passively accepted my role, mistakenly thinking that the solace he derived from me was somehow healing him.

As with my mother, I felt fiercely protective towards my brother. He was terrorised and humiliated on a daily basis by my father who saw him as inadequate and weak. He was bullied by his peers for being withdrawn and strange in his behaviour. Added to this his poor hygiene was a further barrier to prevent people from engaging with him. As an adult he developed schizophrenia which is hardly surprising given the distress and trauma of his early years. On the day my mother gave birth to him she received news from Italy that her father had died of a heart attack. She was distraught and her grief prevented her from bonding with my brother. Now a middle-aged man, he still craves constant affection and reassurance that he's loved. Being a sensitive child myself, it is perhaps understandable why I let him interfere with me. In any case the sexual intercourse was sanctioned by my father who encouraged him to 'use' me, a pre-pubescent girl, rather than getting someone of his own age pregnant.

Being abused as a small child creates a multiplicity of physical and emotional discord. There is a betrayal of trust and grief at the loss of innocence. On the one hand there is shame and guilt; on the other passive resignation. There is the extreme pain of penetration and then the premature awakening of sexual organs. Anger too must play a part although I was not in touch with this till much later in my life. It is a complex trauma to make sense of and even more difficult to live with. In my case both male members of my family were abusing me. Whilst I knew instinctively it was wrong of them, it became routine and natural to expect it and also to comply. This compounded the feeling of my having colluded and somehow brought it all on myself.

When the chips are down

When I was seven years old something else happened which confirmed for me the 'fact' that it was my fault. One Saturday evening, as I was returning home for tea from a friend's house, I stopped off at the chip shop and bought a small bag of chips to eat when I got home. As I hurried through Claremont courtyard—a well known shortcut—with the chips tucked under my arm to keep them warm, I became aware of a gentle whistling sound. A young man was sitting on the railings trying to attract my attention. He stopped whistling, smiled and waved at me. As a polite child does in response to such a gesture from an adult, I smiled and waved back.

I skipped down the stairs to get to the street below and was startled when the man suddenly leapt off the railing, landed squarely in my path and forced his hands around my neck and mouth. Next thing I knew he was dragging me into a tenement stair. He thrust me against the wall and pulled a knife to my throat. "You scream and I'll kill you" he said, the knife in his hand trembling against my neck. I can't remember what went through my mind at that moment, only that I was mute and frozen with fear.

He proceeded to unzip my jeans and interfere with me. There was no penetration but he rubbed himself against me and I became aware of how thin and bony he was. I could smell hunger and desperation on his breath and the frightening physical sensations in my own body were overtaken by a protective instinct towards him. Young and all as I was, I understood that this man was not going to kill me; further, that he was in deep emotional distress, frightened and hungry. I reasoned that if I gave him the chips this would calm him. When I did so he looked as though he would cry.

He asked me to put his 'thing' in my mouth which confused me as I was not familiar with oral sex but at that moment I would have done anything so I opened my mouth tentatively as he guided my head towards his penis. Of course my mouth was too small and he seemed suddenly to be jolted by this into releasing my head and zipping up his jeans. He held the knife at my throat again and warned me not to tell anyone about what "we" had done saying he knew where I lived and would come after me in the night and slit my throat. Then he picked up the chips and held the door open for me to leave.

I walked along the road away from him, not looking back, not fully understanding or even registering what had just happened. I was in a daze all the way home feeling strangely disconnected from my body.

When I got in the house I told my sisters in a detached fashion what had happened. It was as if my voice was not my own. One of them got angry and said "Imagine making up a thing like that" and I crumpled into hysterical tears. They realised then that I wasn't lying and rallied round to comfort me.

My parents were downstairs and we knew that my father would be preparing to go to the pub. My sisters reasoned that it was best not to tell him or he would become angry and end up frightening me even more. After he left the house my sisters decided to phone the mother of the friend I had been visiting to warn her not to let my friend out that evening as there was a dangerous man in the neighbourhood. They were also probably seeking contact with a responsible adult—in such situations my mother was considered redundant.

As soon as they explained to my friend's mother what had happened she took the reins and ordered them to phone the police. What followed next is lost to me but I must have been hyperventilating because I was taken to the Sick Children's Hospital. I have a terrifying vision of my father brandishing a spanner from his tool box in the air, bellowing "no cunt violates my daughter". The doctor said I was in shock and my parents were told to take me home into their bed to comfort me. I remember wishing with all my heart they would keep me at the hospital but it was not to be. I was taken home that night and violated by my father.

Next day—a Sunday I think—I was taken to the police station to give a statement and look through mug shots to identify my attacker. I remember deciding that if I saw his photo I would not let on. After all it was my fault. I had smiled and waved at him. I had given him my chips. I had let him do those things. I had made him cry.

They took me down to the scene of the crime and I was horrified to see that the empty chip packet was still there on the ground. I hadn't told the police about the chips, it would have been tantamount to saying I had brought it on myself.

Uncle Giovanni

Another key event, or series of events, happened in my seventh year. My mother's eldest brother, Uncle Giovanni, who with his wife and family ran a chip shop/cafe in Portobello, killed himself by jumping from a top storey window to the garden below. He had been ill on and off for years with schizophrenia and had been recently discharged from hospital.

I was balancing on a bike against the wall of our upstairs hall when the door bell rang. I answered it to find my cousin and her fiancé standing there ashen-faced asking to speak to my parents. When they broke the news my mother's hysterical cries seemed to rip through the fabric of the building and I knew listening from my room upstairs that something was terribly wrong.

My mother worshipped her eldest brother. It was he who sent for her from Italy and, with my aunt, had always looked out for her. When her father died after she arrived in Scotland my uncle had become the family figurehead in her eyes. Though troubled and vulnerable himself, he represented for my mother a symbol of strength and protection in a foreign land—a comforting male presence in her life especially when things were bad at home.

The days and weeks that followed his suicide were intensely uncomfortable in our house. Various relatives came and went, plotting vengeance with my father on the hospital which they blamed for having discharged him prematurely. My father had suddenly become the hero of the hour and he puffed up to the challenge. As a native Scot he was able to advise the Italian relatives on matters of protocol on raising a complaint. It became a vehicle for his bilious fervour and an opportunity to redeem himself in the eyes of his in-laws who despised him for his treatment of my mother.

The script was now re-written as he tearfully recounted how he had faithfully promised my dead uncle, as head of the family, that he would protect my mother from all worldly evil. You could almost hear mythic pipes playing in the distance as his voice broke telling us that my uncle and he had had a cigar together 'man to man' and with that he had entrusted his sister, my mother, to my father's care. It was a complete sham. The only person who bought this display of sentimental trickery was my father himself, whose capacity for self-delusion was legendary. His in-laws allowed him to go on in this fashion because they needed him on board to try to exact retribution on the hospital authorities whose neglect, they felt, had led to my uncle's suicide.

Meanwhile, my mother moped around the house, a wounded animal, so broken by the enormity of her brother's death that every hour was a curse upon her shoulders and every chore a form of torture. She retreated into herself till at last I woke one morning to find she was gone. I searched the house inside out to find her, panic tightening my throat like a noose. We were well used to her spontaneous disappearances but this time I knew something was much more serious. I cried my heart out all day long till news finally came that she was safe. The police brought her home trembling and bedraggled. They had fished her out of the Water of Leith where she had tried to drown herself. After we were permitted briefly to see her she was bundled off in a police van to the Royal Edinburgh Hospital where she spent the next three months doped on tranquilizers during her respite from my father and her four distraught children.

Going, going, gone

Even had she not been fleeing the terror of my father's reign, my mother's disappearances would have been understandable given her own bipolar affective disorder, an illness which made her jittery and unpredictable. It was impossible for my father to pin her down for any length of time or to bend her exactly to his will. Even we, her children, despaired of her chaotic forays into anxiety, mania and crippling depressions. Much as we hated our father for his brutal control over her, there were times we just wanted someone to exert some definitive influence on her moods and behaviour.

My sister remembers her taking overdoses but my prevailing preoccupation was her random disappearances. She would take off usually early in the morning whilst we were still asleep and end up in homeless hostels or Women's Aid refuges, or at my aunt—her sister's doorstep. Although I didn't appreciate waking up to find that she had gone at the time, I now feel proud of her resourcefulness in managing to get to safety when she felt overwhelmed and desperate. What for any woman in an abusive relationship would be difficult, for my mother with her many additional obstacles — her mental illness, her feeble grasp of English, her illiteracy and inability to use the telephone — must have been an almost insurmountable task.

Nonetheless as a small child it was devastating for me to wake up and be confronted with the reality of her disappearance and the possibility she might never come home. Being left with my father's rage compounded the trauma. Though she was ineffectual over influencing him, my mother's gentle presence was a source of great comfort to us as children. The fact that she had gone seemed to multiply my father's extreme behaviour for he was a jealous, possessive husband and couldn't bear it when she was out of his clutches for long. We had somehow to appease his fury as he stormed about the house blaming us for driving her away; and more so for our not being able — or willing as he saw it — to get her back.

My mother always did come back. My father tracked her down each time and wept like a foundling in her arms protesting that he couldn't live without her and that things would be different now. Of course she knew from bitter experience that nothing would change but he manipulated her pity to the extent that it was impossible for her to refuse him. Had she done so he would have found some other way to get her back. The most effective weapon in my father's arsenal was me. As my mother's trusted confidante and raison d'être I must surely be able to influence her. So my father set about brainwashing me with the intention that the message would filter through.

Refugees

In the months preceding her suicide attempt, my mother had left and was living in a shared refuge for battered women. She missed us terribly and decided that she wanted us to leave my father too and join her in the refuge. This was also in my seventh year.

So on a Sunday morning we got up to go to Mass as usual, piled into my father's room to say goodbye (he never joined us at Mass) and kissed him on the cheek — which I would later come to associate with

Judas' betrayal of Jesus — and set off up the road with bags of clothes. My sisters hadn't told me we were leaving home. Being so young I couldn't be trusted to keep it secret; and so when we got to the church I was surprised and delighted to see my mother there. In a covert operation, pre-planned with the priest, we slipped during Mass into the Sacristy and followed the concealed route behind the altar through the back of the church out into the light of day. There were fluttering wings in my tummy as I took in all the ecclesiastical paraphernalia en route: cassocks, lecterns and crucifixes; the intoxicating smell of candle wax. I knew we were doing something illicit as my mother was beside herself with a mixture of fear and excitement. The priest's aide who rushed us through seemed nervous too. I remember thinking it was like the nail-biting escape scene from the Nazis at the end of The Sound of Music. When we got out to the street there was a car waiting to meet us.

We were sped off to Burdiehouse, a suburb in South Edinburgh where we went to live with my mother in the Women's Aid refuge. All five of us had to share the one room. There were bunk beds for my sisters, a single bed for my brother; and my mother and I shared the double bed. There was another bedroom also in the house with a young family staying in it. I am not sure how many months we lived there. I was transferred to the local primary school, this having been arranged by the priest, though the new school was not Catholic, and my brother and sisters attended the secondary school nearby. Though it was a relief at first to be away from my father, it was an alien place and we did not acclimatise well. We were used to the bustle of the city centre, to having our own rooms, and the familiar chaos of our ramshackle house. Besides, every day we grew more and more anxious waiting for my father to find us, as inevitably he would.

At the new school I had an alarming accident that nearly cost me my right eye. I had tripped and fallen head-first into the milk crate, so had to be rushed to the Sick Children's Hospital for emergency treatment. The doctor who treated me said I was 'a very lucky girl' not to have lost my eye. I remember feeling far from a lucky girl. In the days that followed, the tissue around my eye swelled to a flagrant purple bruise and I felt very self-conscious at school. My teacher there was nice to me and she let me sit with her in the classroom during break while she marked our jotters.

This incident coincided with the court proceedings taking place to determine who should have legal custody of us. We were bought new clothes for the occasion and taken to the Sheriff Court with my mother. Her solicitor, a young suited lady with a briefcase — who was nice to my mother but irritable with us — seemed tense and cross with me about the bruise on my eye. I remember her muttering that it would make the panel think that our mother hadn't been looking after us properly.

We were interviewed separately by a panel of three adults — two older gentlemen that reeked of tobacco, and a lady. They asked me questions about my new school and how I had got the bruise, and various other things about life at home. Then came the question that loomed like a hatchet over me: who did I want to live with? I knew that I wanted to be with my mother but I was concerned the judges would think I was being unkind to my father, so I added with a meek apology "I love him too".

Shortly afterwards my father who had re-established contact with us through my brother (he had not yet been given access) persuaded my mother to come home. It was with a mixture of relief and grudging resignation that we left Burdiehouse and returned to the squalor of East London Street. Within a very short time the familiar beatings and tyrannical rages of my father had resumed and it was like we had never been away.

At school I wondered if the teachers would start being nice to me knowing as they now would that there had been trouble at home. But it was not to be. Nobody mentioned my absence and I was met with irritation because I still couldn't tell the time or tie my laces — neither of which I learnt to do till I was in secondary school. I think I resigned myself then to the fact I would never be liked, that I would always be a failure.

Survival of the littlest

As I progressed through primary school a certain quality of willfulness grew in me. I was still quiet and reserved, kept my counsel as I had to, but there were various examples of my standing my ground in conflict situations.

In Primary 4 I confronted the class bully, gently but assertively asking her to stop picking on people. Fury flared in her eyes with indignation at the small scrap of a girl, the runt of the class, daring to challenge her dominion. As if delivering a sentence of death on me she pressed her finger to my chest and said "You! Out the back, after school!" This was code for the severe beating I would later receive as what seemed like the entire cohort of children from our school stood and egged her on chanting "Pagger! Pagger!" (slang for *bring on the fight*).

It was useless to try to defend myself so I stood rigidly waiting for my fate. I managed to maintain some sense of dignity by asserting "I won't fight, I'm a pacifist". This was a new word I had learnt. Naturally she tore chunks out of me as I cowered in a foetal posture to mitigate the impact of the blows. It was a humiliating defeat but somewhere deep inside I felt proud of myself because I knew I had stood up to her for the sake of my peers. Ironically all of those peers ganged up against me, hedging their bets on the side of 'might not right'. Everyone left in dribs and drabs, muttering to each other that it was boring because I wouldn't fight back. And so the torture ended and I limped down the road home to lick my wounds in the sanctuary of my room. John Wayne would have been proud of me nonetheless!

Another example of my emerging determination was an incident in the classroom where the teacher sought to make an example of me. We were breaking up for the Easter holidays. As was her custom at this time of year, our teacher asked us to stand by our desks and wait for her to come round with a box of Cadbury's Creme Eggs which she proceeded to dip into and give to each child. She wore an expression of lofty benevolence as though she were handing out the crown jewels. When she came to me she stopped, looked down at me gravely then walked on to the next child without giving me an egg. I felt a stab of shame because this was her way of saying to me in front of the whole class that I did not deserve a treat. It felt cruel and unnecessary and I did not think I merited such treatment. Although I knew she didn't like me and that I had performed poorly in lessons all term, I had not misbehaved. I was angry and resolved not to crumple as she expected me to.

She stood at the door and held it open for us to leave, gaily wishing each child a happy holiday. When I reached the door she blocked my exit then lifted the last Creme Egg out of the box and handed it to me deliberately as if to say "you do not deserve this but I am going to give it to you anyway because I am kind and merciful". Understanding her intention to compound my shame, I looked her directly in the eye and said "No thank you Miss. If you wanted to give me the egg you should have given it to me with the others". She was stunned at my precocity. Her little display had backfired and I, an eight year old child, was making an example of her. She knew I was justified. Flushed and flustered, her voice breaking into shards, she said "Take it!" forcing the egg into my hand and practically pushing me out the door.

Looking back I think my fierce resolve had developed in response to the poor treatment by adults all around me. In particular my father's reign of terror at home had built up an intense anger in me, and although I wasn't yet able to articulate it, I felt aggrieved on behalf of my mother and brother whom I perceived to be the most vulnerable in our family. I felt I had a duty to protect them from my father. Gradually my fear of being beaten whenever he blew up was overtaken by the instinct to challenge him for picking on them. It created a changed dynamic between us. He responded not by hitting back but by resorting to more subtle tactics. He knew my Achilles heel was my sensitivity and tendency towards guilt and self-blame. This was something he had effectively instilled in me from the outset and so he turned the tables to make me appear the aggressor. When he caught my mother weeping by my bed at night over how unhappy she was with him, he would point the finger and say "Look what you've done to your mother, you've made her cry again" Of course I internalised this and did indeed feel responsible for her suffering. It was a clever strategy.

Still my instinct was to fly in the face of his rages against my mother and I would sometimes even physically place myself between them to prevent him hitting or verbally abusing her. My father therefore came to see me as the greatest impediment to his authority and a symbol of resistance between him and my mother. He would blame me for trying to wreck their marriage. He told me I was a 'bad Catholic' for trying to turn my parents against each other. He accused me of trying to control and manipulate her to my own ends, saying that I wanted to be the 'man of the house', the 'head of the family', that my intention was to divide and conquer the whole household. Effectively he projected his unsavoury motives onto me and, being still a young child, I believed what he said. I came to see myself as an evil monster and thought I was going to go to hell.

It is not hard to see this as the origin of my adult psychosis. When I am ill I become fixated by the belief that I have caused genocide all around me, that I have murdered people, driven them to suicide, sexually abused young children; that when I am in public places I have a bomb in my bag waiting to go off. This rapid descent into madness has many times in the past led to suicide attempts. I cannot cope with the terror and guilt and feel I have to be punished—stopped in my tracks before I cause any more harm. Though I am loath ever to hold him directly responsible for my mental illness, I know my father's behaviour has a lot to answer for in terms of my shattered psychological development.

Siblings

Though damaging in many ways, my early childhood was not a complete catastrophe. As the youngest I was cosseted and fussed over and referred to lovingly as 'the baby'. There was a strong bond between me and my sisters. They were closer to each other in age but they never made me feel left out. I enjoyed watching them prepare for discos and dates with boyfriends. As they grew towards independence they took on part-time jobs and had the means to buy their own clothes and make-up, and to treat me too. My sisters were pretty and popular among their peers. I wore their proximity to me like a badge of merit, flaunting every opportunity to drop anecdotes about them into conversations at school. They were indulgent of my endless fascination for details of what they got up to at parties, and I would plead for them to take me out with them on a Saturday night till my tears fell like apples. Of course sometimes I took it too far and got in the way. Then they would leave irritated that I had held them back. I would mope all night in a pool of rejection, devastated that my big sisters didn't love me anymore.

With my brother it was I who took on the role of older sibling though he was nearly eight years my senior. I mentioned earlier that he was withdrawn and troubled. He would brood in his room for days. I would try to engage him in games to distract him from his melancholy. Sometimes we played table tennis or Connect Four. He always beat me, at which I was secretly pleased. Because of the age gap we never crossed paths at school but I knew that he was bullied and shunned for being 'smelly' and 'weird'. This distressed me greatly. I would have given anything to be able to help him integrate with his peers. Sometimes he took advantage of the tenderness of my feelings for him and, of course, there was the regular sexual contact between us. He also cheated me out of money and sweets and could, at times, be mean and spiteful. At Halloween when we went guising he would divide the spoils grossly in his favour. I didn't feel able to complain even though I had put all the effort into preparing our costumes.

My crowning ambition for him was that he would one day find a girlfriend who would love him and make him feel special. Once, I took it upon myself to give him "a makeover". I reckoned that if I could spruce up his wardrobe and buy him some deodorant he might have a chance of attracting friends and maybe even a girlfriend. For this reason I saved up my pocket money for several weeks with the intention of going shopping together when there was sufficient for me to buy him some new clothes. He entertained my project though refused to go along with my suggestion that he too should contribute some pocket money to the fund. One day, when I had almost enough to buy him a 'T' shirt, he broke my heart by stealing the money and spending it on cigarettes.

Santa Claus is coming

As for every child, Christmas was a special time of year for me. The anticipation was exhilarating. My favourite part of the season was the build up: Christmas carols, tinsel, exciting TV and, of course, planning what presents I would buy for people with my meagre allowance. With a week's pocket money I felt like a millionaire, eking out every last halfpenny to maximum potential in Poundstretcher. It was a marvel how many cheap pairs of socks or synthetic chocolates you could get for a pound. I even once managed to make lucky bags for every child in my class by splitting a pack of plastic animal shapes, some 'scrap' stickers and three tubes of Smarties. Like the Tooth Fairy I sneaked in and placed them on everyone's desk then waited for the gasps of awed delight. In fact I think the only person who took any pleasure in these inappropriate gifts was me. Because I was not a popular child the gesture must have seemed all the more desperate to my peers. Certainly it did nothing to endear me to them.

As for the presents I received, my mother pulled out all the stops to get me a toy or board game and a selection box. We didn't hang stockings in our house; it was an alien concept, a middle class pretension. Perhaps it just wasn't customary in Italy where my mother had grown up; certainly my father wouldn't have thought of it. He did, however, grudgingly consent to buy us a new jumper, blouse or pair of shoes—whatever we needed most badly. Christmases and birthdays were the only time we ever received a new item of clothing. The rest of our sparse wardrobes was made up of cast-offs from cousins, handed down the line to each of us in turn. My father, whose own clothes came from Burton's, always bought our things from Asda. Needless to say they were the cheapest items and the dredges of the reductions. It didn't matter that the fabric wasn't warm enough or the colour didn't suit. It was a case of 'like it or lump it'. We always wrapped them up when we got home so that we would have some presents under the tree even though we knew what was in the parcels and even if we didn't like the contents. In a house where there was so little to spare we learned to make an occasion out of every opportunity.

My favourite night of the year by far was Christmas Eve. The ritual of Midnight Mass was one of those exceptional treats you could look forward to all year and didn't have to feel guilty about enjoying. I could never get to the end without falling asleep. Ensconced in the warm bosom of a packed congregation, I felt drunk on incense and prayer. I was transported by the choir singing descants in Latin, their cherub voices soaring and the haunting melody of *O Come O Come Emmanuel* with its rich velvety timbre bleeding in minor key. The music swept me in its arms and made me feel a part of something cosmic that could only be divine.

Traipsing home, especially in pristine snow, we were beside ourselves with the anticipation of ripping open the parcels under the tree, even though we had had to wrap them ourselves. We teased the magic out of every moment knowing it would all soon be gone.

The biggest anti-climax was Christmas day, not the least because on that occasion my parents always argued their larynxes dry. The main source of tension was that we were regularly invited to have dinner with my mother's sister, her husband and their two daughters. My father never wanted to go. He wielded the threat of missing auntie's Christmas lunch — a meal which made our eyes pop — to maximum effect. Everyone knew we weren't really wanted at their house but my aunt, a kind woman, felt duty bound to invite us because she knew we would have a miserable, spartan Christmas on our own.

We always arrived late and tucked straight into the chicken. My father didn't like turkey and so no-one had it. We licked our fingers to the bone and forgot to use our napkins. Our table manners were feral and we lacked the art of appropriate conversation. Between courses we would either snigger nervously or sit in mortified silence.

The look of disdain on my uncle's face could have turned ice-cream sour. He hated my father and he resented the fact that he and my aunt had to grimly pick up the pieces every time my mother left him. My uncle was a man of few words but he cherished his wife and daughters. He considered my father despicable for not providing for his own family in the same way. It felt to us, as children, that our poverty and reliance on them for scraps of charity was an insult beyond forgiveness.

The meal would pass with an air-shattering frostiness. Then there was the drive home with my father's beaten up old Renault 4 stalling at every traffic light. When we got home my father's temper had reached breaking point because the pubs were shut on Christmas day and it would always end as it started, in argument.

Hogmanay was a more congenial affair. At least then it was socially acceptable for my father to drink himself to blazes. We were permitted a half lager shandy to see the bells in, all the time knowing that it would be another dismal year.

The trauma of an empty purse

One of the most challenging aspects of our home life was the threadbare budget on which my mother was expected to feed us. We received state welfare. My father was clever at eliciting the maximum benefits from the system but he spent it almost entirely on himself. While we ate pasta with chicken fat and carrots, or shared a single tin of Campbell's Meatballs among five of us, he would dine every night on beef. While we were squeezed into worn clothes and shoes too small for our feet, he would have his tailored suits and was clad in a sheepskin coat. We went without holidays or recreational opportunities while he would drown a small fortune each day in beer and cigarettes. It was grossly unfair and we hated him for it.

My mother had to beg, borrow or steal (all of which she did) to provide for us. She was given a small daily allowance by my father because she was impulsive with money and couldn't be trusted not to waste it all on fripperies. The money he gave her was enough to buy a minimal amount of staples such as milk and bread. It was a constant source of stress for her to find the extra money needed to put a meal together.

She would get up every morning at the cusp of dawn while we were still sleeping and scour the streets for discarded pennies. My mother had excellent eyesight and, borne of necessity, was well used to spotting the odd silver coin glinting on the ground, or that rarest of finds — a banknote waiting patiently to meet acquaintance with her purse. Her chances were maximised if she went out early before the street sweepers started their shift. She wandered near pubs where the night before men had spilled out careless with drink and dropped their change on the ground. Once she found a £20 note lying crisp on the snow like an invitation and we dined like gods for a week.

Such diamond finds, however, were rare and my mother had to resort to begging or running errands for the neighbours. We had a very kind lady in the house next door who was in a wheelchair and couldn't get out to do her shopping. My mother would help her with this and other chores for which she was rewarded handsomely. This neighbour took my mother under her wing and spent many hours listening to her tales of woe. She encouraged her on many occasions to leave my father and provided her with support to do so. She was also generous and warm to us children—one of the few adults ever to take an interest. I used to walk her dog—a big wiry mongrel, stubborn but affectionate, with the strength of a stallion. We must have been a farcical sight, tearing down the hill past Gayfield Square with me desperately clinging to the lead as he pulled with mustang power.

There were a number of well-to-do Italian families living close by in grand houses who my mother knew by acquaintance. They were local business owners who'd come from my mother's town in Italy. There was an unspoken expectation that they would help 'their own'. My mother used to take me to their homes. She would press the doorbells incessantly till they were reluctantly opened and we were ushered through to wait in the parlour while they put money in an envelope to discreetly pay her off. Few words would pass between them but the look of shame on my mother's face told me all I needed to know. The arrangement was a one-way transaction. We had nothing to offer in return. It was common knowledge that we had to beg. I remember seeing curtains twitch as we walked past and people pretending to be out. I was a proud child and this felt especially difficult. Even now I find it uncomfortable to accept gifts or receive payment from people.

The Catholic Church was another source of charity for us. The St Vincent de Paul Society volunteers would come round to our house with boxes of groceries for my mother to stock up the cupboard—tins of Spam, processed peas, pilchards and the like. Although we were poor we were fussy and were always disappointed by the contents of the boxes. Occasionally a particularly kind priest would give my mother a portion of his personal stipend. She once bought a black velvet jacket with gold trim from Littlewoods with money he gave her. It was the only 'luxury' item I ever saw her buy for herself. She probably fantasised about an occasion to wear it to but of course there were none.

A little gift from me

The only chance my mother ever had to go out by herself in the evening was to the Union of Catholic Mothers meeting on a Tuesday. Of course she was not allowed to go on a regular basis because that would mean my father had to stay in and miss the pub for the early part of the evening. The UCM was a source of fellowship and pride for my mother. The other ladies would have to have taken her under their wing for it was unlikely that she would have been able to understand the proceedings. One of these Tuesdays while my father was sitting on his throne with the TV at full blast, I crept behind the settee, took my pants down and emptied my bowels on the floor. I think I was around eight or nine years old at the time. I'm not sure why I did it or if anyone even noticed.

Never Never Land

I have some happy and relaxed childhood memories and one is of playing with my dolls at 'schools' or 'houses'. I particularly enjoyed being the teacher, instructing them in whatever I had just learnt at school. The essence of these lessons was the attention I would lavish on my 'pupils', It was sometimes punitive if they were naughty, but always delivered in a loving, generous and appropriate way. I think it was a form of wish fulfillment for the affection I myself lacked at school. Another imaginary game was 'Priests'. I'd dress up in a nightdress of my mother's to resemble a cassock and process up and down the bedroom with a broomstick for a cross. Pieces of paper cut into circles served as communion wafers for my dolls which I'd solemnly place on their lips and say "the Body of Christ" in an Irish lilt. My favourite part of this game was giving sermons to the congregation. Though I struggled to keep up the accent I did try to instil the essence of love and forgiveness in my delivery. The parable of the 'custard seed', as I understood it, was a firm favourite. In these sermons was a precursor of the passion I would later develop for rhetoric.

Children retreat into imaginary worlds to escape or make sense of their own and one of the ways I sought to understand the distress that surrounded me was to enact little dramas about other people's lives. For instance I would recreate the scene at my uncle's chip shop and the conversations he would have had with people before he took his life. Momentum would build as the orders for fish suppers came in from my dolls and my uncle would become so overwhelmed he would storm out and go missing or take to his bed and weep inconsolably. Only years later did I come to experience the hallucinations and voices that were a daily feature of his illness. My 'chip shop' game was a crude representation of the descent into madness which led to my uncle's suicide. Acting out this game helped me to develop a precocious insight into the complex workings of the tormented mind—a subject that would come to dominate my life as an adult.

I also enjoyed going off on little adventures on my scooter, particularly rescuing damsels in distress. At these times I identified with the persona of a boy though I didn't appreciate the usual rough and tumble pursuits of the boys around me. I dressed like a boy though, already showing an early interest in hats and ties which would later become my signature attire.

As a child most of my play life was solitary. I did have one or two friends with whom I played games like hide and seek or kick the can but I was anxious around other children and so my preference was for playing on my own. One playmate of course was my mother with whom I had great fun whizzing down Calton Hill on flattened cardboard boxes, or taking picnics up Arthur's Seat. My mother was in some ways like a little sister to me. Being the dominant one in the relationship, I took it upon myself to explain things to her and generally bossed her about with rules and instructions. She was extremely acquiescent which

I enjoyed at one level because I always got my own way in the choice of games we would play, but it also disturbed me and made me feel guilty because it confirmed my father's accusation that she was under my control. If my mother had been capable of being an authority figure like other parents perhaps I would not have grown up feeling like such a bad person. In many ways the lack of boundaries I had as a child made me feel dangerously out of control—and still does to this day.

Chalking up the years

My mother's illiteracy and lack of numeracy affected our household in many ways, particularly since my father kept himself absent from domestic matters. It meant we got no help or encouragement with our homework and there were never any bedtime stories. We often had upset tummies because mum couldn't read cooking instructions. Being unable to count she couldn't budget and there were often embarrassing instances of being sent from shop counters to put groceries back on the shelves. We helped her as much as we could but we weren't always on hand and many of the things that other children took for granted were problematic for us.

I had overcome my own dyslexic problem sufficiently to read and write. To my naive ten year old mind the solution was simple—I would teach mum to read, write and count. I set about making a classroom in the kitchen with a doll's blackboard, a wooden abacus and the dining table as a desk. Every evening for a week at 9pm I would ring a little bell to signify that lessons had begun. I put my poor mother through her paces until, exasperated by her lack of progress because I could teach her nothing, I would end up getting angry and shouting "It's easy. Why can't you get it?" The week of lessons I inflicted on her was torture for us both. It must have caused her stress all day and made her feel terrible about herself but, as in all things, she went along with it to please me right up until the last night. Having failed once again to recognise 'the cat sat on the mat', she started to cry. It was then I realised what a tyrant I had been and threw my arms around her and sobbed out every last 'sorry' that was in me. To this day the episode fills me with shame and regret.

Marie Antoinette had nothing on me

Another source of shame for me then, as now, is food. I have always had a voracious appetite, undoubtedly borne of emotional need. In a house where there was not enough to go round it was an unhelpful trait. However little food there was, my mother tried to ensure that her 'baby' had a stash of sweets and biscuits. I cannot imagine how she managed to keep up the supply. My sister remembers me sharing my sweets with her but that is not what I remember at all. In my memory I guarded them jealously and was demanding of more. Whatever the reality of the situation there was a dichotomy in my mind: my desperate craving for sugar — versus the irreconcilable guilt I felt that my mother, brother and sisters were going without other food because of me. I also recognized that I was manipulating my mother's desire to comfort me with food. She knew I was deeply unhappy and it was her way of showing love. She even gave me the biggest portions at meal times though I was by far the smallest. It is hardly surprising that I still battle with a compulsive eating disorder.

There must be many other things from my childhood which might explain some of the unhelpful coping mechanisms I have now. In the face of such dysfunction I also managed to develop some compensatory skills. I displayed wisdom and empathy beyond my years, a growing inner strength, resourcefulness and the capacity for further growth.

In spite of the horrors of my childhood I somehow knew I was loved. But my wings were clipped before I had the chance to fly.

Up, up and away...
ADOLESCENCE | 1983–1989

If my 'latent' years were starved of innocence, adolescence was characterised by a burst of guilty pleasure in the longed for kindness of adults. Leaving primary school my teacher wrote in my yearbook "Go placidly amid the noise and haste" but experience had led me to expect the worst. My life so far had not prepared me, in the words of C.S Lewis, to be suddenly 'surprised by joy'.

Saint Tam's

I started St Thomas of Aquin's High School a couple of months before my twelfth birthday. The first few weeks were spent in an old annexe of the school, an imposing prison of a building that belied the warmth within. The annexe was affectionately known as 'Jimmy Clarke's'. It reminded me of Colditz standing as it did on a precipice opposite the cliff of Salisbury Crags.

I don't remember much from Jimmy Clarke's but there are two images that stand out. The first is jogging with my classmates in the rain round Arthur's Seat in the park at our doorstep, and the other is a rather strange snapshot of me standing in the middle of the playground transfixed by the breathless struggle of wasps in their late summer throes. Perhaps their death was like the shedding of my old familiar skin, the melancholic brooding at my dismal lot.

Now a golden age was dawning in the sanctuary of secondary school. I wouldn't say I'd become popular but I no longer felt an oddity among my peers. Still quiet and unassuming, or given to wandering off on my own, by now my sensitivity was tolerable to other children and would come to be an asset in attracting friends.

As for the teachers, I got the distinct impression that they actually liked me. I was still wary of them turning on me, but slowly I began to trust that I would not be shunned or humiliated for being slow and awkward. It was just accepted that I needed help with doing up my laces, much as reaching for a text book on the highest shelf.

Within a few short few weeks Jimmy Clarke's was closed permanently and we were transferred to the main building on Chalmers Street at the edge of a sprawling new natural playground — the Meadows. The main school, which consisted of a row of converted tenement houses and prefab huts, was an even friendlier affair, and it was there that I really began to settle and feel at home.

We were a relatively small community for an inner city secondary school, six hundred pupils in all, and right from the start it did feel to me like a community. Being one of only three Catholic high schools in the city, St Thomas' had a large catchment area that took in a wide social demographic. It meant I had peers from professional families and blue collar backgrounds, or, like my own — what might be deemed as underclass — with parents who were chronically unemployed. This is one of the many things for which I am grateful in my education there — the melting pot of social groupings and the opportunities available to us all. Blending in is always easier when you're not the only one on free school meals, and there is the bonus of exposure to social diversity.

As far as I can recollect, there were never issues of snobbery or serious bullying in the school. Difference was accepted much as oranges and apples in a fruit bowl. We didn't co-exist in neutral ground but rather complemented one another. As a microcosm of society our school perhaps was an atypical example of harmonious living, though at the time some may have taken it for granted.

One of the defining factors in making St Thomas' such a special place for me was the kindness of the teachers. They were good-natured, approachable and warm. Friendly banter was encouraged in the classroom which made lessons on the whole relaxed and fun. I think the bar was set by our headmaster, Mr Dames, an exceptionally pleasant man with a twinkle in his eye and a genuine love of the pupils and staff in his charge. His wife, who taught Religious Studies and Learning Support, was the perfect consort in our little kingdom. She too was gentle, kind and so warm-hearted that it seemed she'd like to take every one of us home and spoil us with a limitless supply of treats and affection. The Dames' also had children of their own who attended St Thomas' which gave it even more of a family feel. Indeed there were a number of teachers whose own children attended the school—testament I think to what a fine establishment it was and the quality of education one could expect there.

No doubt the rosy picture I have painted would not be the impression of every former pupil. Perspectives, being unique, are coloured by a myriad of interpretations. My own fond glow might not have been so vivid were it not the first place I felt happy. If all you've known throughout your life is famine, when even common fayre arrives it is a banquet worthy of the gods.

Sit Nobiscum Deus

Religion featured barely on the curriculum but, being a Catholic school, our faith was celebrated and affirmed at communal gatherings—not the ram-it-down-your-throat religion of our parents' generation but a faith that was enquiring and generous. School assemblies and public events were accompanied by prayers—more it seemed as a bonding experience than a rigid statement of belief. Indeed there were many in our school who probably did not believe in God and nothing was demanded of them in the way of spiritual observance but a willingness to come together as a community.

Each day at lunch time, Mass or a short communion service was held in the small school oratory. This was a very informal affair in a room the size of a family lounge. A handful of people attended, many of whom were teachers, but also the odd bright-faced pupil, like me. Daily Mass was an important part of school life for me throughout my time at St Thomas'. As there was no expectation from my parents to attend church Sundays remained the day of sloth and we treasured the sacred lie-in. I did go sometimes with my mother on a Sunday but it never became routine like daily Mass at school which I loved. My main motivation was the opportunity for closeness with the teachers. I craved attention and affection from adults to the extent I'd give up half my lunch time every day to drip-feed on their presence and, of course, approval.

Behind the bike shed

My ego wasn't stroked by exceptional grades at St Thomas'. In first year I extended my primary school track record for being mediocre but slowly and surely, I blossomed under the nurturing charge of the teachers. Maths, Arithmetic and Science continued to be my Achilles heel, and I showed scant aptitude for P.E., Technical Drawing and Woodwork. Home Economics was a drudge beyond compare, aided only by the knack I quickly acquired for getting a boy who fancied me to do my share of the cooking. Peter—a doe-eyed ape of a boy—became my boyfriend, and we snogged behind the science block till our tongues turned blue.

I later attracted another boy with a racy message in the school valentines magazine. He also was willing to be roped into helping me with wood and metal work. He was appropriately chisel-jawed, sultry and brooding like the archetypal teenage rebels I had seen in films. Needless to say, he was far too cool for me and the 'relationship' didn't last long.

When I look back at pictures of myself I realize I was bright-eyed and pretty but then nothing could have seemed to me further from the truth. I was shy and felt unattractive—not aided by the fact I looked much younger than all the other girls in my year. I took my time in reaching puberty. There were other boys who I collared into being my latest beau but my appetite for boys was not so much to do with lust as a desperate bid for approval. In the scramble to be popular it somehow eluded me that I was the only girl in my class who regularly had a boyfriend, and these 'couplings' seemed more odd at such an age than evidence of status in the pack.

Another boy, called Fabrizio, was lassoed into going out with me because I, somewhat ironically, felt pity for him and thought I could rescue him from being a social misfit. He was a good-looking boy but sidelined because his manner was unfortunate. A week into our wooing I persuaded him to come with me to Arthur's Seat. He broke my heart on the brisk climb up by dumping me as though I were dead weight. In adulthood Fabrizio and I would meet again as fellow patients in the psychiatric hospital. He developed schizophrenia and spent his final years wandering like a bearded prophet round the hospital bargaining with the terrorists in his head. I sometimes went to see him in the long-term rehabilitation ward and he would dazzle me with fast-tripping talk and bizarre frenzied sketches. Then we would go to the Morningside Deli and he'd lard his lungs with greasy burgers till the fat ran out of him and, still a boy in many ways, he died.

A number of my peers ended up in the Royal Edinburgh Hospital as adults, all of them with whom I've reminisced about how sad it was the good times spent at school had to end. There are casualties in every institution but never do you think it will be you.

For pity's sake

There was a teacher whose sensitivity used to make me cry. He couldn't control his classes and would snap closed his book and storm out the door. He had a passion for his subject and for imparting it to us but, like a scattering of birdseed on a pond, his lessons sank beneath our wisdom. I loved this man in secret, till a girl called Tess with mischief in her sights, blurted out to him what everybody knew. The shame of being 'found out' was only second to the realisation that it came as no surprise to anyone, least of all to him. The tell-tale signs were there all along: lingering behind after class to catch the ember of a smile, saving questions that I knew the answers to already, handing in my homework earlier than due. As with the other men in my life I fancied I could see into his pain and be the one to set him free. This pattern repeated itself well into adulthood and got me into many scrapes.

Curriculum on fire

The subjects I fared better at were History, English, Spanish and Biology. Our first year Spanish teacher, Mr Walls, brought the language alive with his hearty laugh and avuncular warmth. It was a joy to learn exotic words and phrases from this tender bear of a man. Mr McNairn, my Biology teacher, was a shy, sensitive man, extremely kind and committed to his pupils and his subject. I was very fond of him and he managed to do the impossible for me: make science interesting. In History I was entranced by Mr Hume's dramatic accounts of the altercations between Mary Queen of Scots and her nemesis, John Knox, with his damning polemic The First Blast of the Trumpet against the Monstrous Regiment of Women. Mr Hume was a charismatic teacher with a mischievous glint who loved delighting us with his quirky twists on the syllabus.

English didn't come alive for me till third year when I was taught by our guidance teacher, Mr McPartlin, an extremely popular man with hippy leanings and a natural affinity to teenage rebels. As such he didn't have much time for a goody two shoes like me. He was friendly to me as he was to everybody, but I always felt invisible to him. Indeed he has passed me as an adult once or twice without a hint of recognition. It caused me grief as a child because I liked him very much and, as my guidance teacher, I had the expectation that he might come to ask about my home life: my heartfelt wish was to be rescued from my situation. I think, like many others, he just didn't think to look beyond my stoic smile.

But his gift for teaching English did inspire me and I flourished in his class. He was overtly left-wing in his politics and he instilled a sense of outrage in us with his impassioned interpretation of Wilfred Owen and Siegfried Sassoon, and the closing of steel mines and erosion of workers' rights featured in Billy Joel's *Allentown*. Music was his favourite vehicle for teaching. He played us songs by Bruce Springsteen and Billy Bragg among others, using the lyrics to convey themes of injustice and oppression. It was he who introduced me to Simon & Garfunkel whose tender harmonies touched my soul with a feather's ease. We also studied standard texts such as Shakespeare, and Harper Lee's *To Kill a Mockingbird*—a book which had a profound impact on me by first opening my eyes to racism. Indeed it was these classes which awoke my political consciousness and affirmed values I still hold dear. I will always be grateful for this radical edge to my education.

Holding a candle

My most visceral awakening was in second year, when first introduced to my new Spanish teacher, Miss Dugan. The crush I developed on her swamped me like a cart of delicious fruit. It was the most raw, the most alive I had ever felt. Not only was she pretty, clever and charming, an exceptional teacher and a lovely person, but I also felt a very personal connection with her. She was the first adult in my life, other than my mother, to make me feel special. Her praise and encouragement buoyed me to bursting point. It was a revelation that anyone could have such regard for me. Naturally I blossomed in confidence and sought to please her in all things. I didn't just do the exercises she set us for homework, I wrote a whole book—in Spanish! Of course it made no grammatical sense but the hours I spent lovingly weaving the basic vocabulary I had learned into the story of my sister's recent holiday to Spain were rewarded with the requisite approval. Miss Dugan exceeded the imperative of kindness by reading the book in her own time—all 14 chapters!—and corrected every one of my mistakes with a faint pencil.

My desperation to please Miss Dugan led to some embarrassing incidents which drew the attention and derision of my peers. On Monday mornings, periods one and two, we had P.E. followed by Spanish. In the changing rooms after badminton or gymnastics there was a habit among the girls of stalling so as to be late for Spanish.

Though it bothered me I was swept up in the culture, not having the courage to buck the trend. We would meander across the playground in a lazy straggle and pretend we had been held up by our P.E. teacher. Unbeknown to us Miss Dugan could see us taking our time from the window of her classroom. One day, as we drifted in, she dished out punishment exercises—but not to me—dropping the bombshell that she could see very well what they were up to. The girls got wise and resolved to avoid her all-seeing eye by going a different route. I saw the opportunity to redeem myself in Miss Dugan's eyes by tearing at break neck speed across the old route through the playground just so she could see me and know how keen I was to get to class on time. It was a shameful display of sucking up and I got my comeuppance by being mercilessly teased by the others in the changing rooms for being a 'lemon' and other things too graphic to mention. This was the girlish equivalent of wet towel slapping but, unpleasant though it was, it didn't deter me from currying favour with my teacher.

Teacher's pet in the corner

Another incident I remember as though it were yesterday, was the devastating experience of being given detention by Miss Dugan along with three other girls. The class had been split into two sets for turns to go to the language lab with Cristina, the young native speaking Spanish student on placement at St Thomas's. My half, which included some particularly naughty girls, seized the opportunity for mischief with the gullible young Spaniard—only a few years our senior. They stood up on their chairs and started stomping their feet and playing imaginary musical instruments. I was initially frightened that a teacher would hear, but gradually drawn in to the fun. Normally I would have felt too guilty but they coaxed me to join in the frenzy of disobedience so I got up on my chair and started playing air guitar. This rare display of anarchy was intoxicating. Just as I was strumming a particularly convoluted chord, the door flung open and in walked Miss McMillan, the German teacher. The silence was palpable. The inevitability of our being reported to Miss Dugan was written like a grave inscription on her face. As Cristina, flustered and embarrassed, tried to resume the lesson, her words washed over me. My stomach was knotted like a fist and I thought I was going to be sick.

We trooped back into class like condemned cattle, knowing word would have already reached Miss Dugan. Once seated at our desks, we were asked who the ringleaders were. The others, including a close friend of mine, stood up, brazen rather than meek. It was unbearable for me to watch them shoulder the blame while I got off scot-free. With my heart in my mouth and my cheeks the colour of cabbage, I slowly stood up and hung my head in shame. Though I couldn't see her face as I stared hard at the floor I knew Miss Dugan was baffled and disappointed. This would have marked the incident more for her than anger. At first, she was persuaded that I had nothing to do with it; that my admission of guilt was an act of martyrdom. "Sit down Joanna" she said firmly "I know you are just trying to rescue the others" This made me feel like the biggest heel that ever walked the earth. "No Miss" I insisted in a quiet voice, "I did it too".

There was a moment's silence—then "I see. Well I would have expected this behaviour from you three but as for you Joanna, I am very disappointed." She told us to report back for detention during the last half hour of lunch then dismissed the class.

At break time I felt as heavy-hearted as a lark without its voice. The others bragged about the incident, conferring kudos on me too for having the guts to join in but I couldn't care a pickle for being welcomed to their merry band. I had upset the person I loved most in all the world and I was inconsolable. I couldn't show it to the others though, for fear of a double whammy—being teased for being a 'lemon' and a 'sook'.

At lunchtime, before detention, I went to Mass as usual—full of contrition for my sins. As the queue edged forward for Communion, Miss Dugan, who also attended every day, stopped to let me go in front of her. I knew this was a conciliatory gesture. Still I kept my head down, knowing I did not deserve her kindness.

I resolved after school to go back to her class and apologize.

When I knocked on her door she welcomed me with a wide smile as though she had been expecting me. "Ah come in Joanna" she said in a strawberry tone, and before I could utter the word 'sorry' she launched into a speech about what a pleasant girl I was, how I always brightened up her day and that she was so sorry that she had had to put me on detention. I was astounded and still couldn't look her in the eye. I tried again to say sorry, but she intercepted with "Everything's okay. Now off you go home and don't worry about a thing". Then the miraculous happened. She gave me a hug.

I dined on the experience all evening and, if truth be told, for many years, deliciously savouring her words in stolen moments and re-living the effervescent shock of being clasped affectionately in her arms. And so was learned a lesson early on in how calamity can quickly turn to joy.

'Here comes Fizz'

Another of my favourite teachers, and one who also made me feel rather special though I had little aptitude for her subject, was Ms McGhee, the Geography teacher. She was a stunning woman with beautiful, big eyes, a model's figure and poise, and jaw-dropping style. She had a quirky sense of humour and a natural ease with her pupils, and it is easy to see now why she was so popular. Her lessons were always something to look forward to, though paradoxically I had decided early on that Geography was not for me. I perceived it to be too scientific and I had no confidence in this area. Ms McGhee did her best to persuade me that I was good at Geography, and certainly good enough to take it up to 'O' grade. I think she was always a little disappointed that I never quite believed her.

That said, for someone who 'didn't like' the subject I spent an inordinate proportion of my homework time on Geography assignments. Ms McGhee once gave us a project to do at home on different ecosystems of the world. I think she intended each one to cover a half page or so: a short description and a picture of some animals or plant-life there to be found. Over the next few evenings I became so engrossed in this project that mine ran to sixty-eight A4 pages! Of course most of it was hijacked from a single book (I had not yet developed the technique of drawing from a number of sources) and there wasn't a shred of analysis in what I wrote. My project was beautiful, at least to me, illustrated as it was with pictures and an abundance of fancy lettering. How I wish that now I could apply myself with such enthusiasm to things I 'don't enjoy'!

Ms McGhee rewarded my efforts with the anticipated appreciation, bestowing on me a week long Cheshire smile which was duly returned. These were the triumphant moments of adulation which spurred me on to do my best. Though I didn't feel yet that I'd be an outstanding pupil in any discipline, I had made a meteoric leap away from being a 'dunce' as I was considered at primary school.

Ms McGhee was also generous with tangible rewards for our work. One Halloween we asked her if we could have a dooking party at the end of class. She thought about it briefly and said "only if you don't make too much mess", knowing that of course we would. She was even sporting enough to put her own head in the basin and fish out a Cox's pippin, adding with a wink, "Apple for the teacher!" I wrote a poem—my first ever—to record the event.

One day Ms McGhee let slip her impending birthday. Of course I wasn't going to let that one pass. The next few days were plump with the joy of preparing home-made surprises for her. We were making weather vanes in Wood and Metalwork so mine—or should I say that created by whichever boy I'd coaxed into doing it for me—was lovingly engraved with "Ms McGhee". A watercolour of the Pope was duly painted—as she too came to Mass every day I figured she'd be impressed by this. It had the desired effect—another heart-warming smile from my teacher who was very touched by the gesture and still remembers it to this day.

A year later, in third form—after I had dropped Geography—I was hanging out with friends in A-block trying to look nonchalant and cool, when Ms McGhee passed by and greeted us cheerily. She called me aside. "Joanna" she said, "Do you still have a copy of that great wee poem you wrote? I can't find mine and I wanted to keep it."

This drew restrained sniggers from the group and my face turned Frisbee-red. Even in a nice school like ours it wasn't the done thing to give your teachers presents and you were in for a real joshing if you did. Unaware that the others had heard, she went on her way and the pressure valve burst. Everyone except me fell about laughing. "Oh, very funny" I huffed and puffed, trying to backtrack on the gesture, "I only did it for a laugh". But the damage was done. This confirmed the verdict that I was definitely "gay"—the obvious conclusion for such a wanton display of sookiness towards a teacher of the same sex. To compensate, I tried to make a big deal out of various crushes I had on male teachers, dropping heavy references here and there about how 'tidy' this or that one was.

Daughter in the house

Home life was still in many ways bleak and troubled, but now I had a tangible means of escape in the form of St Thomas'—something which had not been the case for my first eleven years because primary school had been just as dire as home.

My father continued to cast his toxic spell over the house, still aggressive, manipulative and quixotic in his moods. My mother remained unhappy and tried often to leave but always my father managed to entice her back by appealing to her pity. My sisters, now in their late teens, were both consumed with boyfriends and work, and were getting ready to flee the nest. As for my brother, his brooding got worse and he veered even further out of orbit from his peers. Now that I was approaching puberty I wouldn't let him have sex with me but his appetite seemed to grow and I was forever having to fend him off. My father didn't have the same access to me now that I was too old to sleep in my parents' bed, but he continued to touch me inappropriately and leer at me which I found repulsive.

The weekly shopping trips to Asda and visits to my paternal grandmother on a Saturday remained a fixture until the family unit broke up. By now it was only me and my middle sister, Paula, who went with my parents. We were excruciatingly embarrassed by my father's gross behaviour in public. His voice would boom out over everybody else's. He barked out orders and reprimands, expounding in his arrogant way the inalienable truth of everything as decreed by The Big I Am. If anyone seemed to look at him the wrong way he'd glare at them threateningly. But, as with most bullies, he never crossed other men — unless they were acting under the constraint of official capacity. Woe betide any till operator perceived to have short-changed him — they seldom had — or the unfortunate waitress in any café which ran out of bacon or who served his toast a fraction underdone.

Sometimes my father could be awkward simply out of spite. There was a precedent in our school that every child in first year would be taken — two classes at a time — to Newtonmore in the Scottish Highlands for a week's residential trip. The theory was that some children would not be able to go on subject-based trips later on in school because their families couldn't afford to send them and there should be an opportunity made available in first year for everyone to go. Because of this, there were fundraising activities throughout the school to subsidise the expense for poorer families like my own. However my father objected to my going. I would be the only child, from our year of 120, left behind. I was devastated. Not only was this to have been my first residential school trip, but I had never been on holiday in my entire life — not even for a weekend away with my family.

My father seemed to take curious delight in my distress. The teachers battled hard to persuade him to let me go but he drew out the process till the eleventh hour, only relenting (as I believe he had intended all along) the day before we were due to leave. The reprieve was delivered by such a narrow margin that my father managed to emerge heroic as I clasped him tight in tearful gratitude before we set off. Of course he didn't have to pay a penny because the school had funded my place. They must have considered his behaviour cruel and unnecessary but they had to tread softly in their negotiations since his metronomic temper might swing either way.

You may think me cynical for assuming my father's performance was calculated but supporting evidence had manifested itself five years previously when the same scenario was enacted over my sister's first year school trip to Kinharvie. He must have elicited such pleasure from the drama that he decided to repeat it.

The holiday was a bittersweet experience for me. I was thrilled to be away from home but never quite trusted that I wouldn't be dragged back early. I somehow didn't feel I had a right to be there.

Pack up your troubles

My father had his tender moments too, and in a curious volte face I was permitted in second year to go to Belgium with the school History department for an excursion to the battlefields of World War 1. I still don't know who funded the trip but it was the most exciting thing in my life so far—my first trip abroad. The night before we set off I was beside myself with anticipation as my mother helped me pack my suitcase. I remember *It's a Knockout*, the 1980's game show with obstacles and flumes, flashing on the television as my mother prepared meat paste sandwiches for the trip. My father was in the pub as usual and so we had free rein to sing and dance around the room. My mother was just as excited as I was. Though she would have missed me terribly while I was away, she must have gained immense pleasure in knowing I was having fun. Whether it was the school which provided the funds or my mother from scrubbing neighbours' floors and early morning raids on my father's hung-over trouser pockets I will never know. In any case I got to go and had a wonderful time.

The coach trip to Dover was the best bit and I have always loved travelling by coach since. Before we set off, Mrs Dames, the headmaster's wife, came to wish us a happy holiday. On the bus she called out my name and I froze, thinking that perhaps my father had changed his mind. However she approached me with a warm smile and handed me a small parcel. "From Señorita Dugan" she winked. This was the crowning glory of the whole trip and we hadn't even left the school! I opened it up like illicit treasure, and found—to my delight—a box of Lindt chocolate teddy bears—*ositos de chocolate*! It was a reference to a conversation a few months back when she had asked me what my favourite chocolates were. She had remembered! This lovely surprise was well worth the mild teasing I incurred from my fellow passengers for being 'teacher's pet'.

Throughout the week-long trip I felt as if a weight had lifted—the cumbersome drudge of being at home. The weather wasn't always nice but in my heart the sun was bouncing off the pavements every day. Of course the subject matter was grim: so many millions losing their lives in a horrific futile war. But there was a sense of redemption in the air as birds sang around the uniform graves, and the names carved on stone arches took on personalities—men, and boys not much older than us, writing letters to their sweethearts, sharing swigs of rum and playing cards. It was better not to concentrate on the severed limbs or choking lungs. We fingered the rusting shells more like toys than implements of war to rip through heart and liver or gouge out teeth and eyes. We heard about the cruel injustice of soldiers, frozen with fear, being tied to a stake and shot for cowardice by a firing squad of reluctant peers; how on the night before the execution they got blitzed on booze, and of the Padre offering comfort and salvation to hysterical wrecks of men. The most moving part of the whole trip for me was in a museum courtyard listening in bowed silence to the Last Post on the bugle followed by the haunting prayer: *At the going down of the sun... we shall remember.*

One incident I recall with a mixture of embarrassment and delight was on the coach at Ypres when there weren't enough seats because one had to be given up for the tour guide. A good-looking male teacher, whose name I can't remember, but who had a reputation for being unapproachable, said I could sit on his lap for the journey. It was the obvious solution given that I was the smallest child there. Nowadays such a thing would never happen, but then it was perfectly acceptable and there was nothing sexual in his gesture. Of course I was too mortified to enjoy the experience at the time but I pored over it afterwards, my fantasies of being adopted by a handsome father taking flight.

Secret longing

I often had fantasies about being rescued. One of my favourite and most elaborate whilst a pupil at St Thomas' was that I would be taken hostage along with all the teachers. In my mind with the backdrop of the Falklands War it didn't seem too far-fetched that the school might be invaded by an enemy. I glossed over the details and logistics. We would be held hostage and the teachers would now have to act in loco parentis for me—much like the arrangement of officers still being in charge of their troops in a prisoner of war camp. *The Bridge over the River Kwai* was my inspiration. Our captors would take a hands-off approach but the threat of danger lurking over us would make the teachers extra protective, especially as I was the only child. It was the ideal outlet for my desperate need to be cared for in a way which made me feel nurtured and safe. This scenario must have represented the brutal reality of my home life, and it allowed me the freedom to fully immerse myself in the fantasy of normal parenthood and family life.

How sad now to think that so much of my creative energy as a child was given over to this desperate and unfulfilled wish. I would like to be able to say that I outgrew such fantasies in adulthood but sadly this has not been the case. Throughout my life, and to this day, my dominant 'driver' (in the language of Transactional Analysis) both conscious and unconscious, has been to find an alternative experience of being parented in an appropriate, loving and safe way. To quote myself from a recent poem, I feel

Trapped in a woman's body;
waiting for childhood to begin

This limbo has been a source of both grief and shame. I have always found comfort when surrogate attachments form but have not in the past always made best use of such relationships. I have now progressed to the point where I am able to reconcile this part of my development with my instinct for survival and see it as a healthy, natural response to the parental deficit in my early life.

Growing up, my rich fantasy life was more of a breathing apparatus than a crutch. I do not think I would have survived such trauma and neglect were it not for my capacity to transport myself through imagination to alternative realities. The other oxygen supply of course being secondary school. Unfortunately, the latter came too late to rescue me from the emotional damage to my psyche, something which would not become apparent till I started university.

The first cut is the deepest

The rocky terrain of adolescence was tough to navigate through its triumphs and disasters — in retrospect minor and petty, but mammoth in scale at the time. The biggest disappointment — such a bland word does no justice to the heartache I felt — was when our Spanish teacher, Miss Dugan, the centre of my universe, announced to us at the start of third Year that she was leaving St Thomas' for a year to take up a sabbatical post with the Education Department. I believe it was to develop learning materials but I did not really take in the details. Sitting in my usual spot at the back right hand of the class, I felt in that instant as though a catapault had hit me in the face. Everything else she said swam in some bubble around the room. I stared straight ahead as her words echoed like droplets, the tears in my eyes more stunned than sad or angry. Those emotions would come next.

Leaving class at the end, we each filed passed as she wished us goodbye at the door. When it was my turn I refused to look at her. "Joanna" she said, lightly touching my arm to draw me back but I steamrollered on to the next class with the heavy clunk of footsteps reverberating in my head.

I don't recall how, or if, I got through the next lesson without breaking down. I do remember that when I got home I crashed on to the bed and cried for six hours solid — not for the last time in my life, and always over a woman on whom I depended leaving. It was as if the soul of me had drained with the tears, and when I emerged from my room, puffy-eyed and hair tangled with snot, the house seemed emptier than ever — even emptier than the times when my mother left. It was dark outside. My father would be drunk in the pub, my brother masturbating in his room, my mother picking fleas off the cat downstairs and my sisters out in the world being independent, doing what they had to do to keep their worlds from crashing as the centre imploded from mine.

Next day I had composed myself enough to face Miss Dugan and wish her all the best. I felt such love for this woman it was one of the hardest things I have ever had to do, especially since I didn't believe she would come back the following year as she promised. But she did come back. Something astronomical had shifted though: nothing would ever be the same again. I now knew what it was to be broken-hearted.

The next few months went by like bland supermarket music as I tried to pick my life up from the shelf. It was hard to eat, sleep or concentrate. All I wanted was to die. Had I known then my life to come would be littered with the bones of unrequited love of women, I might have given up before I had the chance to experience mutual longing for a man. My interest was awakened by the plump flowering of puberty and I began to see boys not just as objects of pity but as vessels of desire.

I didn't have a boyfriend in fourth year as my 'O' grades took priority. I was sitting ten 'O' (ordinary) grades when the official maximum allowed by the school timetable was eight. The extra two were extra-curricular, one being Italian which I studied at an after-school class attended along with four Scots-Italian boys in the year below. The other was an adult evening class in Religious Studies at which I was the only student of school age. As I hated being at home, taking these classes was a calculated measure to spend more time away.

When I was at home every hour not eating or sleeping was spent in study. I developed a system to help me revise. Each subject was divided into units — on which I'd prepare detailed questions to quiz myself to ensure that I had learnt my topics inside out. I am not a natural learner of facts. On the whole I prefer theory and analysis and this system forced me out of my comfort zone. It was not the most creative approach but it meant my study was systematic and rigorous. I applied myself with gusto to the task. As ever, the holy grail of approval from my teachers was there to spur me on.

Fleeing hell

Shortly after the start of fourth year my mother left us again. This was to be her longest absence. My eldest sister had moved out two years prior to establish a family of her own and so it was just me, my brother, my other sister and my father left at home. My mother had gone to stay in the Victoria Hostel, a run-down hovel of a dwelling for homeless women in the Grassmarket. The other residents were mostly people with chronic alcohol problems who had certainly seen the rough side of life. I worried initially that my mother, who was gullible and weak, would be taken advantage of. In fact my prejudices proved to the contrary. The other women felt protective towards her because of her vulnerability and though always fighting with each other, they rallied round to support her.

There was an old blind cat in the hostel and my mother was appointed the task of feeding it for which she was paid £2 a week. She was so excited when she told me about this, referring to it as her 'job'. I think she saw it as a symbol of independence from my father. When we used to meet covertly after school she would tell me this and other details of her new life with such giddy pleasure that she forgot to ask about me. Naturally I interpreted this as her not caring though I knew deep down she was just so drunk at her new found freedom that she had no space in her head to worry about me.

Meanwhile my father's abusive behaviour became more extreme as it always did when she left him. He drove my sister Paula out of the house with his violent rages, and she went to live in a flat with friends. I was now left at home with just him and my brother. As in the past, my father blamed me for my mother's having left him, saying I had driven her away. He said

I was the only person who could bring her back. Though I never tried to, it was probably true as I knew she would do almost anything for me. It was a terrible burden, the choice of inflicting hell on my mother by asking her back or this miserable status quo without her which was hell for the rest of us. I chose the latter, knowing I couldn't live with her unhappiness on my conscience. Because my father knew I was going to Mass every day at school, he resolved to use my piety as a means to manipulate me, saying that I was a 'bad Catholic' for splitting my parents up. Though I understood at a rational level what he was doing, I internalised the guilt and I was on my knees day and night begging forgiveness for what I had done to my family.

My brother, now in his twenties, was beginning to experience the onset of schizophrenia and was in extreme distress. He had started attending the Royal Edinburgh Hospital as a day patient but was finding it increasingly difficult to manage at home, especially with my mother gone and my father's behaviour being so destructive for us all. I was up with him through the night trying to keep him from slashing his wrists or overdosing on his medication which he was on the precipice of doing. Exhausted and worn I was struggling to cope at school and desperate for someone to notice what was going on and take me out of my situation. I must have seemed fine to other people because no one intervened. I did have one or two close friends whom I confided in and they were supportive but it wasn't within their power to do anything. I really needed an adult to step in.

The only grown-up I disclosed anything to at this time was a priest in the confessional box, because I thought I was to blame. He did his best to reassure me it was not my fault and he gave me emotional support when things were particularly bad, like the time I turned to him after my father came home drunk and hit me over the face so hard I fell to the floor.

Defying Daddy

Shortly after this incident I tried to leave home, turning to my elder sister, Lena, to take me in with her husband and two small children.

I was 15 and I had left without my father's permission. The following day he came to the school and told the headmaster I had been disobedient and was causing trouble at home. Mr Dames had to call me out of class and take me to see my father who then put me through a humiliating lecture on how much I had worried everybody and that I had better start behaving. He was canny enough not to blame me for my mother leaving in front of Mr Dames. I was ordered by my father to come home there and then. Mr Dames, not knowing what was going on at home, had to agree. My father could be both aggressive and extremely persuasive. He was also adept at discerning when to switch from one to the other.

The journey home in the car was unbearable. Hardly a word was spoken between us. I hated my father for humiliating me in front of Mr Dames and for putting him in such a difficult position too. My sister tried to convince my father that I should stay with her to study for my 'O' grades, but he was having none of it. A few days later it was my birthday and he gave me a Walkman, something he knew I had wanted for a long time and always thought was out of my reach. He told me he loved me very much and only wanted what was best for me. I believed him.

After that his campaign to get my mother back intensified and I was subjected to more urgent persuasion—tears one minute, insults the next. The worst kind of pressure wasn't the physical or verbal abuse but the way he manipulated my emotions. To see your father sobbing hysterically that he doesn't want to live any more, is a genuinely distressing sight, and I did indeed feel sorry for him. Sometimes I would hold him in my arms like one would a distraught infant but always, when he had me where he wanted me, he would spit out angrily "you don't really love me, if you did you would get her back". My first loyalty however was always to my mother because I knew she was the more vulnerable and needed me to be strong. My father finally realised I wasn't going to give in. In fury and disgust he went into my room, scooped up some clothes and books in a black bin liner, and threw it and me out the front door, slamming it behind me with the words "You're not my daughter anymore". I think this is when I finally realised I was a commodity to him, only useful as a pawn to get my mother back.

It was night time and winter. I didn't have a coat or money to take a bus to my sister's which was quite far out of town and so I set off for my mother's flat in Infirmary Street. She had moved into it a few weeks prior and was sharing with another lady, who like herself, needed support. My mother was delighted to see me. She didn't realise the implications for her. I stayed the night there, and next morning, having been reported to the landlord by her flatmate, my mother was visited by the housing officer and told that she would have to leave if she wanted me with her as there were no dependents allowed in the flat. My mother's social worker contacted Women's Aid and explained I had been thrown out by my father. I was at an awkward age, almost officially an adult but still at school and so it must have been difficult for them to know what to do with me.

My mother wanted us to be together so we were offered a room in a refuge in Gilmerton and moved in that day. I collected belongings from my father's house in dribs and drabs over the next few weeks, arranging with my brother to let me in when my father was out. I felt very worried about my brother, and guilty for leaving him behind. Not long afterwards he was admitted to hospital where he remained for the next 15 years.

It was difficult to study in the Women's Aid refuge. My mother was like an excitable child and required a lot of support and attention from me. There was another woman living there with two young children who made a lot of noise too and so I tried when I could to go to the Central Library on George IV Bridge. It was close to my school and open till late in the evening. To my mother, having me there without my father was a fantasy come true. She saw it as an opportunity to confide in me all the more. My head was bursting with her tales: having had her teeth punched out by my father when they were first married; my grandmother calling her a 'foreign whore', and all the other stories I had heard a thousand times before I even learned to speak. Sometimes I felt like a tape machine with her voice going round in a loop. I developed a sort of 'trauma fatigue' like a soldier beaten down with the sound of gunfire. Even at school I had no relief as she developed a habit of randomly turning up with sweets and asking the teachers to take me out of class. It was embarrassing but my mother had no awareness of the effect she was having on me. To her it was all just a big adventure.

One day at school our headmaster, Mr Dames, called me out of class and stunned me with a gift of £50 in an envelope for me and my mother. He quickly explained that it was from the school hardship fund; that it was quite normal and appropriate for families who were going through difficult times to receive assistance from the school and so I should not feel embarrassed accepting it. I was so touched I didn't know how to respond. I understood the gesture to be more than monetary. It was his way of showing that the school was on my side. At such a troubling period of cares too heavy for my years it made all the difference.

Rising high

In the weeks preceding my exams we secured a Council flat in a high rise block in nearby Moredun where my sister lived. I was delighted to be leaving the refuge as I had felt very self-conscious being there with young children and, rightly or wrongly, I felt that the support workers blamed me for my mother's situation. Certainly none of them ever offered me a listening ear. They were evasive and so protective of my mother that it felt as if they were being hostile to me. This is a sense I have absorbed from the people around my mother all my life. She is so vulnerable that the people supporting her are wary of others around her. As a child and teenager this was particularly difficult as it made me feel, not only that my needs weren't important, but also that I was part of the problem. Moving into a flat of our own and having space for myself was therefore welcome and seemed like a positive turn in our fortunes. Then something happened which set us back to square one.

My father always managed to track my mother down. When my paternal grandmother died my mother took him back out of pity for his loss as much as from his powerful persuasion. I say 'took him back' because this time he moved out of East London Street and came to live with us in the high rise. This happened in the middle of my exams, and while part of me wanted to support my father and was relieved to have some of the intensity of my mother's presence lifted, I also felt angry with them both for all the upheaval during my exams. I couldn't articulate this to anyone because my grandmother had just died and everybody else in the family seemed pleased to see them back together. Inevitably I felt guilty for being selfish but I was now beginning to realise just how selfish they had been with me all my life.

Nonetheless, I was welcoming and loving to my father and, though I never liked my grandmother, went through the motions of grief for his sake. In a rare display of assertiveness my mother insisted she would not go back to East London Street and so my father sold the house and bought a flat for the three of us in Dalkeith Road. We moved out of Moredun and went to live there. As the house in East London Street was in such disrepair, it went for a fraction of its value and we could only afford a small flat with one bedroom for my parents and a tiny box-room for me.

9 out of 10 stats

I was disappointed with my 'O' grade results though had passed nine out of the ten, narrowly missing Maths by 2%. It felt churlish to dwell on the level of my grades which I felt could have been better when everyone else was delighted with how I had done. My brother and sisters had not been academic at school and so my achievements seemed outstanding to the family.

I went into fifth year choosing Highers in English, Spanish, History and Biology, and to re-sit 'O' grade Maths. On my 16th birthday my elder sister, Lena, and two little nieces bought me a beautiful tortoise-shell cat called Sacha. She was the sweetest most affectionate cat I have ever known and I loved her with all my heart. She used to come into bed with me, her body under the covers, head on the pillow next to mine and her paws round my neck as though we were lovers. She got jealous when my attention was on study and would sit on top of my papers demanding with a purr that could waken an elephant that I stroke her.

It was that year, 1987, that I started going out with a boy in the year above called Niall. He was in my Higher History class and set about wooing me with aeroplane love notes and footsie under the table. We went out for four months. It felt like my first serious relationship with a boyfriend and I fancied him like my pants were on fire. We would mostly hang out in his bedroom at his parents' flat. The heavy petting felt like torture, stopping as it always did before we went too far. That Christmas I bought him a green stripy granddad shirt from Burtons which was the most grown up thing I could think of. I had a part-time job as a bar supper waitress in the Grange Hotel which meant I could afford the little rites of passage towards becoming an adult: 18 certificate films, underage drinking, deodorant, and buying clothes for a boyfriend.

Teenage kicks

Niall dumped me not long after Christmas which upset me so much that I asked his friend Connor out on a date! We arranged to see *Fatal Attraction* at the ABC on Lothian Road and I had the audacity to turn up almost an hour late to find him standing there in the rain—the queue long gone—with a wilted red rose in his hand. He wasn't the slightest bit angry. In fact he looked as if all his Fridays had come at once. To my great surprise I felt the first stirrings of ardour. Of course we had missed the film and so we went across the road to the Burnt Post for a Jack Daniels and Coke. I was 16, he was eighteen months older and the pub was our oyster. We cuddled up with the sound of cupid singing in our ears. He walked me home through the Meadows gallantly piggybacking me over puddles and ditches. I was so happy my pink stiletto heels felt like magic slippers. When we reached my doorstep he kissed me softly on the lips.

Connor became my boyfriend for the next eighteen months, seeing me into my first year at university. When it was time for him to leave school (the year before me) I accompanied him to the sixth year prom feeling terribly proud of myself — the only fifth year girl at the party! I wore my sister's knockout silver satin dress and the customary pink stilettos. My perm was backcombed and set with a whole can of hairspray into a dome resembling a stone poodle. It was the 80's and I looked a zillion dollars! Connor wore a rather stuffy pin stripe navy suit and red bowtie. I was secretly disappointed that he didn't have a black 'tuxedo' like all the other guys. His business-savvy father had thought it more prudent to buy him a functional suit that would do him for work too.

Connor's father was in fact exceedingly rich and the family lived in a grand old house with a tower set in nearly 8 acres of land with a quarter mile driveway up to the door. We jokingly referred to it as 'the castle'. Connor's bedroom was in the turret. He was a strapping lad of 6'2", broad shoulders, dark haired and quietly handsome. He had no idea what a catch he was because he was just too darned nice. He never flaunted the family wealth or judged other people on that basis. Add to that he was a drummer in a blues band — be still my beating heart! I wondered what such a teen idol was doing with plain mousy me.

For the first year of our relationship I got on well with his family. I dined at the castle and they took me out for fancy lunches. They suffered my eccentric parents with politeness when they met, and Connor's mum, a lovely woman, often took my mother out for coffee and cakes. I must have seemed a dismal catch for their son. They were an extremely devout family. Each of the three boys remained altar servers into adulthood whereas my family only sporadically went to Mass on Sundays. None of us fasted during Lent or observed Holy Feast Days. We didn't even know when they were. Although I loved attending Mass with Connor's family and was moved to tears by the hymns, had they known about my somewhat over-ripe appetite for heavy petting with their son they would have found me a far from suitable girlfriend.

Although we never went 'all the way' I think it is fair to say that I led Connor astray. He was generous and obliging, and in every sense met his duties as the perfect 'trophy boyfriend'. Indeed I think some of my girlfriends at school were quite envious of the fact I had managed to bag him.

Unravelling

During this time there were the Higher exams. I was studying diligently with Sacha the cat—when I wasn't devouring Connor in his gothic tower! The situation at home had improved somewhat and there were moments of real levity when I entertained my parents with caricatures of Italian ladies from my childhood. 'Maria Foch' was a particular invention. She had a fur coat, thick accent and no inhibitions! In what seemed like no time at all my personality had transformed from a quiet downtrodden girl to a fast-talking headstrong young woman confident of her abilities. Little did I know it then but this was an early sign of the bipolar affective disorder which would dog my life as an adult.

During my Highers the cracks started to appear though not in any way I could then recognise. I was irritable and moody, which had not been my nature up till now, and somewhat reckless—getting drunk and staying out all night. I even walked out of my Higher History exam half way through the first paper because I couldn't concentrate. My teacher was furious. I had been his star pupil and was tipped to win the year prize for History, but now I'd blown it all in what seemed to him like a gung-ho show of teenage rebellion. I couldn't articulate to him, far less to myself that my tightly coiled mental state was beginning to unravel. To the rest of the world around I must have seemed high-spirited. It was exhilarating to have this new found confidence at my fingertips though I felt a little frightened of the monster which was being unleashed.

My Higher results came. I had done quite well and even managed a C in History. Under my belt were secure unconditional offers for the five top Scottish universities. How the girl who had left primary school with the taint of the dunce still on her head had come into her own! I elected to study Joint Honours in Spanish and Italian at Edinburgh University, a choice governed by my fear of not being able to cope or make friends in a new city. My unconditional acceptance meant that my sixth year at school was academically pressure-free. I took full advantage of the opportunity to laze around all year, studying for only one Certificate of Sixth Year Studies in Spanish, and a re-sit of Higher History to upgrade it to an A.

Practice makes prefect

On October 11th 1988 — my seventeenth birthday — Mr Dames, our headmaster, came into the common room and said "Congratulations Joanna, you have been elected Head Girl". I was ecstatic. In truth I had fantasised about this moment from my first day at St Thomas' back in 1983. Being voted Head Girl by a consensus of the teachers and my peers seemed the ultimate endorsement and I knew my parents would be immensely proud of me. I couldn't wait to rush home and tell them. I bunked off school early and raced across the Meadows to our house. When I broke the news to my parents my father's chest puffed up like a swan and tears welled up in his eyes. My mother threw her arms around me and cried "My baby, my baby!" It was the proudest moment of my life and, I believe, theirs. One could almost forget what a traumatised dysfunctional family we were.

A week or so later came the school prize-giving at Methodist Central Hall. This was the first public event at which my friend Freddie and I were to officiate as the new Head Boy and Girl. When the headmaster called on us to give thank you speeches, the audience started cheering as we floated up to the stage like pop stars on a red carpet. My new found flamboyance suited such occasions well. When it was my turn to speak I held on to the microphone a little too long and enjoyed the moment more than I should have as a trusted public 'servant'. I think Freddie was a little irritated by the way I hogged the limelight. It wouldn't be the last time I'd put a man's nose out of joint by being too full of myself.

The remainder of that year proved a showcase for my burgeoning celebrity. In Spanish I won the school prize, became Editor of the magazine, and was asked by Miss Dugan to host the Spanish evening at which there would be 200 or so parents, teachers and pupils. My sister's silver dress was duly taken down from the hanger; the perm back-combed and sprayed into its 'poodle' and the microphone took flight as I dazzled the audience with my witty banter and general wonderfulness. It is excruciating now for me to reflect on the vanity of my Cilla Black moments but such inflated egos are the stuff of hyper-mania, as of course is the inevitable come-down and the mortified insight that follows.

Up and down like a Jo Jo

What I haven't explained yet is that my moods are generally rapid-cycling. At the onset of my illness I experienced this as a particularly alarming assault on the senses. It would take many years to develop the insight and experience to recognise the peaks and troughs for what they were. The hallucinating to come would tip me off the edge of the see-saw.

Mr Walls had ears

I mentioned that I was studying in sixth year for CSYS Spanish. Miss Dugan was still my teacher for the bulk of my lessons, but now Mr Walls — who had not taught me since first year, but whom I had always held in high regard, offered to take me for Spanish literature. He chose the work of Federico Garcia Lorca and we set about unpicking his rich imagery of gypsy feuds and shotgun weddings in rural Spain at the time of the Spanish Civil War when he was writing. Mr Walls was a shrewd and gifted teacher and a seer into the human soul. He knew I think before anyone else did, how much I was suffering inside and he used the yearning heartache of Lorca's poems and plays to tap into my hidden pain.

Soon I began to open up and confide in him some of the terrible secrets buried all these years in the guise of 'good little girl'. He was visibly distressed at some of the things I told him, and being a caring man and a conscientious guidance teacher (though not my own), he realised he had a duty to intervene. I will always be grateful for his courage in being the first person to stand up to my father, and for his deep humanity and kindness to me.

Though the abuse at home had ended Mr Walls could see that it was toxic for me to be in that house with my parents so he set about applying to get me a Council flat. Meanwhile he referred me to the Royal Edinburgh Hospital's Young people's Unit (YPU) where I started to see my first psychiatrist, Dr Lomax, for weekly sessions. It was spring 1989, a few months before I was due to leave school.

Dr Lomax was in her mid twenties, extremely pretty and stylish — not at all what I had expected a psychiatrist to be like. I quickly developed an intense attachment to her and it was liberating to be able to talk so freely about my inner turmoil with someone who really seemed to care. But our sessions were painful too. I began to see from her reaction just how dysfunctional and damaging my upbringing had been and that my troubled mental state was far from normal.

Bad apple

Connor had told his parents that I was preparing to move into a Council flat and his father, horrified at the thought, or moved with pity — I'm not sure which — insisted that I go to live instead with *his* mother, Connor's grandmother, in Claremont Crescent near my old family home. I had been accepted for Mylne's Court halls of residence on the High Street following a special request to Edinburgh University on my behalf from Mr Dames. I was due to move in at the start of my degree in October. Lodging at Connor's grandmother's house was to be just a temporary stopgap over the spring and summer. 'Nan Fifi' as she was known in the family, and I was encouraged to call her too, was extremely kind to me. She had a gem of a cat called Piddles, black and soft as a bunny, which would wrap his paws round my neck and let me carry him round the house like a baby. I felt happy and safe for the brief time I was there.

Connor's family also invited me to go on holiday with them to Mallorca in June. The holiday was a disaster. As my moods rollercoasted and the traumas being unearthed in my psychotherapy sessions with Dr Lomax threatened to overwhelm me, I became increasingly obstreperous and difficult to manage. Poor Connor was a receptacle for my distress and he tried hard to comfort me as I groped around in a quagmire whilst trying to make sense of the blizzard in my head. The distress played out in flagrant sexual behaviour under his parents' noses. We would 'creep' into each other's rooms and thrash about so that everybody could hear.

The atmosphere became frosty and terse. In a last ditch attempt to curb our behaviour, Connor's father dispatched his daughter and her fiancé to speak to us, reckoning that they would be more influential as closer to us in age. My reaction was like a volcanic eruption. I stormed off telling them to mind their own business. In truth I was ashamed but I wasn't going to admit it. I was too proud to apologise so I dug my heels in and continued to flaunt our wanton behaviour. Connor was confused and hurt, torn between wanting to obey his father and yet not wanting to infuriate me by withdrawing intimacy when I was so volatile. The holiday came to an end in a bitter stalemate. Connor's father, his sister and her fiancé refused to acknowledge me and when we got back to Edinburgh it was made clear to me that I was no longer welcome in his grandmother's house.

Having arrived like Oliver Twist at my rich benefactor's home a few months earlier and opened the window to a street full of singing, dancing possibility, I was now sent packing in utter disgrace to fend for myself. School may have ended but my education had yet to begin.

Preparing for the Fall
UNIVERSITY | 1989–1991

Following my nose dive from grace I went back to live with my parents for the summer till the start of university. I worked from June to August as a waitress in The Pancake Place at the West End. The hours were long and tiring and I struggled to keep up, particularly because of my dyspraxia (then undiagnosed) which meant I was forever being told off for being slow and clumsy. Eventually I was fired, or rather, politely advised that maybe the service industry wasn't for me.

Meanwhile I was seeing Dr Lomax for weekly sessions at the Young People's Unit (YPU) who was delving deeper into my childhood trauma. I don't remember much from those early sessions other than the comfort and relief of having somebody kind to talk to at a time of such upheaval in my life.

Connor and I were still seeing each other without his father's consent, but the relationship was just limping towards its inevitable end. The shame hanging over us proved insurmountable and we broke up at the end of October.

Fresh-faced and raring to go

October was also the month I turned 18 and, more significantly, the start of university. I arrived at Mylne's Court halls of residence on the Royal Mile at lunchtime on a Sunday, full of trepidation and excitement to be leaving home. My parents dropped me off in the car with my bags containing everything but the broken toaster! They left tearfully soon after — a mixture of pride and grief in their hearts to see me start on this brand new chapter of my life.

My room-mate, a tall leggy blonde called Greta, was enrolled to study Medicine. She seemed to have it all: beauty, brains, affluence, and an ease of manner which suggested she had glided through her life up to now with minimum effort. Greta was extremely friendly and I couldn't believe my luck in landing such a decent room-mate.

The next few hours were buzzing with new arrivals, some of them freshers like me, others seasoned travellers on the path to their degrees. Two second year students occupying the two rooms next to ours (only first years had to share) arrived in the flurry of activity within an hour or so of each other. Annalise — spelt with two A's — turned out to be a straight A scholar. She was a softly spoken English girl, posh and pretty with a waist size to die for. The other student was Marcia (affectionately known as the Marchioness) who would become hugely significant in my life and remains a close friend to this day.

To the manor born

It would not be overstating the case to say I fell madly in love with Marcia from that first moment she said hello. She was tall, a good foot taller than me, with long hair which was thick, black and wavy. She was elegantly clad in racing green trousers with a wine coloured waistcoat — dapper you might say, though very feminine. She struck me immediately as being a classy lady who stood out in many ways from her peers. I was dazzled and when she introduced herself it felt like she was offering an invitation to the palace of Versailles. I took every opportunity to be in her company. I might as well have camped outside her door for all the blatantly contrived excuses to knock on it. I even stooped to borrowing a cup of sugar though I take my coffee without!

That first Sunday at Mylne's Court a group of us from my floor initiated a bond by going out together to see a film: *The Dead Poets*

Society. We walked through George IV Bridge and across the university campus, heading for Clerk Street to the Odeon. Sitting through the film, I felt as though a weight had lifted. Robin Williams' golden words pirouetted in my head: *Carpe Deum, Carpe Deum*—time to grasp this new adventure, to boldly leap into the future without parachute or the fear of going back.

Student life at first did not disappoint. The exhilaration of freshers' week provided a welcome veneer for my ongoing inner turmoil. But soon old demons were to rear their ugly heads. My first year subjects were Spanish, Italian and Linguistics. With a combined total of 15 hours for lectures and tutorials I had lots of unstructured time between classes. This 'free' time became a necessary evil in terms of my crumbling mental state and I found that I couldn't keep up with what little academic demands there were.

Breaking up with Connor that autumn was painful. It felt as if the decision had been forced on us and, though we both knew it was for the best, it was difficult to say goodbye. Of course there were the usual platitudes about staying in touch but our lives were going in different directions and the night we tearfully broke up turned out to be the last time I ever saw him. I will always remember him with deep affection.

Meeting Marcia was like switching television stations from drama to thriller. Soon she became the focus of my every thought and all my time was channelled into being around her. She was in the Savoy Opera Group (a student Gilbert & Sullivan society), and the Officer Training Corps (affiliated to the Territorial Army). She was also a member of the Mylne's Court branch of Scripture Union. So naturally I became a member of all three, even though I couldn't sing, didn't approve of the Army, and the word 'scripture' frightened the BeJaysus out of me!

Scripture Union was on a Tuesday night. We were a peripatetic little gathering of modern day apostles each taking turns to host in our rooms. We'd sit on the floor round a candle with guitars and tambourines passing round the bible like a newborn babe. I remember a lanky bespectacled guy with long hair called Richard who seemed to have taken it upon himself to lead the informal worship. He would address his prayer to 'Father God' which, as an inhibited Catholic, always used to make me giggle. The presence of the Marchioness, with whom I was now consumed, added a frisson to the muted disapproval in the room.

Marcia, God bless her, never complained about my following her around her extra-curricular clock, though I often wondered if it irritated her to find a doting little sidekick tucked under her arm wherever she went.

Tripping hither, tripping thither...

My status in the Savoy Opera Group was as something of a 'groupie'—always tagging on to post-rehearsal chill outs in the pub; lending my services for flyering, or just turning up at parties uninvited. Of course I enjoyed the music and lyrics (how can one not be utterly charmed by Gilbert & Sullivan?) and it was the spark which ignited my legendary 'love of the arts'. Before university I had barely set foot in a theatre. However the main attraction on-stage and off was the Marchioness. I will never forget sitting third row from the back of the Churchill Theatre watching her in full regalia play the Faerie Queen in *Iolanthe*. How I wished I were one of those faeries 'tripping hither, tripping thither' to her every whim.

Another significant figure to enter my life at this time through the Savoy Opera Group was Michael. At 6'4" Michael towered over me, a sturdy oak of a man with a gravelly voice that belied his tender years. He was only eighteen months older than me. Sensing my need for a protective influence, Michael became infatuated with me. I became very fond of him too though could not return the ardour of his feelings as I was so fixated on the Marchioness. Nonetheless he persisted, enticed by my unavailability, and our friendship blossomed.

My memories of hanging out with the Savoy crowd are among the happiest of my university years. Being accepted into the bosom of bohemia opened up a whole new sphere of influence. I was hugely inspired by these bold, generous spirits some of whom later gave up their careers in Law and Medicine to pursue a life on the stage. When Michael became President of the Savoy one year later, my membership by proxy was confirmed. The next step was to don the greasepaint and tights and strut the boards myself.

Reluctant recruit

The other society I followed Marcia blindly into was the Officer Training Corps. This involved a gruelling 'familiarisation' weekend at Warcop barracks in Cumbria to assess whether I was fit to wear the Queen's khaki. The things I did for love! The basic fitness test (BFT) I had to pass was as far as I can remember a 2.2 mile run in under 19 minutes at the end of which I was practically horizontal with breathlessness. Getting up at 5am for star jumps and tag proved a bit of a chore too. I enjoyed drill though because military etiquette dictates that an army should march 'at the pace of the slowest man'. In case of doubt, I was always the slowest 'man'. Because I am so small my leg length was shorter than average. That meant I had to practically jump from one foot to another to qualify at a reasonable pace. Not only did this look untidy but I just couldn't keep up and so I reverted to my pint size dawdle which made me very popular with the other recruits who could now legitimately slacken their own pace.

I also had to give a 5 minute lecture as part of the assessment—to evidence I had the makings of an officer. This was the only test of the whole weekend in which I managed with any competence and which was to swing it for me. In the OTC leadership potential is everything. The rest they can drum into you.

The most memorable part of the weekend however—for all the wrong reasons—was my inept attempt at the assault course. I would have run a mile were I not frog-marched by the Regimental Sergeant Major (RSM) through each obstacle. When presented with the first of these, a twenty foot scramble-net climbing frame, I winced in horror. I confess I actually started to cry, bleating to the RSM "I can't do it Sir, I'm scared of heights". "Miss McFarlane, you WILL do it!" came the resolute reply. He detailed four beefy men to take position around me, one in front, one behind, one on either side. They practically shouldered me like a hovercraft over the frame while the RSM barked orders from below.

Next came the 'Burma Bridge' — two narrow planks of wood, one in front of the other with a 2 foot gap between them suspended high above the ground. I might have fainted at this point had the RSM not slapped my back in a gung ho attempt to keep me upright. What I haven't mentioned yet is that the whole regiment of 200 or so was assembled along the sidelines to cheer me on. It had become something of a circus and they were all chanting "Come on Munchie (short for Munchkin — my new nickname), you can do it!" Of course this only added to the torture. The RSM took my hand and led me whimpering up the ladder to the first plank of wood. He ascended first then coaxed me gently on beside him. We sidled along shakily hand in hand with the crowd below hushed in trepidation. Then it was time to step-leap over the two foot gap to the other plank of wood. For the life of me, I don't know how I managed not to fall. My balance is generally very shaky. I suppose with a grimacing sergeant major, 200 baying wolfhounds and twenty feet between me and the ground, adrenalin at last came into play.

I don't remember the next few obstacles, just the Tarzan rope on which I had to swing across a ditch of mud to reach the finishing line. By this time I couldn't have cared less. Grasping the rope with puny strength I kicked off and fell straight into the mud. I had to be dredged out and taken back to do it again. Realising I had no upper arm strength of my own, the RSM climbed on the rope with me and, after locking me in a very compromising hold, we swung like lovers on the vine to the other side. I then had to blaze my trail of glory for the last hundred yards to the finishing line whereupon I crumpled in a heap on the ground and sobbed with a mixture of pride, self-pity and relief that it was all over.

Spit and polish

Also during the Warcop weekend my friend, Bruna, entered my life. It was in the billet that I first saw her. She was bulling her Size 6 combat boots — rubbing spit and polish with a rag in tiny circles on the toecap. Bruna is one of those people whose face reeks of mischief even when she's doing something innocuous like preparing her kit for inspection. Her chocolate tousled curls were scraped back into the obligatory netted bun revealing the barely suppressed expression of someone about to explode into giggles. What was she laughing at, I wondered? Then I saw it: a plastic jobby on my pillow!

Soon we were both crumpled in hysterics and that set the tone for our long friendship. Had I known then she'd become my best friend over all these years I would have somersaulted for joy. She was quite simply the most audacious, fun-loving person I had ever met. During the entire weekend we stole every opportunity to mess around whilst under the scrutiny of Miss Runcie — a somewhat stern 2nd lieutenant who had won the Cane of Honour at Sandhurst and who amused us immensely with her marble-mouthed delivery.

When it was time to return to the OTC base at Forest Hill I had come to the conclusion that — despite all the trauma of PT and press-ups, spray starch and drill — with a chum like Bruna to see me through, this military fandango might actually turn out to be quite a lark. So when I was accepted I eagerly took up the offer of a place in Kohima Platoon alongside Bruna, seven other female recruits, and 16 men. The following Wednesday, our weekly night for meeting, I was sent to the quartermaster to collect my kit. Proud as Munch I was in my dinky uniform and size 2 boots. The enemy would wet themselves when faced with such a terrifying sight!

I could regale details of covert military operations and nocturnal manoeuvres, being deployed to war zones around the country and holding out under enemy fire… but it is more entertaining to focus on the scrapes and japes I got up to with Bruna!

Bruna was a genius in the art of evasion, always finding shortcuts and excuses to get out of trials and chores. At the end of a weekend away we'd have to 'hand over' the barracks to the hosting regiment in pristine condition, which meant a flurry of scrubbing floors and polishing banisters on Sunday morning. It was sacrilege to shirk duty. Bruna, however, figured that if we marched up and down the corridors with a purposeful air people would think we had already been detailed to perform some or other task and would leave us alone. Bruna had primed me to say "We're on an errand for the Colonel" if anyone asked what we were up to. Nobody would argue with that. Once or twice we were even brazen enough to hide under the bed in an unused billet and nap till all the cleaning was over. There was also the smug satisfaction of rolling out of bed with our PT kit still on from the night before to save time in the morning. We were always getting into trouble, Bruna for her blatant disobedience, me for my unwitting incompetence.

There was a sound dictum which ascribed teamwork over self-advancement. We were told in no uncertain terms that we were expected to help each other, particularly the slower or weaker among us. As the slowest and weakest member of our platoon this worked very much in my favour!

A competition was held each year culminating in Recruits' Cadre to determine the Best Female, Best Male, Most Improved Cadet, and the Best Platoon. The stakes were high. In the competitive environment of ambitious eighteen year olds everybody wanted to win. To win meant going out of your way to impress the sergeants and officers. Obviously I could not compete but became part of the equation as a useful prop for all the other girls to demonstrate acts of self-sacrifice in the cause of the greater-good. In other words they were tripping over themselves to help me. In the morning I'd have several girls fussing over me with kirby grips for my hair and sellotape to de-fluff my beret. I was never short of a helping hand to dismantle my sub-machine gun or fix my gas mask—all done in full view of the officers. Of course it was a symbiotic relationship and I lapped up all the help I could get.

There was one person who disapproved thoroughly of this unspoken arrangement: my section commander, Miss Runcie. She had ambitions for me to win the 'Most Improved Cadet' award—the only award realistically available to me—and she took it upon herself to make a proper soldier out of me. This was most inconvenient from my point of view as it meant I was forever being punished for falling short of the mark. If she caught me with my epilettes askew or my laces undone, I'd get an extra stint of guard duty. A more serious misdemeanour like forgetting to fill up my water bottle before a military exercise— being dehydrated is in nobody's interest—meant a curfew from the bar or, worst-case-scenario, a severe 'beasting' in front of the platoon. Beasting, now outlawed in the British Army, was a process whereby you were driven to physical and emotional extremes by having orders and insults screamed in your ear while being forced to do press-ups or run uphill at superhuman speed. Basically anything short of physical assault was permitted in order to break your resolve. It was a terrifying prospect for a lily-livered mite like me.

Most of the sergeants and officers took pity on me—one of the rare occasions when being 4' 10" was advantageous—and our platoon commander, Mr Shipley, used to consistently turn a blind eye to my insufficiently polished buttons and 'tramline' creases. One of the other recruits, a rather ungallant young man, complained about this blatant favouritism and Mr Shipley replied "Oh come on, could you send Munchie to gaol?" (gaol being another term for a beasting).

Miss Runcie however was having none of it. To her I was neither cute nor vulnerable, just a wayward shirker to be knocked into shape. Everybody knew I was frightened of her and it became a sport among the girls to wind me up about it. I was well-known for my gullibility and some of the others were ruthless in exploiting this.

Ranting Runcie

One dismal Friday night in December we were heading in a truck on exercise to a training camp at Garelochead near Faslane nuclear base in the West of Scotland. The air was doom-laden as we knew this was going to be our toughest challenge yet—a simulated war between the platoons, open range blank fire, full camouflage and camping out in sub-zero conditions.

The atmosphere in the truck was so heavy that we needed a clown to cheer us up. One of the other girls, Dot, notorious for her pranks, suddenly piped up "Munchie did you remember to pack your swimming costume?". "It wasn't on the kit list" I replied earnestly. "Oh my God" said she in horror, "you mean you didn't see it?". "No" I laughed nervously "It wasn't there". Surely they wouldn't have us swimming in these temperatures, I thought. She must be kidding me on. "Oh Munchie" she lamented gravely, "Miss Runcie's going to kill you. You'll just have to wear a black bin liner in the river." I searched the others' faces for confirmation that it was a joke, and they too were full of concern. I started to panic. "Are you sure?" I said, "I definitely didn't see it on the list?". "Don't worry Munchie. Maybe she won't be too hard on you, since this is war. I went completely quiet in a concerted effort to hold back the tears. I was in for it now!

Of course there was no swimming but I still managed to fall foul of Miss Runcie's temper that weekend. We had been told the Wednesday before that we would need thermal underwear and it should be green 'army issue'. As there hadn't been any left when I reached the quartermaster at the start of term, I decided to make do with the next best thing: skin tight pyjamas. Only they were white, with pink teddy-bears. "Ach well, no one's going to see them", I thought, "We'll be camping out all weekend without a change of underwear".

When we arrived at our position we were told to pitch our bivouacs and bed down for the night. We would be taking our usual turns to do guard duty, and some of us would be detailed through the night for reconnaissance on the enemy platoon. It was so cold (we were literally lying on a sheet of ice) that I didn't get a wink of sleep all night. My body was bumping and rattling off the ground with shivers such as I'd never known before. And so when at 2.15am Miss Runcie tapped on my shoulder and gave me the signal to join the reconnaissance party, I was for once glad of the opportunity to get up. I picked up my personal weapon, a sub machine gun or SMG (everything in the army is ascribed a TLA — three letter alphabet!) and groped through the dark to find the others. We stalked like panthers a hundred yards or so, weapons poised to fire, till we came to a barbed wire fence, about five feet in height. As always I was the last to climb it, struggling to get my legs over the top without touching the wire. I gingerly lowered my bottom and tried to jump the distance, but my combat trousers ripped on a spike which had penetrated the fabric though thankfully stopping short of flesh. I was stuck like that dangling on the fence for a few moments, whispering "help!" to my comrades up ahead. Miss Runcie stomped over to me, rather loudly, I thought, and not very tactical. She yanked me off the fence. The seat of my combats came right off exposing my pyjamas. Miss Runcie shone her torch on my derriere to assess the damage.

"Teddy bears!" she had to stop herself from yelling. "The enemy will see you a bloody mile off!"

As you can imagine, and pun entirely intended, I was the butt of jokes for the rest of the weekend. This episode competes with being locked up two years later in the Intensive Psychiatric Care Unit as the worst weekend of my life. At least it was warm in the IPCU!

Bad table manners

What this comedy of errors belies is the bleak mental state into which I was plunging deeper. I had become affectionately known as the regimental 'mascot' because of my morale boosting powers—attributable to the hilarity I brought to others over my ridiculous height and farcical incompetence rather than by dint of any virtue. Dot, whom I mentioned earlier, sometimes took the ridicule too far. At mealtimes if there were no officers around she would get me to stand on the table, just stand there, while everybody pointed at me and laughed. Because I was so dependent on them all for help I felt I had to go along with it though, to be honest, my low self-esteem meant I probably would have anyway. It bothered Bruna. She became fiercely protective towards me, especially as she knew I wasn't well.

Before I continue with more army tales I will go back to my psychiatrist, Dr Lomax, for a 'check up from the neck up'. I had started feeling suicidal and was struggling to get up to face each day. Disturbing thoughts and flashbacks were getting in the way of study and I was forgetful, anxious and confused. Dr Lomax asked me to do a Beck's Inventory — a questionnaire that assessed levels of clinical depression. I scored very high and she decided to start me on Amitriptyline, a tri-cyclic anti-depressant that was in common use back then. I was reluctant to take them as they made me foggy and sluggish but Dr Lomax encouraged me to persevere and soon I started to get some relief if only because my senses were so dulled that I had a layer of insulation from intrusive thoughts. At this point I hadn't started hearing voices or visually hallucinating. That was to come the following year along with more extreme mood swings and crippling paranoia.

My friends in Mylne's Court were starting to notice how troubled I was, in particular Marcia, with whom I had become obsessed, and who became the conduit for much of my distress. I started to see her as the cause and answer to all my problems. If only she would love me back everything would fall into place. I became particularly fixated on sad music, associating it with the hopeless nature of my love. Albinoni's *Adagio* and a borrowed Paul McCartney album from my roommate, *Give My Regards to Broad Street*, stand out in my memory during this time. I would play the tracks *Here, There and Everywhere* and *Yesterday* as expressions of devotion and of my desperation for the pain to go away. Marcia told me years later that she could hear the songs playing over and over from her room and it disturbed her to know I was thinking about her with such morose longing.

Going through the motions

As if to relieve the intensity of my obsession, a man called Steven came into my life. Steven was a senior cadet in the OTC who took a shine to me from the start and set about wooing me by bestowing favours he had access to by dint of his senior rank. He had aspirations to join the military police following graduation and cut a dash among his peers, looking toned and handsome in his uniform. It was really exciting being pursued by someone so sexy and desirable. He was five years older than me and seemed suave and worldly. I remember being particularly impressed by the fact he had a car with a personalised number plate and that his father was a Harley Street eye surgeon.

Steven owned a flat in the New Town which he shared with two female students. He was somewhat narcissistic and always liked to surround himself with women. I never quite understood what he saw in me but in those days I had quite a few admirers—all the more curious given my disturbed mental state. Perhaps I hid it all a little too well from other people. The relationship became physical and I recall that he was a very generous lover—a department in which he did not enjoy much return. I had developed vaginismus, a condition caused by fear of sex which constricts the vagina and prevents penetration. There are a number of explanations for the condition. In my case it was probably a combination of them all: the trauma of childhood abuse being revisited in my sessions with Dr Lomax; the recent shame of my sex life with Connor played out publicly to the disapproval of his family; and finally my depression and medication both of which drastically reduced my libido. Nonetheless Steven persevered. Perhaps his ego responded to the challenge.

I don't have many happy memories of that relationship. To be fair to Steven, this was caused more by my depression than any fault of his but we were never natural soul mates. My obsession with Marcia left little room in my consciousness for a boyfriend, even as considerable a catch as Steven. One night, on the dot of twelve, he sprung to his feet and declared "I'm taking you on a mystery ride". Wow, what an allegory that turned out to be! We leapt into the car half-naked and drove to the Forth Road Bridge, which might have been romantic were it not for my recent preoccupation with jumping off that same bridge. I hadn't yet told Steven about my depression, the medication or seeing a psychiatrist, but the look of petrified horror on my face as we stood looking down to the water probably told him all he needed to know. We got in the car and turned back home. Parallel thoughts of dumping and jumping hung in the silence between us.

In terms of study I was only just managing to meet essay deadlines. I have always been fastidious about punctuality; it would pain me to hand in an assignment late. However, that does not say much for the quality of what I was producing—at least by my own reckoning. Because I had got an 'A' in Sixth Year Studies Spanish I was placed in the top tutorial group (there were six in all). I was not happy about this as I didn't feel up to the level of the other students. I asked to be moved down but my Director of Studies insisted that I was advanced enough to remain. Indeed she told me that she expected me, or at any rate thought that I was bright enough, to get a First class Honours. All I had to do was put the work in. Therein lay the rub.

My extra-curricular activities, the Savoy and OTC, not to mention my relationship with Steven, took up a lot of time—all useful distraction when my head just wasn't in a place to study. My roommate, Greta, a medical student, by contrast had to work late every night on top of a full timetable of classes. I would saunter in from the pub at some ridiculous hour to find her sprawled on the floor with anatomy charts and bones littered about the room. It was hard not to trip over them, especially after a few vodkas and Coke! She became irritated by my laziness and this sometimes soured the atmosphere between us but generally we got on well. Perhaps this was because our lives didn't coincide beyond meals or bedtime.

Social class 3

Greta had a twin sister called Trudy. Like me, they were cradle Catholics but had missed Confirmation in childhood and were now about to be confirmed as adults in their home town of Prestwick. I was surprised and honoured when Greta asked me to be her sponsor. After the Mass we stayed overnight in her family home which I found difficult. Greta's parents were educated and well-off, a far cry from my own, and I felt intimidated in their company. They were perfectly nice to me but I felt I didn't have anything interesting to add to the conversation so I was shy and awkward. This was a situation I commonly experienced when with university friends. Although I espoused equality at a moral and intellectual level, my troubled working class background left me feeling unworthy.

Marcia had also invited me home overnight to her parents' house in Lenzie which I enjoyed. That was the first time I had been to Glasgow on the train. Her family were friendly and warm; down to earth yet exotic in their choice of puddings. They introduced me to Ice Cream Mars Bars which I became rather partial to thereafter; that and granny Macrae's secret recipe 'bombe'—an explosion of whipped cream compacted into a ball. Marcia and her younger sister sang and played the piano for our evening entertainment. The absence of such harmony and cultured pleasures in my own upbringing left me feeling very emotional. Of course it all added up to the ideal in my head which I had built around Marcia's background. She never fell from her pedestal—much as she would have liked to renege herself of the responsibility. The distance between us would become wider before I could overcome my infatuation and finally relax and call her an equal friend.

That first Christmas holiday from university was a challenge as I had to vacate Mylne's Court and stay with my parents till the start of the new term. They were delighted to have me home and I entertained them no end with my demonstrations of saluting and vast military knowledge. Little did they know I was considered an empty-headed space cadet.

I have not yet mentioned my nieces but all this time they were a great source of pride and delight to me. They loved it when I donned my OTC uniform and marched up and down the garden for their amusement. I had also memorised some funny songs to teach them from *Iolanthe*, quite determined as I was that they should benefit from my burgeoning repertoire. Perhaps the most enduring legacy from my undergraduate years at Edinburgh University was my initiation into the arts, and of course the friendships I developed through the OTC with Bruna and Mylne's Court with Marcia.

Staring into the abyss

In the run up to end of year exams my mental health deteriorated markedly despite increases to my dose of Amitriptyline. Dr Lomax was monitoring me much more closely now that my suicidal urges seemed likely to materialise. One night in April when my roommate, Greta, was home for the weekend, I did take an overdose and curled up in bed convinced that I would not wake up. But I did the next day, groggy and disorientated, unable to stand without falling over, and my speech was slurred to the point of being indecipherable.

Marcia got in touch with Dr Lomax who told her to bring me over to the Sick Children's Hospital where she was doing a clinic. There she informed me that I was to be admitted to the Royal Edinburgh Psychiatric Hospital. I protested vehemently. I tried to enlist Marcia to argue my case for being supported through the crisis by my friends at Mylne's Court but Dr Lomax was having none of it. She felt I needed 24 hour supervision which could only be provided in hospital and she threatened to detain me legally if I would not go in as a voluntary patient. Furthermore, she said I could not sit my exams which were in the next few weeks. If I wanted to continue with my degree I would have to re-sit First Year which she advised me to do.

I was horrified at the thought of going into hospital, especially as I was to be confined to the ward for the initial assessment period. My uppermost concern was being separated from Marcia. In the event she ended up coming to visit me almost every day in spite of her own exams which were underway. The hospital frightened me because I associated it with my mother's being there when I was a child, my brother who was still there, and my uncle who had completed suicide.

In the trenches of my logic

That first time I was only kept for three weeks. I was angry with Dr Lomax for making me miss my exams and yelled the roof down every day to get out. My Consultant Professor, who was a somewhat complacent and matriarchal figure, refused to listen to Dr Lomax. Dr Lomax had known me intimately for a year and thought that I should be transferred to the Young People's Unit for inpatient treatment. I refused to go and it fell on Professor Keene, as my Responsible Medical Officer, to make the final decision. Somehow I managed to seduce her into thinking I was well enough to be discharged.

The OTC was due to go for summer camp to a military base in the North of Germany and our Commanding Officer who did not know I was unwell had asked me to stay on afterwards to interpret for two NATO exchange visits that were taking place between our hosts and the Italian army. I had managed to convince him that I was fluent in Italian but in reality had just completed my 1st year beginners class. I knew Professor Keene would be impressed by this information so I used it to bargain my way out of hospital. Persuaded by my pretence of feeling 'much better' she said "Splendid!" and discharged me with a cheery smile.

Dr Lomax and I parted badly that summer. I felt I had paid her back for forcing me into hospital by manipulating Professor Keene to override her recommendation, while she was angry with me for pulling the wool over everyone's eyes and for running away from my problems. I can see now how much she stuck her neck out for me and I wish I had listened to her. Perhaps if I hadn't left and gone abroad my subsequent admissions would have been shorter.

In any case it was certainly clear that I was in no fit state to spend the summer playing soldiers with the army in Europe, especially as they knew nothing of my depression and could not have provided any support if I was in danger. The military is an alien environment when it comes to expression of sensitivity and feeling. It is not the done thing to admit to being emotionally vulnerable; it would jeopardize the career of anyone who chose to do so. At least that was the case back then. Had I disclosed my recent hospital admission I would have been discharged on medical grounds with immediate effect and indeed this happened to me the following year. At that point however, I did not feel ready to let go of my OTC connections, not least because I needed the income to supplement my student grant.

Enemy within

The first two weeks of my time abroad were with the whole OTC on our annual Summer Camp in Hohne military base just outside Hamburg, where we were being hosted by 40th Field Regiment Royal Artillery. Bruna got me through this in more ways than she could imagine — practically, emotionally and by sheltering me from the onslaught of other people's expectations.

A military metaphor is the most apt I can think of to describe the war zone in my head. It was not a benign melancholy but a splintering of faculties, a torture even to exist. The rapid gunfire of destructive thoughts supplanted my will to survive. On the shooting range I would have turned my rifle on myself but for the fear of botching it up. In Nuclear and Biological Warfare training I considered inhaling gas by taking off my breathing apparatus but I didn't have the stomach to withstand the burning in my throat and eyes. There just didn't seem an easy and fool-proof way to do it.

Really, I should have cut my losses and come home after the two week camp was up but there was a stubborn part of me that compelled me to sink my teeth deeper into the raw experience even if it threatened to rip me apart. And so I stayed on in Hohne for the next phase, along with Bruna and six fellow members of the Scottish Country Dance Team. At the time I had been asked to interpret, someone — probably Bruna — had persuaded the Commanding Officer to allow the dance team to join the trip to Italy and perform for the Italians as part of the cultural exchange. After all, the NATO visits were as much an exercise in diplomacy as anything else, and who could fail to be charmed by a Strathspey?

We spent the first few nights before the journey in the Officers Mess at Hohne, the most luxurious quarters we would ever be exposed to as cadets. I felt a bit calmer at that stage as there was less pressure and all our time was spent relaxing before the long bus trip to Italy. The weather was hot and we lounged about in cotton shirts and dresses. In the evenings after supper we played croquet on the lawn. There was a grand piano in the Mess, and the multi-instrumental Bruna entertained us.

I have a particularly vivid memory of her playing Scott Joplin's *The Entertainer* at break-neck speed with her head thrown back in hysterics and her fingers barely touching the keys. Yet the notes came out perfectly.

I was still anxious and troubled at times but Bruna's antics provided a soothing distraction. It was a physical relief as much as anything to laugh. My nerves had been jangling and knotting for months and the laughter was a release. Bruna seemed instinctively to know this and persevered with the 'laughter therapy'.

We departed the halcyon haven of Hohne for the long trip to L'Aquila near Rome with the dancing team and B Company 40th Field Regiment. It took over a day to get there — a hot sticky journey, unrelenting but for Bruna's ability to keep me afloat with 'pure knicker-drenching humour' — a phrase she coined on the trip.

On arrival we were met by a serenade of cat calls and wolf whistles from the Italian soldiers on balconies who watched us alight from the bus. It didn't need translation to know that their suggestions, which were clearly not directed towards the male squaddies, were highly improper and made us feel besmirched while we squirmed in our crumpled and sweaty uniforms.

We stayed in L'Aquila for two weeks — two weeks of wining and dining on grappa and peaches, prosciutto and parmesan. There was a daily itinerary. Some activities were cultural and fun like the day trip to Rome where I went off wandering round the market to look for hats and scared Bruna half to death when she thought she'd lost me. Others were more mundane, like the whistle stop tour around the parts of a gun. It was my job to interpret. My efforts mainly involved adding an accented 'a' or 'o' at the end of English nouns, the occasional made up word and a lot of lucky guessing. Every Italian there could speak better English than my Italian which compounded my feeling of being an imposter.

Fanjobbery

Bruna and I got into the habit of making each other laugh so much we would wet ourselves. The silliest things would set us off, like spying the profile of someone's chin between the seats of the bus, the sound of a toilet failing to flush, or ice-cream melting so quickly you had to lick it off your fingers. We developed a new language—indeed a whole new philosophy called Fanjob—a combination of our pet names for each other. I was Fanny, and Bruna, after her prank with the dog's mess, became Jobby. Fanjobbery came to describe the helpless state of laughter that even the slightest crude reference or observation could reduce us to.

There was the famous 'pee in the bag' incident when we were heading on the back of a truck up a winding road to some shooting range or war memorial. Bruna banged on the front for the driver to stop because she urgently needed to pee. He showed no sign of stopping. My pidgin Italian might have come in handy but at this point I was too busy laughing. She reverted to the time-honoured solution of peeing in a poly bag while we all closed our eyes. Unfortunately the bag had a hole in it and to stop the contents dripping over our legs as the truck jostled and veered round the bends of the road Bruna tossed it out of the back of the truck. It hit the windscreen of a car which had just caught up—the car of one of the officers in our entourage! The repercussions cannot have been too serious or I would remember them equally with the incident.

Generally, over those few days everything was bliss because the sun was shining and we were on a paid holiday. Aside from my 'interpreting services' the only thing we had to do to earn our keep that fortnight was to perform Scottish country dancing on the last night in front of all the British and Italian soldiers. We made sure we were sufficiently inebriated to fly through it with minimum effort and the Italians were charmed by our bobbing tartan sashes. The men in their kilts even caught the wayward eye of a soldier or two. All in all it was a successful trip and, most significantly for me, Bruna had managed to keep my black hounds at bay.

We journeyed back to Hohne with trousers sticking to leather seats in the cloying heat of the sun, perspiration dripping from brows and frequent beer stops for the lads. When we got back there was only one more night together in the Officers' Mess before Bruna and the others had to return to Edinburgh, leaving me behind. I was signed up for another two week trip to Italy in another week's time. I would have to entertain myself as the only female in the Officers' Mess and there would be no distraction from the demons in my head. I was crippled at the thought of saying goodbye to Bruna and panicking that I might not get through the next three weeks without her.

Black Forest Chateau

As it happened Marcia was spending the summer working in a guest house in the Black Forest region of Germany. She suggested since we were both in the country, albeit a few hundred miles apart, that it would be a missed opportunity for me not to visit her there for the few days before my next trip to Italy. Desperate to escape the Officers' Mess, I set off for the bus on the next day. It was the first time I had ever attempted a long journey on my own. I was a nervous traveller, a situation compounded by the fragility of my mental health.

Although I longed to be in Marcia's company again, the journey was a nightmare of strangulated thoughts and fantasies of suicide—something which distressed me greatly because I didn't want to become a burden on Marcia. When I arrived in Baden Baden where she was staying, I was relieved to find it a peaceful place and this helped to settle my mind. Marcia was the most relaxed I had ever seen her and we spent an enjoyable few days together chatting in our beds till late at night, sipping beer in quiet cafes and going for long walks in the forest. This tranquil time spent with Marcia gave me ballast for the tortured weeks ahead.

When it was time to leave I was tearful and morose, thinking I would never see her again. Always in my mind was the heavy feeling that something awful was going to happen and I worried that I might succumb to the suicidal impulses which regularly plagued me.

Received Pronunciation

The Officers' Mess, ornate and comfortably appointed, was an environment lacking in warmth. The officers were polite yet somewhat distant. I interpreted this as their response to my lack of 'breeding'; I couldn't hold my KFS (knife, fork and spoon) correctly let alone negotiate the niceties of high brow conversation. I spent most of the next ten days in my room once again listening over and over to Barber's *Adagio for Strings* which had been recommended to me by my beloved Miss Dugan. The music brought me to tears every time I listened to it and I would often spend the whole day snivelling into a hanky which left me self-conscious about going for meals with puffy eyes.

Then on the last day before I was due to travel with 40th Field Regiment back to Italy for the second NATO exchange in Rimini, a broad-spoken Irish Major, newly arrived at Hohne, stopped me as I crossed the compound. "You look a bit lonely" he said cheerily. "Have you been to Belsen yet?" Belsen Concentration Camp was next to the compound, looming like an ugly spectre that no-one ever talked about. I was relieved to be having a conversation which was not about polo or hunting. We continued chatting and he invited me to come with him on a visit to Belsen.

I was moved by what I read on the museum plaques, and particularly appalled by the mass graves — huge mounds covered with grass which belied the scale of the human sacrifice. Our experience there was bonding. How can you not feel close to someone under such circumstances? We went afterwards for a drink. He told me he was a children's writer when he wasn't firing guns. I said I wanted to be a poet and he promised that once I had written my first book he'd help me to get it published. "I feel very protective of you" he added tenderly, "you need a father figure and I'm going to adopt you!" I was not experienced enough to know what that meant so when he asked to come back to my room for a night cap I trusted him. It was a relief to have the company and I was beginning to feel that some spiritual connection had brought us together. Maybe he was my father in another life and the experience of going to Belsen together was meant to show me how blessed I was to be alive.

All too soon his fatherly role became clear. He stretched me out quietly on the bed. I didn't want this but I felt unable to stop it; my passive childhood role had reasserted itself. He seemed totally oblivious to the fact that I was crying. I held my breath all the while, staring glassy-eyed at a crack in the ceiling while he did what he had to do. I'm not sure how it ended because I wasn't really in the room. Somehow it was over and I never saw him again.

The next morning I felt dirty and hysterical to the point of hyperventilation. I ran a bath and scrubbed every trace of him from my body. If only I could sterilise my thoughts so easily. I was desperate to go home and speak to Dr Lomax but I had to polish my boots and put my professional face on for the next leg of the journey. There was nobody here to help me.

The day of the jackals

The journey to Rimini can only be described as hell on Earth. I was the only woman on the trip. There were no officers. In theory they would have been a 'civilising' influence. Whoever could think it acceptable to leave an 18 year old girl unsupervised on a bus full of rampant squaddies in holiday mode? It was bad enough to be the butt of relentless innuendo but the laddish license they felt to paw me all over amounted to nothing short of molestation. I tried to protect what little modesty was left to me by curling into a foetal shape on the floor while they continued their cruel sport.

This was compounded by the crude welcome from the Italians as I dismounted the bus. As the sole female I had to run the gauntlet across the length of the quadrangle without my band of protective friends. In an effort to avoid contact with my tormentors I spent every evening of the next two weeks in my room alone. During the day I was on automatic pilot doing the minimum to justify my presence. Some of my duties included translating the menu (where I relied on my mother's cooking as a reference point), accompanying British soldiers to the sick bay and interpreting within my meagre repertoire at formal functions where a speech or presentation had to be given. All of this could have been done more ably by any of the Italians who had tried out their English on me.

One day in the sick bay I met a lovely Italian doctor, a young captain, who immediately put me at ease with his gentle manner. Given my recent unpleasant experiences and the fact I did not have any friends to confide in, I was ready to seize on any display of kindheartedness and respect towards me. We chatted many times over the following days and I felt safe enough—in no small part because he was a doctor—to confide in him about my depression and recent hospital admission. He was very sympathetic and reassuringly indignant when I told him of my treatment at the hands of the soldiers. Even today I don't see how I could have communicated more clearly that what I valued about our friendship was trust and safety. But my mistake had been to open up to him for he was not what he seemed. However, I was oblivious to this at the time. Here I was with a handsome protective authority figure who had been showing an interest in my welfare and also appeared to find me attractive for myself. For some perverse reason he must have been titillated by the vulnerability of my situation.

On the last night there I was persuaded by the sergeant in charge of our troops that it was my duty to join them for a drink in the bar. On their return to Hohne these men would be deployed to the Gulf where war had just broken out and they could do with a little female company 'to send them on their way'. Reluctantly I acquiesced, smiling as required through their boorish songs and crude jokes. I left the bar as soon as I could politely relieve myself and on the way back to the compound through the beach I ran into the Italian doctor. We went for a walk along the deserted shore. I felt disarmed in his charming company which was a welcome antidote to the soldiers in the bar. As we were talking he suddenly grabbed me and pinned me down on the sand. He did not meet much resistance. By now I was well-enough versed in my rag-doll compliance to know what was expected. As he tried to penetrate me roughly I lay crying, swept away by the sound of the waves to a childhood memory of being sexually abused by my brother. I am not sure if the doctor even registered my tears.

Perhaps he confused my compliance with consent. Yes it was a beach at midnight and by now I should have known better. I told myself I had known all along but didn't care anymore; in fact I wanted to be violated by another man. Such were the distorted thoughts of a teenage mind systematically damaged by childhood abuse.

Hard on the heels of the incident with the Italian doctor was the repeat experience of the journey back to Hohne where the soldiers sitting round me pawed my body spurred on by their jeering mates in spite of my obvious distress. By the time I touched down two days later at RAF Brize Norton my self-esteem was rock-bottom. I don't remember how I got back to Edinburgh; perhaps serial disassociation had bleached my memory.

Do the sexually abused send out unwitting signals of their vulnerability or do predatory men have a sixth sense which helps them to identify their prey? Either way, when you have been groomed from an early age to subsume your needs to serve the sexual appetite of deviant men, compliance becomes a survival technique. Passivity does not imply consent. During these incidents my distressed body language should have been enough to show I did not want sex—something that decent men would recognize and respect.

I should have been able to go back to the reassuring arms of my boyfriend, Steven, in Edinburgh but, sad to tell, since my hospital admission he had been treating me with revulsion and contempt. He ended our 8 month relationship but continued to seek out my company and seemed to take a perverse delight in humiliating me. He would ply me with drink till I could hardly walk, then take me home and insult me for being in such a state. Next morning he would throw me out of his flat and slam the door behind me, yelling that I was a pathetic excuse for a human being.

I didn't go back to Mylne's Court for my re-sit year. Instead I was invited to share a two bedroom flat with Annalise and Marcia. I was surprised and delighted that Marcia was prepared not only to share a flat, but also to be my room-mate. Within days of moving in it became clear that my mental health and my fixation with Marcia were only going to get worse. We all bitterly regretted the naive assumption that good will and the strength of friendship could cure all ills.

In the gutter

The next few months saw a rapid decline in my functioning, personal hygiene and behaviour. I became withdrawn, troubled and paranoid—which manifested itself in aggression towards Marcia, Annalise and Dr Lomax. I started hearing voices telling me that Marcia and Annalise were plotting to get rid of me and trying to turn everyone against me. I'm not sure if I even told Dr Lomax about the voices; it was so difficult to trust anybody. I was terrified of ending up back in hospital as I thought it would spell the death knell for my association with Marcia. I was torn between my crazy obsession with her—a possessive longing to be near her all the time—and my anger towards her for my deluded notions of her rejection and betrayal.

The atmosphere in the flat became so unbearable that I started going out most nights and getting drunk on snake bites, crawling from pub to pub on my own, or swigging from a bottle of Buckfast in graveyards and lanes—anywhere concealed where I would be left on my mission to self-destruct. Some nights I slept out to avoid going back home. Yet still I feared being thrown out, banished from the person who was keeping me alive and simultaneously trying to kill me.

It was nigh impossible to study at this time but I saw a degree as a passport out of my mess. I fiercely clung to the semblance of normality that my student status gave me. In effect I was living a Jekyll and Hyde existence.

A liability with wings

By now I had officially joined the Savoy Opera Group. Their next show was *Patience*. I was cast as a cherub which didn't appear in the libretto but was a device by the director to add visual effect to the pre-Raphaelite theme. I was the only person on stage for the entirety of the show and didn't have any lines or songs. However it was an elevation from my status as groupie. All I had to do was stand at the side of the stage as stationary as possible in a cupid's pose with bow and arrow. Occasionally I had to turn some placards over on an easel which changed depending on whether 'Ye Dragoon Guards' or 'Ye Lovesick Maidens' were on stage. I somehow managed to botch my simple task confusing the order of the placards to somewhat comedic effect. Even more disastrously I let a placard fall into the orchestra pit where it landed on the cellist's head and interrupted the musical proceedings. However my worst faux pas was visibly shaking with barely suppressed laughter while the leading lady was singing a poignant love song. The elicited tears from the audience came from laughter at me! The catalyst for all the hysterics was Bruna who was in the front row doubled up at my hammy ineptitude.

I had unintentionally sabotaged the whole show and the director was understandably furious. It is to everyone's credit that I was forgiven and no grudges were held. At the after show party I was too busy getting drunk in a corner to try to redeem myself. I justified my drinking, especially the solo binges, as a means of getting rid of the voices in my head and the distressing visual hallucinations. Of course it only served to make them worse.

What was not apparent to anyone but Marcia and Annalise was that I had tried to slit my wrists a few hours before the show because I felt overwhelmed by the pressure of holding everything together for another night. Marcia and Annalise both had lead parts in *Patience* but were preoccupied all night with worrying about what I was going to do next. My behaviour was so unhinged that I was clinging to reality by a thread. It must have been unbearably stressful for them both, especially as they were only 20 years old at the time.

Nobody to trust

The following week auditions then rehearsals were starting for the next Savoy show, *Camelot*, which would be performed at the Edinburgh Fringe. Of course by this stage, given my appalling behaviour during

Patience, there was no hope of my being given a cameo part. But I still doggedly turned up at the pub every evening to join the others after rehearsals. The terror in my head made it difficult for me to be on my own. I seized on what company I could and then, when I was drunk enough, I would crawl off by myself to wander the streets or go home and hide paranoid under my bed. When I was with the others in the pub, nursing my vodka—which I saw as a more respectable choice of drink to consume in company—my inner voices would be whispering "She's going to throw that glass in your face", or "He wants me to kill myself".

Marcia and Annalise were constantly on tenterhooks. One night in Oz Bar, a favourite watering hole after rehearsals, as I became increasingly drunk I was aware of them exchanging covert glances. Naturally I took this as evidence of a plot to get rid of me. The voices were having a field day. As I ordered another vodka Marcia and Annalise told me I had had enough to drink and they wanted me to come home with them. Now! Something was building to an inevitable climax; tonight they were going to throw me out. I just knew it. Of course I refused to go with them. There was a tussle of wills. Then, sensing that other people could hear the commotion, they cut their losses and left. I was so charged with paranoia by this stage and frightened to go home that I wandered off into the night. I knew I had to face the music eventually. I decided I would just refuse to leave.

Eventually, dead on my feet, I returned, falling in the door like a parody of my father after a night at the Cask & Barrel. Marcia and Annalise were still up, clearly waiting for me. They ushered me into the living room and broke the news that I least wanted to hear: "We want you out of the flat tomorrow. We've spoken to your Director of Studies and to Dr Lomax, and everything has been arranged". The words came like furious fists. I should have been sufficiently anaesthetised with alcohol not to feel the impact but instinctively I buried my head in my hands and howled like a wild animal as they tried to reason with me. There is no rational response to madness on the boil particularly if fuelled by alcohol.

From the hysteria welling in me they could see that I was going to do something self-destructive or violent towards them. They tried to coax me into bed but in my mind I was already half way up Salisbury Crags about to leap into the scream. I ran at full pelt out of the door, almost tripping down the stairs, across Dalkeith Road and into Holyrood Park. Like the archetypal drunk chasing shadows in the night, everything was spinning and voices were screaming in my ears. Marcia was hot on my heels, with Annalise not far behind. Marcia eventually caught up with me just as I reached the foot of the Crags and was starting to ascend. She pinned me down and practically sat on me to prevent me from wriggling free. She then called for Annalise to go to nearby St Leonard's Street police station and call for help.

The police arrived and took us to the station. A psychiatrist was sent for to assess whether I should be in hospital, which was clearly the opinion of Marcia, Annalise and the police. But the psychiatrist was dismissive. He had come cold to my case. He was sure he knew better than everyone and thought that all this patient needed was a proverbial boot up the backside. During the interview I was rocking back and forth like an autistic child with my head buried in my arms to muffle the intrusion of bright lights and voices. I just wanted them all to leave me alone. I was terrified and couldn't utter a word in answer to the psychiatrist's questions. This annoyed him. Thinking that I was being deliberately obstructive and that the crisis was a charade to attract attention, he concluded "There's nothing wrong with her. You can take her home." This was certainly not what Annalise and Marcia wanted to hear. They were left to carry the can. Angry, and frightened for my safety and their own, they hailed a taxi to take me the few hundred yards up the road to the flat because I was proving too difficult to drag.

I was aware of myself making alien animal noises while I rocked back and forth to soothe the fear and the pounding of voices battling against each other in my head. Sometimes "Open the fucking window. Get me out of here" would filter through. I was hell-bent on suicide that night. Because Marcia and Annalise wouldn't let me out of the door I resorted to trying scissors on my wrists under the bed. Whatever I tried to harm myself with, they took from me. Eventually they called the police again. They came to the flat and threatened to lock me in a cell overnight if I didn't calm down. Finally I was so exhausted I collapsed into a jagged sleep, the rocks of Salisbury Crags hurtling towards me in a never ending fall.

I woke dazed with a thumping headache the next day. I found the front door locked and no one else in the flat. Marcia and Annalise had gone to see Dr Lomax to hasten my admission to hospital—something they had already discussed and agreed the day before. I managed to find a spare key. I escaped and ran to the nearest place selling aspirin and outside the shop took an overdose. I had the persistent thought of Holden Caulfield in *The Catcher in the Rye* when he went to visit his sister Phoebe at the end of the book. I became very emotional thinking of my own brother who had been in hospital for four years now. I wanted to say goodbye to him and tell him I loved him in spite of all that he had done to me. So I went to the Thomas Clouston Clinic where he was a patient and hugged him so tight with tears in my eyes that it confused him. I couldn't tell him I had taken an overdose and so he was left wondering at the intensity of emotion being thrust upon him.

The aspirin was beginning to take effect. I felt nauseous and increasingly weak. As the symptoms grew stronger fear kicked in—fear of hell and writhing agony. In a last ditch attempt to pick up the pieces before the wind blew them all away, I called Marcia from a public telephone box and told her what I had done. She came in a taxi to collect me and, on instruction from Dr Lomax, took me to the Royal Infirmary to have my stomach pumped.

Physically it was one of the worst things I have ever experienced. They put a hose down my oesophagus and pumped saline water into my stomach till all the poison was flushed out in vomit. I felt like a suffragette. I was pinned to a bed to stop me from pulling out the hose. Fortunately this method is no longer used. New antidotes have come on the market which can counter the effect of some drugs even after they have entered the bloodstream. I've heard it said the old stomach wash was used as a deterrent from future overdose attempts. It must have been awful to administer; seeing fellow humans screaming and retching like animals with saliva, vomit, mucous and tears streaming down their faces.

I spent the next day recovering in the Royal Infirmary. It was there I met the hospital chaplain, Norman Macrae, who would become a lifelong friend. Norman sat by my bed and like a bandage to my soul he blessed me with such tenderness that the guilt of having tried to take my life seemed insignificant to God. All that mattered now was opening my heart to the love that would follow. I was transferred to the Royal Edinburgh Hospital. I was about to enter the world of tough yet kind professionals who would be prepared to hold my hand and, when necessary, hold me down as I fought my way through the battleground of mental illness.

Plummeting

THE HOSPITAL YEARS | 1991–1995

The period from 1991 to 1995 covers the largest concentration of my time spent in hospital—4 years more or less continuous though it was split between the Young People's Unit (2 years) and the adult acute wards.

First impressions

The Royal Edinburgh Hospital's acute psychiatric division which was housed in The Andrew Duncan Clinic (ADC) comprised four wards each covering a geographic quadrant of the city. I was admitted to Flanders Ward. One of the first things I noticed on the way in was the lift situated just outside the ward boundary where everybody seemed to congregate. "That might come in handy if I need to make a quick exit" passed through my mind. The brisk tone used by nurses in the Royal Infirmary suggested a not so welcoming reception here either. Was it because of the overdose? I consoled myself with the thought that I would probably only be kept in hospital for a few weeks. After all my first admission to the Professorial Unit had only been three weeks long.

The nurse who escorted me to Flanders Ward told me to wait in the communal lounge while they sorted out a bed for me. I was horrified by the sight of a drooling man rocking back and forth, picking his nose and muttering to himself. There were other characters dragging on cigarettes or slurpping from chipped mugs as they stared vacantly into the distance. The TV, which nobody was watching, blared at full volume and the air was dense with smoke and the smell of cheap perfume. I noticed a heavily made-up woman in skin tight jeans sitting in the corner grinning to herself as though she held the secret to the cosmic joke of existence. My time in the Professorial Unit, which had been mainly reserved for university students needing respite from exam stress, did not prepare me for the assault of institutionalisation that this place suggested. These patients seemed to have been here forever. They could have been lifted from a poorhouse scene in a Dickens novel, so extreme were their bizarre movements and ungainly features. I was later to learn that the drooling and fidgeting were unwanted effects of antipsychotic medication: the 'Largactil shuffle' reduced people to pacing the narrow corridors like caged animals, or added a sudden frenzy to their limbs.

I gingerly lowered myself into an armchair which was shabby and stained. (Incontinence also featured among the pick and mix of side effects). A morose looking woman still in her dressing gown at 4 O'clock in the afternoon asked me if I could "gie her a spare fag". "Sorry I don't smoke" I replied—a refrain that would pass my lips a hundred times a day. Cigarettes were the unit of currency which came to dominate everyone's life in here, even if they weren't smokers when they first arrived. I managed to avoid picking up the habit mainly because in this place it required sharing cigarette butts and I have an aversion to other people's saliva.

After an interminable few minutes sitting there among the statues I was summoned to follow a nurse to my 'room'. It consisted of a partitioned cubicle with a single bed, side cabinet and wardrobe. There were four others each separated by a flimsy curtain. The term 'cheek by jowl' might have been coined specifically to describe our living quarters. "You'll get used to the place soon enough" said the nurse, registering my disappointment.

Life on Mars

I did indeed become quickly accustomed to life in the ward. The bizarre characters I first encountered there soon were companions in the wilderness of my despair. Gradually I came to see behind the shuffling limbs to the restless souls within and I could identify with the ghostly pall of their demeanour. I too wanted to disappear outside my body, to fly away to some exotic place and be a stranger to myself.

There were other patients on the ward who seemed more grounded in the present. They were the ones who suffered most of all; casualties you might meet on the street whose only claim to madness was the battle scarring that had brought them here. Psychosis hadn't claimed them yet. They seemed quite normal, seeking camaraderie in one another, sharing life stories into the night. Of course their stories found an uncomfortable home in me by sparking memories I wanted to forget.

The ward routine revolved around meal times and the dispensing of medication. In between were ad hoc appointments with doctors or medical students where I felt I had been plucked from a conveyer belt of random goods to be the prize exhibit in a show. Then the questions. Questions. Questions. Questions. How was I sleeping? How was my appetite? Any more troubling thoughts of suicide? There were times when it was all I could think about. So they dampened the intensity with Chlorpromazine—the catch all cure that supplemented everyone's drug regime regardless of diagnosis. The willy nilly way they prescribed it made me wonder if the doctors were on commission. Chlorpromazine had a sledgehammer effect on me. For the most part it was a welcome relief to be chemically flattened.

After a month or so on Flanders Ward they served me an invidious choice: be transferred to the Young Peoples' Unit (YPU) for inpatient treatment or be discharged. The options were presented by Dr Lomax who feared that I was becoming institutionalized in an environment which would contain me without offering any sense of hope. The YPU on the other hand, she explained, was a psychodynamic environment where I would be challenged and supported to move forward through individual and group therapy. The emphasis there was on personal responsibility—achieved through a mandatory routine of shared activities, meetings and chores. I had heard this speil before and I was less impressed hearing it the second time round. I knew that the average age in the Unit was 15 and at 19 I would be by far the oldest. I refused to go. However discharge was not a viable option.

I had been kicked out of the flat I shared with Annalise and Marcia. There was nowhere for me to go other than my parents' house which was not an option conducive to recovery. In the end Dr Lomax forced my hand knowing I did not feel well enough to try and get a flat on my own.

I didn't ask you to come into my life with your Size 999's

When the day came for transfer I scowled all the way across the hospital grounds to the grand old building on Tipperlin Road which housed the YPU. However the defiance I was projecting gave way to self-pity and when it was time for Dr Lomax to leave me there I started to cry. My new key workers, Jill and David, tried to comfort me. I shrugged them off preferring to maintain an air of dogged independence. Jill's eyes were soft with the realisation that I really wanted to be held. I could see it was unbearable for her not to put her arms around me but I wasn't ready to succumb. She let it be known I could take my time settling in. Like a protective father David stood behind her echoing her gentleness with reassuring tones. He was a tender-hearted lion with a mop of reddish hair and a shy unassuming smile. To me he was just the enemy—Jill less so because she was a woman. At 5'2" with Shirley Temple curls and a bosom which could house a village, Jill was far from threatening. However I still wasn't ready to relinquish my defences.

That first afternoon I hung around like a restless cat by the door with my bags, to let it be known that I wasn't planning to stay, but after a few hours I let Jill show me to my room. I would be sharing a dormitory with five other girls. What a horrific realization for me to get my head around—five teenage brats. I wouldn't even have the privacy of my own room. It was a Tuesday, traditionally the evening that all the young people went out together unsupervised on an activity of their choice—invariably to the cinema as it turned out. It was expected that I would go with them. I refused to spend my evening going to see a rubbish film with a bunch of loony kids. That was to cause the first of the fights.

The Charge Nurse, Bryan, who was doing the sleepover shift, told me that activities night was a mandatory part of the programme and that I would have to go. I had no choice in the matter. Eventually I came to realize that Bryan was a kind and genuine man and became very fond of him, but at that moment I decided I hated him. Because of his status as Charge Nurse he epitomized the authoritarian excesses of my father and I was damned if I was going to let him tell me what to do. "It's not happening" I said in a low voice, warning him to back off. Bryan was canny enough not to force the issue; it represented a battle of wills and for the sake of my pride he allowed me to be established in the place before I would accept being ordered around. So he flushed and said "Well as it's your first night you can spend the evening unpacking your things and settling in. In future you *will* go out with the others on a Tuesday. That's non-negotiable." My sneer said: *yeah right mate*!

It was the first of many clashes between Bryan and me. We developed a love/hate relationship with a kind of grudging mutual respect. Each was top dog in their own domain—he was kingpin among the staff, as I became so among the young people. However our wariness of each other that first evening was to set the tone for what would, at times, be an uncomfortable dynamic. As he was the only member of staff on that night we were alone in the big house and both judged it best to steer clear of the other. He stalked the corridors below to indicate that he was available if I wanted to talk. He knew of course that I did not. Meanwhile I fizzed in the upstairs dormitory constructing mental effigies of him to rip apart limb from limb. "That bastard won't get the better of me" I thought. The night passed without incident. By the time the young people trooped back from the cinema I was tucked up in bed pretending to be asleep—anything to avoid having to interact with them.

Rude awakening

I have never been good at getting up early. After a month of languishing in a chemical haze all day in my bed in Flanders Ward I was hardly likely to make it down for breakfast next morning. I listened to the girls busying about me scooshing deodorant and closing drawers. None of them dared waken me. I waited till they straggled downstairs before I opened a lazy eye to survey teenage debris on the floor and closed it again. I turned to go back to sleep but heard Bryan knocking on the door and thought the better of it.

By the time I arrived at breakfast the cereal bowls had been cleared and the last pieces of toast and butter were being slurped down with tea. There was a frosty silence among my peers who knew there wasn't a legitimate excuse this side of being dead for turning up late for breakfast.

"You're late" said a woman with long dark hair seated by Bryan's side. "I take it you're Jo. Pleased to meet you. I'm Sue. But please bear in mind that breakfast is from 8am to 8.30". I cast her a look that could curdle cream. Who the hell was she to tell me what to do? "Actually I don't eat breakfast".

"Nonetheless you are required to join us between 8 and 8.30. Now please help to clear the table. It's your turn to dry the dishes. One of the others will show you where the plates and cutlery go. Then you can go and get ready for the community meeting at 9." "I am not drying dishes that I haven't used" I spat back indignantly, "And you'll have to excuse me from the community meeting. I've got important stuff of my own to be getting on with" by which I meant packing my stuff to leave. "Would you mind coming through to the office for a minute" said Sue. I followed her lazily through the kitchen and round the corner into the gold fish bowl, the office where the big fish swam. I was in no particular hurry.

"Joanna" she began, a little more hesitantly than before, "I know you don't really want to be here but while you are here you need to follow the same routine as the other young people. It would hardly be fair if you didn't. Now let's not get off to a bad start. The morning and evening community meetings are an important part of the programme here. They're where most of the therapeutic work gets done actually. You really don't have a choice but to come to every meeting if you want to stay here." "But I don't fucking want to be here!" I snapped back. "Well you need to go away and have a think about that" she replied softly and ushered me out of the door. Her quiet delivery came with the assurance that we both knew very well how the decision would fall. I needed a roof over my head and so I had to agree to the rules of the house however much I disliked them.

Part of the furniture

The matter was not to be settled outright there and then of course: it was going to take a long time to tame a spitfire like me and they acted as if they had all the time in the world. However the clock was ticking away and I would not remain a young person much longer. The upper age limit of 21 was to dangle ominously throughout my time at the YPU. The staff were sensitive in not making direct reference to it as they did not want me to feel out of place amongst the younger patients. Ironically I was probably the most immature person there in terms of attitude. For the time being it seemed that I was here for the duration unless I could curb my tongue and toe the line. If I managed this just enough then I could persuade some friends to share a flat with me and be done with the place once and for all.

I rubbed abrasively against the staff in this manner for the coming weeks, trying to appraise how much I could get away with without being kicked out before I had somewhere alternative to stay. Sometimes I refused outright to co-operate and had to be forced by the collective will of the staff team into doing the minimum to justify my presence as part of the YPU community. I did not feel a part of it. I was always the outsider. I was not prepared to relinquish my independence. It was all I had to cling to because at some level I never felt that I would be accepted.

I could not miss community meetings or therapy sessions—that would not be tolerated. I sat through them with my shoulders hunched in protest emanating the odd barely audible grunt when anybody asked me a question. It's easy in hindsight to dismiss my behaviour as teenage stroppiness. Looking back I am appalled and ashamed to reflect on how rude I was. Actually my mental state was very troubled throughout this time with wild mood swings that made me feel dangerous and out of control. I flared up at times and had to be medicated or sent to my room to calm down. I'm not sure what was worse — the hallucinogenic highs fuelling me like a monster with invincible power or the devastating depressions where I was harangued by voices and consumed by suicidal intent. The landscape in my head was sheer hell. I would have given anything to find a little peace if I thought it existed anywhere within my reach. Existence was torture and everyone around me was an enemy who could not be trusted. I was trying to survive in the only way I knew how and it made me a horrible person to be around.

With that Armageddon in my head, the effect of the boundaries I was now subjected to created a schism in me that I could not reconcile or make any sense of. On the one hand I wanted to feel safe and cared for but the caring environment only served to highlight the deficit in my childhood and the heartbreaking grief that could never be made up for now. On the other hand I wanted more than anything to be dead, or rather just to find some peace of mind, and I was angry at being forced to stay alive and engage with the fallout of problems which other people had created in me. I became engaged enough in my therapy sessions with Dr Lomax to realize I had had a very tough start in life. In some ways this helped to relieve some of the burden of guilt I had always felt but I did not feel able to channel my anger appropriately and so instead I took it out on the staff because they were able to absorb it. Unpleasant as this must have been for them, they understood my situation and gave me as much leeway as they could to express my pain. It was humiliating for me to regress into childhood and it made me feel vulnerable and scared. Unfortunately my behaviour was so feral that, much as the adults around me understood, they were bound to cast me out sooner or later.

Falling off the couch

Dr Lomax was the lynch pin of my support at this time. I was 19 and had been seeing her for therapy for the last two years since I was at school. She was no longer based in the YPU building but at the Sick Children's Hospital. Most of her patients were now pre adolescent but she had kept me on her caseload. I think this was due to the close attachment she knew I had formed to her. I had projected the role of ideal mother on her which meant she was a conduit for my anger as well my affection: I had primitive outbursts of neediness where I would refuse to leave her office when the session had ended or would crouch with a doll in the sand pit which was reserved for play therapy with young children. Sometimes I had to be dragged kicking and screaming from the room.

I had regressed so far because it felt safe enough to do so. Dr Lomax and her colleagues at the YPU knew this was all part of the process — perhaps more extreme than normal because of the level of my trauma. They did their utmost to alleviate the shame I felt whilst at the same time supporting me to function as best I could as an adult. I would frequently run away, get drunk, take an overdose or slash my wrists and neck when it all became too much. I was sometimes caught up in manic hysteria, laughing uncontrollably or saying and doing inappropriate things to embarrass people like climbing on top of the roof, waving my bra in the air and flashing my breasts to passing members of the public. One day when I had been told off by staff I ran away and had to be dragged back. An ambulance on its way to the hospital asked the two nurses frog-marching me if they wanted a hand getting me back. I took the opportunity to make a scene and embarrass them in public by yelling to passers-by that I was being kidnapped and held against my will.

Throughout this time I had been sporadically attending classes at Edinburgh University, trying to cling on to the last vestiges of adulthood and independence. The staff encouraged me in this. They wanted me to maintain a sense of purpose and pride in my studies as well as the routine that classes would give me. Before long I had withdrawn so far from normal behaviour that I couldn't sustain the façade required to operate in that world. I had lost faith in everything and saw suicide as my only hope of liberation from the cage of my existence and so my attempts became more serious and frequent.

Howling at the moon

I could not now be trusted to go out on my own. I was confined to the Unit and at weekends sent to 'board out' in the adult acute wards. I had been detained legally on numerous short term (72 hour) orders under section 24 of the Mental Health Act. Sometimes these ran into 28 day sections. I was often placed on 'special' observation where I had a member of staff supervising me at arm's length for 24 hours a day—even in the toilet, or sitting by my bed all night.

One weekend I was dragged to the notorious Ward 10, the Intensive Psychiatric Care Unit, because there weren't enough staff on the acute wards to afford me one to one supervision. Ward 10 was dreaded by all patients as the ultimate punishment—much as solitary confinement would serve in a prison. Dr Lomax was reluctant to send me there and did her best to avoid it but that particular weekend there was no other option. The hospital was short staffed and I needed the safety of a locked ward.

I was distraught at having been reduced to this and terrified as they led me through the unknown door. They had drugged me so much beforehand that the weekend passed in a wash of drunken sleep. I remember, though, when I first arrived being led through a corridor of freakish faces peering down at me—distorted like reflections in a fairground mirror. I clung to the nurses from the YPU imploring them not to leave me there. As was mandatory for all patients on Ward 10, I was relieved of my belt, laces, toiletries and anything with sharp edges so I couldn't harm myself. I noticed with some alarm that there were iron bars on the windows which I had not encountered in hospital before.

All weekend, as I drifted in and out of sleep, I had the sensation of being pawed and stared at by menacing figures looming over me. I'm not sure how much was hallucination or what was reality. It was all so harrowing—fantastical and yet vividly clear. The sound of tortured souls moaning through the ward hovered over my consciousness and I seriously wondered if I was in hell. By the time Dr Lomax and one of the nurses from the YPU came to escort me back on the Monday morning I was a gibbering wreck.

The cruelest departure

Soon after, I received the devastating news that Dr Lomax was leaving Edinburgh to take up the post of Consultant Child Psychiatrist in Oxford. I cannot begin to describe the bullet that ripped through my heart at seeing her go. In the preceding weeks it was all I could do to sit in angry silence through our sessions. How could the person I loved most in all the world leave me? Hadn't I been through this too many times before? This felt even harder than Miss Dugan leaving, or the times I woke up distraught at the realization of one of my mother's disappearances. It never seemed to get any easier. Marcia now had nothing more to do with me so Dr Lomax had become the primary attachment figure in my life. Losing her was like having the soul ripped out of me.

In our last session I cried for an hour solid without being able to say a word or even look at her. Dr Lomax surprised me with a gift. It was a floral scented pillow with a little note attached: for Jo—somewhere to lay your head during times of stress. She was clearly emotional herself which I had not expected, and for the first time ever she gave me a hug. The moment was almost too rich to take in but I treasured it for a long time afterwards. That night I had one of the worst migraines of my life and I wailed like a dying animal in Jill, my key worker's arms. The grief could only be expressed in intense physical pain. Jill's own tears flowed freely over me as she rocked me back and forth for several hours.

After that Jill became my surrogate mother. She was the kindest, most nurturing person I had ever met and the bond we developed was clearly mutual. She seemed to feel my pain as though it were her own. She had the capacity to genuinely love all the young people in her care and yet she made me feel special and individually cherished.

Fisticuffs

One significant person whom I have not mentioned was my consultant, Dr Horne. He had the ultimate responsibility for my care throughout my time at the YPU although it was Dr Lomax whom I had always seen for therapy. Now Dr Horne was to take over my sessions. I was apprehensive particularly since he was a man. In addition, when I had first arrived as an inpatient at the YPU Dr Horne had had an initial consultation with me. He had been very frank in telling me that I would have to start internalizing the intense love and regard I projected onto others if I was to get better. I did not like hearing this because it felt too difficult and threatening. I interpreted his words as a warning that the attachment figures I cherished would be taken away from me.

Therefore I was initially hostile to him and therapy was a dreaded weekly encounter. I was reluctant to open up to a man, especially an authority figure. I really put him through the grinder to test whether he was worthy of my trust as much as to put him off. Our sessions were like a boxing match in which he was the undefeated champion and I the battle-scarred contender who was going to knock him off the podium. He had the knack of penetrating my consciousness with an unexpected blow. I would then retaliate with a torrent of furious fists. The analogy of combat is perhaps unkind to Dr Horne, I'm sure this is not how he saw our sessions and in spite of my well-honed defences I could acknowledge deep down that he did seem to care and was trying his best to help me.

One day in his office we were discussing something particularly sensitive in relation to my attachment issues and somehow he managed to hit the jugular. I flew to my feet, ripped off my T-shirt and screamed "That's what you've reduced me to, you bastard!"

Realising from the shock on his face what I had just done I suddenly felt (as indeed I was) naked and exposed. This made me feel like a vulnerable child — frightened and ashamed. I immediately curled into a foetal position on the chair trying as best I could to protect my chest from view by wrapping my arms around myself and I sobbed not knowing what was going to happen next. Dr Horne slowly rose from his chair and, staying a comfortable distance, picked up my T-shirt and handed it to me gently, saying "It's okay Joanna, you're safe here. I'm not going to hurt you. Now please put on your T-shirt"

It was the most touching thing he could have said. In that moment he was my hero and I loved him. Had I expected him to take advantage of me sexually? Not consciously perhaps, but it had become a familiar enough pattern for me to expect that he would. Dr Horne explained through my relieved tears that what I had done was a natural enough reaction because of all the abuse I had suffered at the hands of men and I should not feel ashamed. "I think you just needed to know that you could trust me" he added, "and you can."

Something clicked in our sessions after that and I began to open up more readily. He was kind and tender in his manner though he did challenge me at times. He seemed to genuinely like and respect me. Dr Horne was in some ways a little eccentric although I couldn't put my finger on exactly why. I found this endearing. He had a quirky sense of humour which he brought into our sessions in appropriate and sensitive ways. This made him feel more like a trusted friend—though we still continued to clash from time to time.

Rapid descent

I was in a safe and nurturing environment but my mental health continued to deteriorate. Like a freefalling bungee jumper, I had gradually begun to trust that I was connected to a secure harness. One of the reasons psychiatric patients with a history of severe trauma may not be offered psychotherapy is because it is considered dangerous in the short term to rattle the ghosts in their cages. Indeed there were times when I wished the staff at the YPU had left the ghosts alone. As a teenager, 19 going on 20, and immature at that, I did not have the resources within myself to survive the crisis and it meant staff had to be extra vigilant.

I had refused to eat for several weeks now because I had given up the will to live. One afternoon I withdrew quietly to my room and crawled under my duvet, feeling weak with hunger and yearning to be free. The rest of the young people were at school and so I had the room to myself all afternoon. There was a plastic carrier bag on the floor which I had retained specifically for suicidal purposes. I reached for it, and without thinking too much about what I was doing, placed it over my head then held a pillow on top and applied pressure. Instinctively I struggled for breath but I knew if I held it down long enough I would lose consciousness and suffocate. However a nurse who had been sitting downstairs noticed that I was looking particularly troubled and weary that day. She had a suspicion that I was going to make a suicide attempt and so she followed me up the stairs a few minutes behind to see what I would do. Whilst I was gasping for breath the nurse entered the room and rushed over to my bed, yanking the pillow off my head and freeing me from the plastic bag. She waited for me to get my breath back then said "What the hell are you doing? You almost killed yourself!" We were both startled and disquieted by what had just happened.

After that I was placed on constant observation and Dr Horne made the grave decision to apply to the Sheriff Court to extend my current 28 day detention order to a Section 18 which would run at least another 6 months. It meant I could be held and treated—including drip-feeding if need be—against my will. Realising how ill I was, the nursing staff excused me from community meetings. I was sent to Flanders Ward to rest. I had lost 2 stone, and though not dangerously underweight like the anorexic girls in the Unit, I was heading that way. My muscles were wasting so that it was difficult even to get out of bed, not that I had any reason to want to. I just wanted to die.

I decided to oppose the Section 18 order. The war of attrition in my head between the staff and me could not go on. I was suffering unbearably and bringing everyone else down with me. As the day of the court hearing drew closer I was appointed a solicitor to represent me. We only had one meeting before the hearing which seemed to consist mainly of my having to fill out the required Legal Aid forms to ensure her Firm was paid. She asked in a rather detached manner what I wanted to happen. I said honestly "I just want to die."

"Well you'd better not say that in court" she replied, "unless you really mean it. Remember you will be under oath" Then she continued: "Let me be clear. Are you saying you want to oppose the detention order?" "Yes" I replied. "Very well, I will act upon your instructions."

I thought she would try to build a case in my favour but she didn't ever broach the subject. She knew I had no chance of winning and had little interest in helping me. My long term detention was a foregone conclusion and we were going through the motions. I at least had to try to oppose it. If I could convince the Sheriff that I was well enough to be discharged—even if it meant I had to lie under oath—then I would be on my way out.

Shortly after seeing my solicitor and before the hearing, I was so unwell that Dr Horne settled upon the drastic decision to send me against my will for Electro Convulsive Therapy. Although I have no personal memory of this (ECT commonly erases all short term memory around the time of treatment) a friend who was a fellow in-patient recalls my being strapped to a wheelchair and taken to the ECT suite screaming because I did not want to have it. I am glad I do not remember but trust that, rightly or wrongly, the ECT was carried out in my best interests.

Guilty as charged M'lud

When the day in court arrived I was taken by taxi with Jill and another nurse. We were met inside the foyer by my solicitor who did not smile at me once. I saw Dr Horne arriving, looking smarter than usual in a suit and tie. He was accompanied by the YPU social worker who had been appointed as my Mental Health Officer and whose role it had been to apply to the Sheriff for a Section 18. When Dr Horne saw me he gave an apologetic smile and walked off uncomfortably to go over his notes. I did not see him as the enemy, just a misguided friend who was trying his best to help in an impossible situation.

My solicitor took me into a briefing room from where we would go straight to the courtroom. I was agitated at being separated from Jill. Technically she was on the other side but I needed her support and had hoped that she would sit next to me in court. She later told me that she was angry with the solicitor for separating us. It was insensitive and unnecessary because the Sheriff would have allowed Jill to sit with me under the circumstances. As it was, I felt vulnerable and freakish sitting on my own while everybody in the spectators' gallery gawped at me as though I were a criminal on trial. There was probably no-one outwith my direct care sitting there but my paranoia-fuelled perception was that it was crowded with strangers who had come to condemn me.

The Clerk ordered everyone to rise as the Sheriff entered the room. I thought it a grandiose and anachronistic show of pomp. The Sheriff asked the Clerk to read something out which I took to be the charges against me. It included the words "proceeded to place a plastic bag over her head in an attempt to self-asphyxiate" at which he glanced somewhat contemptuously in my direction. I'm not sure at what point my solicitor said her piece. It could not have taken long or had much substance to it and I have no recollection of it.

However, I do remember Dr Horne's testimony. As he stepped on to the witness stand he took the Bible in his right hand and made an oath to tell the whole truth and nothing but the truth. The words sent a shiver of mortal fear through me and I dreaded when it would be my time to say them. Dr Horne gave the Sheriff some background information about my treatment at the YPU and the recent events leading up to the application for Section 18. He then spoke rather movingly about the traumatic start I had had in life and what he hoped would be the promising future I might have ahead if they could get me through this difficult period. He described me as a bright, intelligent and very likeable young woman. This surprised and embarrassed me because I had given him nothing but trouble. Dr Horne then pointed out that it was a very unusual step for him to detain one of his patients under a section 18 because he did not like to use compulsion unless it was absolutely necessary.

"But I have no doubt whatsoever" he concluded "that this is in Joanna's best interests. She poses a significant risk of self harm and I would be failing in my duty of care to her were I not to pursue this order to help keep her safe."

The Sheriff then asked if I would like to speak. I knew this was my one and only chance to turn around the course of the proceedings. I said yes. I could see my solicitor was cringeing. Once I had taken the oath — skimming over the words conveniently in my head — I had expected to impress the Sheriff with a little speech about how well I was doing at University and this being evidence that I was on the right track and didn't need to be in hospital. But the Sheriff did not wait for me to speak. He stole my thunder with the direct question:

"Joanna do you intend to take your own life?" He fixed his eyes gravely upon me as though balancing the scales of justice towards my eternal damnation. I did not expect the question to come so imminently and stumbled somewhat. I averted my gaze towards the floor and said "No." He slowly took off his glasses and sighed. "Joanna, do you know what it says in the Bible about lying?" Without letting me answer he went on, "you are a Christian girl, are you not? And I am sure you are aware of the Ten Commandments and that you are to honour thy father and thy mother."

I was lost for words but, in fact, he didn't seem to want me to say anything. He seemed intent on giving me a lecture. "Well how do you think your mother and father would feel if you killed yourself?"

I shrunk into my skin sensing venom from everyone's eyes. "Your mother and father gave you life, they brought you up to be a good Christian girl" (had he listened to a single word from Dr Horne about my childhood?) "and now you intend to dishonour them by taking your own life? It is selfish, ungrateful behaviour, is it not?"

I meekly acquiesced accepting as righteous the damnation of the wicked person everyone in the court saw me to be, and indeed, which I knew myself to be. I was thoroughly ashamed and stood, head hung, as he continued to take me to task.

"And what about your doctors and nurses who are doing so much to help you? Do you think they like to see their efforts wasted? You should be grateful to them and do as they tell you. Now then, I am going to grant the detention order and you will remain in hospital for the next six months at least and accept whatever treatment Dr Horne deems necessary for you. I have no doubt that you will get better soon and make your parents proud of you. Now you may sit down."

After that, there were some formalities I did not understand carried out amongst the Clerk, the Sheriff, my solicitor and the social worker. Various papers were passed round to be signed—none of them by me—and the session was closed by the Clerk. The Sheriff swaggered out of the courtroom looking pleased with himself at a job well done. Any anger I might have felt at the way he had spoken to me was dwarfed by my shame. "Everybody hates me" I thought, not daring to meet anybody's gaze. I took the low level chatter around the room to be whispers of disapproval about me. I felt that every insult directed my way was justified. I was a thoroughly wicked and abhorrent person. Jill was trying to catch my attention from the gallery and reached her hand across the divide but couldn't meet the gap. I knew she would be feeling very sorry for me but I didn't deserve her pity. I couldn't look her or anyone in the eye.

Jill knew exactly the self-recrimination that would be going through my head and she did her best to impress upon me that the Sheriff was a buffoon. It was his problem, not mine. She and her colleague bundled me into the next available taxi and whisked me back to the Unit. Dr Horne and the social worker travelled separately. The solicitor didn't bother to say goodbye. It was all in a day's work for her, another paper-shifting exercise; another time-waster to process through the courts.

Back to reality with a hug

When we arrived at the Unit the other staff had been primed to know that I would need extra TLC that night, or maybe to just sit quietly in the presence of people who cared about me. I couldn't help but say sorry over and over again to everyone who crossed my path. I wasn't apologizing for anything specific, just for being alive, and of course for wanting to die.

It was a Thursday, either the first or last of the month—and I can't even remember which month—but I know it was a Thursday because there was a regular Mass to pray for vocations to the priesthood celebrated in St Catherine's Convent. I was in dire need of divine mercy and so I asked if I could go with a member of staff. There was no hope of my going unaccompanied of course. I hadn't been allowed out on my own for several weeks. Jill looked doubtful

"You've had a very difficult day Joanna" she said, "I'm not sure it's a good idea for you to be going out this evening. But let's see what Dr Horne says. Perhaps if we can get two members of staff to go with you…"

Dr Horne asked to see me. It was like a reconciliation between father and child though each felt like the prodigal in need of the other's forgiveness. "Joanna" he said tenderly "I know you are very angry with me just now."

"No" I whispered, genuinely meaning it.

"Well please just trust me now to do what is best for you. We all want to help you get well. What happened today in court was horrible. The Sheriff should never have spoken to you like that and I'm sorry you had to go through that. But I want you to know none of us think you have done anything to be sorry about. It's only natural you should want your liberty and you have every right to fight for it. We all understand that life has become unbearable for you in recent months but I think we can help you get better. I need you to trust us and allow us to hold on to hope for you until you can take it back for yourself. Do we have a deal?"

I nodded. "Now Jill told me you want to go to Mass tonight. I know what a comfort that is to you and I think it's a great idea. I think you'll be okay with just one escort, won't you?" I understood that this was his first step towards renewing my trust in him.

The tables were set for dinner that night and all the young people were touchingly quiet. I scraped my food around with my fork trying to take in mouthfuls as I gulped back tears. I was the oldest and most defiant among us and everybody could see how humiliating it was for me to be reduced to this. In the past when someone was distressed, the others had usually taken their lead from me in how to respond. In truth I had been a terrible role model. Tonight was no different. They could sense I needed a quiet space to lick my wounds. It is heartbreaking to think now of how connected we were in our suffering in spite of our seeming absorption in our own private dramas.

I was excused from washing up that evening so I could set off in time for Mass. Karen, with whom I had never felt a particularly strong rapport, was to accompany me. We walked in virtual silence but I felt compassion emanating from her such as I had not felt before. Something silent passed between us and her eyes were soft and moist. At Mass the hymns set me off crying again—as the hymns at St Catherine's Convent always did. I felt God's love and forgiveness holding me in the prayers contained within the chapel. Silent intentions and petitions of the faithful were offered by familiar strangers. All of us were looking for a little grace; some perhaps like me—hopeless and despairing. It was all I could do to whisper "sorry" over and over again to my God, though we both knew what I really meant was 'thank you.'

A bump on the head

After that I started eating again although the suicidal feelings did not go away. My moods still flared in angry outbursts or in lewd, inappropriate behaviour; but for the most part were manifested in bouts of deflated woe. Up to then I had only been on anti-depressant and anti-psychotic medication but now Dr Horne felt it was time to add a mood stabilizer to the mix. I was started on a low dose of Lithium which would gradually be increased to the optimum level for my body weight. Almost as soon as I started taking it I had an extreme reaction. One of the side effects some people get from Lithium is low blood pressure and fainting. I felt dizzy after my first dose and stood at the top of the staircase watching the carpeted steps sway beneath me. Then my knees buckled and I tumbled the forty stairs to the bottom. I was lucky not to break my neck though I didn't think so at the time. When I landed at the foot of the stairs my head hit a railing and I was knocked out cold. I started convulsing for five minutes or so and, embarrassingly, when I woke up I found I had wet myself. Because there was a doctor on hand he was able to monitor me over the next 24 hours to check for signs of concussion so I did not need to be taken to the Royal Infirmary. The incident left me with a terrible fear of heights and I cannot begin to imagine how, years later, I was able to launch myself from the top of Salisbury Crags.

Success by degrees

Once my Section 18 had expired I remained as a voluntary patient for several months. I even managed to return to some of my university classes. There was no hope of now following the Honours degree in Spanish and Italian on which I had originally embarked because my ill health precluded me from the requisite study year abroad. I had to settle for the easiest route to a qualification. This was an MA General Degree comprising a broad range of subjects studied to 1st or 2nd year level. Having previously been told by my Director of Studies that I was capable of obtaining a First Class Honours degree this seemed a poor substitute but it was my best hope of staying the course under the circumstances.

I was desperate to be discharged and regain my independence so that I could resume a normal student life. Bruna and I were still close friends and she had faithfully kept up her visits throughout my time in hospital. This was despite attempts by staff to put her off. I often found myself laughing helplessly in her company or behaving stupidly. They perceived she had a rebellious influence over me. As far as I was concerned she brought me some semblance of normality and introduced fun where there was otherwise precious little.

I had also been in touch with some of the old Savoy Opera crowd. I re-established my contact with the President, Michael, who still had a crush on me. There were also tentative stirrings towards resuming my friendship with Marcia who, though understandably wary of getting involved with me again, remained open to the possibility.

When Dr Horne agreed that it was time for me to start the process of moving on, the YPU social worker helped me to apply for a one-bedroom flat and I was quickly offered a tenancy with Canmore Housing Association. Initially I started going there 'on pass' at weekends where

I would have previously boarded out on the acute wards. In spite of my initial bravado at going it alone I found these passes challenging. I had become too used to being in an institutional setting where nurses were on hand if I felt unsafe or in need of support, however I persisted. I filled up my weekends with visits to my family, to the cinema with friends or in trying to snatch opportunities for study whenever my concentration would allow. I bought a typewriter and proceeded to type my essays. Most other students had already converted to carbon but I had had to be dragged kicking and screaming into the modern world.

Poetry in motion

One of my projects during this period was to write a book of poetry for Jill's 26th birthday. It is now hard to believe she was only a few years older than me. I hadn't written any verse since schooldays—and even then only a few poems. I now fancied myself as something of a poet and was buoyed for the task by a little fantasy. I would deliver the poems on an old-fashioned tricycle (which I had yet to acquire) with a basket at the helm to be filled with champagne and the book of poems. I would dress up in a top hat and tails and with a monocle in one eye—I often went about dressed like this—and would attach some pink toilet roll to the back of the tricycle with "Happy Birthday Jill" smeared in pink lipstick.

Quite how the image came to me I cannot recall but it is a feature of my condition to be overcome with bizarrely detailed fantasies and the desperate imperative to carry them out. This has landed me in unlikely situations a number of times. Once, during the Edinburgh Festival, I was striding along the Meadows in my top hat swinging a cane with afore-mentioned monocle in my eye when an American tourist stopped me and said "Gee, you look cute! Are you performing in the Fringe?"

"No", I replied, without a trace of irony, "I'm going to see my psychiatrist".

I described my plans to Dr Horne to ride past the YPU front

window in said drag with the toilet paper billowing behind me to the delight of an awed Jill—who, of course, could not fail to be charmed by the gesture. Dr Horne found it highly amusing but concluded

"Well, you know I think the book is a great idea, and you can deliver it in your best bib 'n' tucker—I'm sure she would like that. But I think buying a tricycle is a step too far. And don't you think it would be very difficult to write a message on toilet paper with lipstick?"

I was intent on being discharged therefore eager to impress upon Dr Horne that I could behave in an appropriate fashion. His was a fair point and I accepted the suggested compromise where I might otherwise have forged ahead with my plan regardless. The next task was to actually write the book!

I was able to tick that one off within a week. My Opus Dei consisted of 56 poems—all about my life so far. After all who wouldn't want to read about me! It was entitled *The Little Book of Secrets*. Although I was quite high, or perhaps 'driven' is a better word, the tone of most of the poems was sombre and poignant. I was seeing a lot of my parents at that time and was anxious to please my father so the poems relating to him expressed only tenderness. My poor mother who could not read received somewhat harsher treatment.

One of the poems was called *Cup of Poison*. It dealt with the time she came into my room when I was around 9 or 10 years old and, giddy with excitement, woke me up to tell me that she had poisoned my father with crushed pills in his milk. She said he was going to die in his sleep and we would finally be free to run away and eat as many sweets as we wanted. I tried to shake her to her senses: "Mum, what have you done?" I imagined she would be put away for life for murdering my father. It was an agonizing 24 hours as we watched him slumped like an elephant, hardly moving at all till the next evening when he finally roused. Of course I should have called an ambulance or at least told my sisters but I was paralysed with fear that my mother would be taken away.

As for the poem, it described a recurring nightmare that I was being prepared for execution because, in order to save my mother I had jumped in and confessed that it was in fact I who had given him the poison. This was just one of a number of poems relating in a matter of fact way to events that other people might find shocking. To me they were just a part of the script of my life as told so often to Dr Lomax and Dr Horne in our therapy sessions.

Other poems were about more recent experiences such as watching a fellow patient being forcibly sedated on Flanders Ward. Another was about sleeping rough at 2am one Friday with my head resting on a dried patch of dog urine while a woman set her Alsation on me. Of course there were poems about my attachment to Jill, and to Dr Lomax and Marcia before her. These were gut-wrenching expressions of the hopeless nature of my love.

All in all, it was hardly a worthy present to give someone for their birthday. But Jill accepted my little book of secrets, read it from cover to cover and thanked me for the deep honour I had bestowed on her by dedicating my life story to her.

Back on my hands and knees

Shortly after Jill's birthday I progressed to a two week pass at my flat with daily check-in visits to the YPU. I knew this was the last leg of my journey—and I would soon be discharged. I became so anxious about this and so sad and lonely at the thought of leaving my surrogate family, that I could not face them at all. I did not turn up as scheduled for daily visits, stopped taking my medication, got a part-time job in a bar without permission from Dr Horne, and flung myself once again into the excesses of student life. It was my way of distracting myself from unbearable grief.

Of course this situation couldn't last long. I was recalled to the YPU and told that I wasn't ready to be discharged until I could comply fully with the terms of my treatment plan. I was ashamed at having failed and this cancelled out any relief in feeling safe to be back in the YPU. I regressed into obstructive behaviour within the Unit and my overnight passes were withdrawn. Once again it was a battle of wills between me and the staff. I ostracized myself from everyone by refusing to do my share of the chores and flouncing out of meetings when anybody challenged me. Far from being the older wiser role model I lost the respect of the young people too. They had no qualms in telling me how destructive they found my behaviour and that it was making me a misery to live with. This went on for another 8 months till finally it was decided that enough was enough.

Transition to the adult ward

Once I had reached my 21st birthday Dr Horne told me that I was going to be transferred to the adult acute ward for my sector — 'Bannockburn'. I was devastated to hear this news though I knew it had to be coming soon. I hoped that my rebellious spirit would show them I wasn't yet ready to be an adult. Indeed I felt more like an angry, frightened toddler than a teenager. Far from buying me time my behaviour had pushed me in the opposite direction. Plans were made for a hasty transfer as the staff were concerned about the negative impact I was having on the other young people. My bags were packed for me because I had refused to pack them myself. I was swiftly man-handled out of the Unit and frog-marched through the hospital grounds to Bannockburn Ward. I kicked and swore all the way there. It was a shameful display of infantile fury and utterly pointless. For the fourth time in my life I had been forced out of the nest.

A bitter pill to swallow

When I got to Bannockburn the doors were locked behind me. I was sedated and told I would be confined there until I could control myself. The YPU was a million miles from me now and there was no going back. The nursing staff were brusque and no-nonsense in their manner towards me. If I tried to leave the ward I was forcibly sedated and left to come to my senses. This was repeated until I eventually calmed down. I desperately wanted someone to hold me and tell me it was going to be okay but far from attracting sympathy my behaviour appeared repellant to the staff and patients alike. Eventually, after a day or so of sobbing hysterically on my bed, I gave up the battle with my lungs. The Charge Nurse, Rita, approached me, put her hand on my shoulder and gently patted it. My head was so sore that it felt like a running fever. Rita asked a junior doctor to examine me and I was given some Paracetamol. The effort of fighting the world for months had left me exhausted and I just lay like that for days, totally wiped out and defeated.

As I gained strength I gradually started to join the other patients for meals and in the TV lounge. I sat in what would become my favourite spot — the top of the corridor by the observation post. A nurse sat there all day and kept track of everyone who entered or left the ward. It was the only place you were assured of some attention from staff because the nurse on duty there was essentially a captive audience. It became a habit of several 'needy' patients like me to congregate here till we were moved on. The fewer patients who gathered there the less likely we were to be moved and so there was always a desperate rush to occupy the one or two vacant seats next to the nurse. This was one of the many idiosyncrasies of ward life that would become second nature to me.

I had been in Bannockburn about a week and was beginning to settle though I was still a long way from being resigned to my fate. Every time I asked to go back to the YPU I was met with blank expressions and if I kept asking I would be sent to my dormitory. They no longer had to wield the threat of restraint and sedation. Finally I stopped asking. The yearning to go back and see Jill burned within me. When it seemed I had accepted that I would not be returning they started to let me off the ward for 15 minutes passes which were gradually extended to an hour. This gave me enough time to go into Morningside and buy chocolate, then to stroll back through the hospital grounds and loiter by the edge of Tipperlinn Road so I could observe the YPU building from a distance. I did not dare go any closer. I had been warned they would call the hospital security guard to remove me and take me back to Bannockburn. This meant having my passes withdrawn.

The monster unleashed

One day as I was making my way back to the ward through the car park, I saw Stacey, one of the staff nurses from the YPU, getting into her car. She was the first contact I had had with the YPU in several weeks. I raced over and begged her to talk to me and take me back with her to the YPU to visit the others. She sternly blanked me as she had clearly been primed to do. When I persisted she said "It is not up for discussion. Now please step aside."

I was furious at being cast out again and terribly hurt that this was the strategy they were adopting. It felt cruel to be denied any contact at all when the YPU had been like a family to me. For two years I had shared my most intimate feelings and made myself vulnerable there. Now I was being treated like a non-person. The old rage welled up inside me and before I knew what I was doing I flew at Stacey in a fury of fists and kicking, crying "I hate you, I hate you!"

She put her hand out to stop me and said "Jo! Please stop! I am pregnant!" Her voice was quivering in obvious fear over what I would do next. This jolted me out of my trance-like state and I drew back in fear at my own destructive power.

"I'm so sorry, I'm so sorry" I cried over and over again as she stared at me in horror. Then I started screaming and ran terrified back to the ward, ripping my clothes off as I went. I was half-naked when I arrived at the ward, hyperventilating in-between shrieks of

"Tie me down, I'm a murderer. I've killed Stacey's baby".

The door was locked behind me and I was held down and sedated. When I came round Rita was sitting by my bed.

"Please call the police" I begged her, "I should be in prison for murder." "It's okay" said Rita. "We've just had a call from the Royal Infirmary. Stacey has been checked out and the scan showed no sign of harm to the baby. You are very lucky, they're not going to press charges."

This should have been a relief but I wanted more than anything to be punished for the heinous thing I had done. I was an evil monster and not fit to be among other people, especially not vulnerable people in a hospital. Everything I had always feared myself capable of had come true. As I saw it this was attempted murder—worse still, infanticide.

Of course I hadn't known Stacey was pregnant and there had been nothing pre-meditated in my attack, but I convinced myself that I must have known and I had set out to kill the baby. As far as I was concerned I was a murderer.

That night a trial played in my head and the voices sentenced me to hang. I lay cold and silent in my bed waiting for the execution to be carried out. A day or so later the nurses had stopped coming in to check on me. I tied a bootlace round my neck, stood on a chair and tethered the lace to a beam in the wardrobe. I kicked the chair from under me and fell with a clatter to the floor. The beam had snapped under my weight. "Die Die Die" screamed the venomous voices as the fingers of destiny prodded me over. I crawled back to my bed and hid under the covers. No-one else had been in the room and I didn't tell a soul about the failed execution till many years later.

Cuckoo tries to fly

After that nothing could ever be the same. I had seen and done terrible things and it was only a matter of time before I would be punished for my crimes. I spent the next five months in Bannockburn and whilst there was assigned a new social worker, Kathryn Blythe, who would become my Mental Health Officer. She would work with me for 17 years until her retirement. I wanted out of hospital but was too scared to be released into the community as I knew what I was capable of and couldn't trust myself. Kathryn agreed I wasn't well enough to live on my own though she said she was more concerned for my own safety than what I might do to anyone else. This seemed crazy to me. I was clearly a danger to the public and that was my primary concern. What did it matter if I killed myself in the process? I deserved to die.

Kathryn discussed the possibility of being semi-discharged into supported accommodation for a trial period. The organization she had in mind was Q Housing Association which ran group houses for people coming out of hospital and prison. The residents had a shared budget and communal meals. They were supported by a residential support worker and a senior social worker who worked one to one with them on rehabilitation plans. When I heard that I would be sharing with ex-prisoners I thought "yes, that is where I should be." I assumed from this there would be rigid checks and curfews because of the risk I posed to the community. This made me feel safer.

There was a vacancy in one of the 6 bedroom-houses in S Street in Newington. Kathryn took me to meet the senior social worker in charge with whom I would have weekly one to one sessions. Her name was Candice Wight. She was a formidable woman who was keen to set out the ground rules from the word go. This suited me well. I needed someone who could stand up to me if I became dangerous again. I seriously feared hurting someone. Candice arranged with Kathryn to have me stay on overnight passes at S Street with a view to gradually being discharged from hospital. Though it had been over a year since I had stayed overnight in my flat at C Crescent I still hadn't formally given up my tenancy there. Kathryn hoped that one day I might feel able to live on my own again so she persuaded me to keep my name on the tenancy and exchange it temporarily with one of the residents of S Street who wanted to live in a single flat. This was arranged between both housing associations, though I was only really going along with it to keep everybody happy. I believed I would always need to live in a supported setting because of the risk I posed.

I began to spend the odd overnight stay then full weekends at S Street however I could never fully settle. There were no locked doors there and I could come and go as I pleased. This made me feel anxious. I began to feel unsafe around my nieces and nephew, imagining that I was going to sexually abuse them. I had no desire or impulse to do so but I was fearful for their safety and couldn't trust myself to be alone with children. Kathryn and Candice did their best to reassure me that I was not likely to harm anyone and that I could always go back to hospital if I did. I believed that where I really needed to be was prison, not hospital.

As they slowly weaned me out of the ward and into S Street, my anxiety levels hit the roof. Coupled with this, I clashed pretty quickly with Candice and I found it difficult to live among the other residents so that the plan broke down. I was readmitted to hospital, this time to Flanders—the sector ward for my new address.

Preparing for battle

I was familiar with Flanders as I had boarded out there a lot during my time in the YPU and I got on well with the staff. My new consultant, Dr Skinner, was very kind to me and quite protective in his approach which made me feel safe. He decided to start me on a new anti-psychotic medication called Depixol which came in the form of a slow-release intra-muscular injection called a 'depot'. He said this would increase my chances of being discharged successfully as it was administered by a nurse so they could ensure I was taking it.

Depixol, like most drugs, has negative side-effects. One of which is increased appetite and weight gain. Within a couple of months I had put on over three stone—a large amount of weight for anyone but huge in relation to my diminutive size. It was the first time in my life I had been overweight. I was greatly distressed by it but because I was back on a Compulsory Treatment Order I had no option but to continue with my prescription. I had always binged on chocolate and sweets since my mother comfort-fed me as a child but up to now I had managed to stay relatively slim. Now I was gobbling everything in sight and my flagging metabolism could not keep up.

I made a new friend in Flanders. Selma was only a few years older than me. For the first two months of my stay on the ward she had been catatonic and electively mute. Because her muscles had wasted she could only get about by crawling on her hands and knees and would look nobody in the eye. Having been drip-fed before she arrived, she had now progressed to high-protein milkshakes through a straw. One day as I was studying for my final exams in the dormitory we shared, I heard a rasping sound coming from below. I looked down to see that Selma was pulling herself up on to the bed and trying to get my attention by name. I was completely dumbfounded. I didn't even know she knew my name as we had never communicated. Of course she must have heard the nurses calling me often enough. I helped her on to her bed and listened as she tried to form a sentence. The self-imposed silence had weakened her vocal muscles but within a few hours she was back in full flow and we were conversing as though we had known each other for years. It was terribly exciting and I felt honoured that she had chosen me to break her silence with.

Live wire

As my exams approached I struggled to cope with my anxiety and my mood plummeted. Dr Skinner decided to prescribe a course of Electro Convulsive Therapy (ECT) which I was not happy about. I knew from previous experience that ECT affected people's short-term memory and I was concerned it would impair my performance during the exams; this was my last chance to sit them. Dr Skinner, however, felt the pressure of the exams would tip me into psychosis and he had already decided that as well as having ECT I should not be allowed to sit them. I agreed to the ECT in the hope that I could use my compliance to bargain with him to let me sit my exams after all. He only relented after I had received my final shock. I was given twelve such 'treatments' over four weeks by which time my memory was completely fried and there were only a few days to go. Somehow I managed to pass two of my exams with Merit and the other with a Distinction.

To my father's credit, he had made a passionate plea to Dr Skinner on my behalf to allow me to sit the exams and this seemed to be what swayed it. My father, for all his dark faults, could be very supportive. The fact that I was studying at Edinburgh University was a source of great pride for him and he wanted to see me do well. At my graduation a few months later I rather selfishly complained that it wasn't a 'proper' degree because it was not an Honours degree. I think this hurt my parents and robbed them of some of the pleasure of the occasion. Although I continued to see my degree as a failure for many years I can now acknowledge that it was, in fact, a considerable achievement given my health and circumstances at the time.

Every inch a gentleman

Towards the end of my stay in Flanders, Michael from the Savoy Opera Group, who had written to me every week for over a year, finally broke through with his proposal that we should be more than just pen friends. I was beginning to realize that I could do a lot worse than go out with such a kind, intelligent and funny man. It's true he would never be Marcia, or Dr Lomax, or Jill, but actually I wasn't interested in romance with them. I was deeply attached to them but it was because they represented security owing to the unrequited nature of my intense feelings. Now I suddenly found myself in a relationship with a man — all 6' 4" of him — and I was torn between smothering him with affection and running a mile. In the event, I did both. I phoned him out of the blue, having returned none of his calls or letters for a year, and asked him to marry me. There was a stunned silence at the other end of the line then he stammered "Yes of course, are you sure?" — To which I replied an ecstatic "Yes!" But I was not at all sure. Within a month or so of our engagement (he even bought me a ring) I panicked and realized I was in no fit state to be in a relationship. Besides I was terrified at the thought of sexual intercourse because of my vaginismus. So I broke it off. I felt terrible doing so, knowing as I did how long he had harboured feelings for me and how devastated he would be. Michael was a gentleman, as ever. He said that he did not blame me but now he needed to move on and could not see me anymore. He decided to go travelling and settle in Australia, the subtext of which I took to mean — get as far away from me as possible.

My family was very disappointed when I let Michael go. In my situation I was hardly going to be swamped with other offers and Michael represented a considerable catch for anyone. Once again I felt I had let everybody down. I was nothing but a failure.

Cola has never tasted the same since

Shortly after graduation it was time to prepare for discharge. I made a decision to relinquish the room at S Street and attempt to live on my own at my flat in C Crescent. The usual process of gradually increasing overnight passes followed but the pressure drove me to illness again and I attempted suicide in my flat by downing a large overdose of Paracetamol with a litre bottle of cola. My sister visited later that day and found me in a pile of vomit. She immediately phoned an ambulance and I was taken to the Royal Infirmary where they gave me medication to empty the remaining contents of my stomach. Fortunately the Paracetamol had not yet entered my bloodstream or I would not have survived.

Dr Skinner and my social worker, Kathryn, agreed that I was not safe to be discharged and would need a further period in hospital to help me prepare for life outside. Since my permanent address was once again the flat in C Crescent I would have to be transferred to the ward for that sector. After much protest I was once again frog-marched with my chattels back to Bannockburn. I would remain there for another year. It was perhaps the worst year of all.

Ever decreasing circles

I had lost all confidence in myself and in the hospital's ability to help me. Once again I had lost the will to live. There followed several months of suicide attempts and going missing from the ward only to be brought back by the police. Once they fished me out of the River Forth where my mother had also tried to drown herself when I was a child. Another time I was found in the Meadows, sobbing at the foot of a tree with a snapped branch at my side and a makeshift noose around my neck. Each time I would be placed back on 'special' observation followed by several weeks of general confinement. I was so desperate that I even managed to steal a month's supply of Melleril from the medicine cabinet when the staff nurse momentarily turned his head. I had overheard a medical student say that an overdose of this drug could cause sudden heart failure. It was not to be. I convulsed violently from a grand mal seizure and was very ill but my heart beat on.

My existence was so miserable that I felt the only thing I could look forward to was chocolate. Needless to say my weight continued to soar. I also experienced many other side effects from different medications I was tried on at that time. My new consultant psychiatrist, Dr Kelly, settled on an anti-psychotic depot injection called Haloperidol which gave me Tardive Dyskinesia (involuntary movement of the limbs) and caused my facial muscles to spasm so that I stammered intermittently. I also developed the common habit among long term patients of compulsively rubbing my thighs whilst rocking back and forth. Various anti-depressants were stopped and started. Fluoxetine (Prozac) was settled upon because it had the fewest side effects. Loss of libido and sweating like a greasy pie were a small price to pay for avoiding some of the nastier alternatives. I also had a further course of ECT which gave me the most blinding headaches imaginable, along with nausea and, of course, memory loss.

Needless to say my behaviour regressed and I continued to feel more hopeless, desperate and angry. I was unpopular among the staff who interpreted my constant attempts to escape from the ward as 'manipulative and attention-seeking behaviour'. In turn I felt judged and misunderstood which led to further disaffection and compounded my 'non-compliance'. I also felt targeted by some staff who saw me as a trouble-maker when I challenged what I saw to be abusive practices on the ward. I frequently spoke up on behalf of patients who appeared too intimidated to do so for themselves and at times I got so angry I lashed out and hit nurses so that I had to be restrained and sedated. A friend whom I met on the ward at this time remembers on one occasion how a whole shift of five nurses were standing round me and goading me to provoke a reaction. Eventually I snapped and threw the can I was holding at a window and smashed it. My friend perceived the ensuing restraint, which was heavier-handed than usual, to be a punishment inflicted on me for speaking out of turn. It was also a warning to everybody else to toe the line.

Some nurses, though, treated me with kindness. Among them was the Charge Nurse, Rita. When Rita was on shift the other nurses behaved more humanely because she set the tone for high standards from all her staff. Because I was considered so difficult by everyone else Rita took on key worker role for me. I respected her because, whilst firm, she was fair.

Imminent release

One evening, after I had been out of the ward all day, I returned to the devastating news that Rita had died of a brain aneurism that afternoon. After that the staff became more hostile towards me, perhaps out of their own grief but also because I had been particularly close to her. Within a few weeks I had turned from being an inconvenience into a complete pariah. My voices were feasting on the conflict and I had no-one to turn to but my social worker, Kathryn. She supported me as best she could but she also had to balance everyone else's needs with mine.

Kathryn referred me to an independent advocate, Allison Alexander, who had recently been appointed by the Patients' Council to work on our ward. I aired my grievances to Allison about staff attitudes and conditions on the ward, not with a view to raising a complaint but rather to confide in someone sympathetic. She negotiated my discharge with Dr Kelly, who could see how unpopular I was among the staff. Allison also suggested I become involved in the work of the Patients' Council where I would have a formal platform to discuss these issues openly and find a means to effect change. I started going to their monthly meetings in the hospital board room and soon became hooked.

During the last year I had become very attached to Kathryn. She represented stability, constancy and immense kindness at a time when I badly needed it. She also proved an invaluable source of practical support in helping me secure Disability Living Allowance and a community care grant to furnish and decorate my flat. It had been largely unoccupied and was in dire need of attention to make it feel like a proper home where I would want to live.

I was discharged in July 1995, full of trepidation at leaving the security of hospital which had become my home over the last four years, but also desperate to put all that behind me and start a new life.

Flying Solo

ACTIVIST/VOLUNTEER | 1995–2000

As I settled into my flat, the friends whom I had met in hospital (Kate, Selma, Archie and Marina) became even more important to me. Having been used to constant company on the ward, I was often lonely in the flat, and so having friends who understood what it was like to have a mental health problem and who were themselves adjusting to life 'on the outside' was a rich source of support and companionship.

Bruna, as ever, continued to be my stalwart and my closest friend. I was delighted when she moved into a flat round the corner from me and we seized on this opportunity to spend more time together. It allowed her to keep a protective eye on me as she always had.

Marcia had also come back into my life after the necessary separation while I was in hospital. Our friendship grew and blossomed from this point. We were able to put the past behind us and it is to her immense credit that she was able to forgive me for the suffering and chaos I had visited on her during our student years. She gave me a second chance—with no hint of bitterness or regret. There were aspects of my behaviour while I was ill which caused me deep shame and Marcia's forgiveness of me provided a model for me to forgive myself.

I was still in regular contact with my family although my parents had now split up. My mother had left my father and moved into a housing association flat in Bellevue. As in the past, my father could not accept that the marriage was over and he continued to put the blame on me, my brother and sisters to elicit our help in getting her back.

My sisters were getting on with their busy lives and whilst I was in hospital Lena had had another little girl and Paula a baby boy who were now toddlers. My brother had been in hospital for several years and though he remained quite stable it was difficult to see any progress in his mental health.

My main support, indeed my lifeline it seemed, was my social worker, Kathryn. She went far beyond her remit in providing practical assistance. She helped me manage my tenancy and provided the emotional support to see me through what continued to be a troubled time in terms of my mental health.

I was also attending Randall House, a NHS day centre for patients living in the community. The nursing and OT staff there, along with my consultant psychiatrist, Dr Kelly, were an important source of support too.

"Disorder" not a word to heal our pain

I was particularly attached to Dr Kelly who was kind and pleasant in her manner towards me. However it was she who had been instrumental in changing my official diagnosis to Borderline Personality Disorder. BPD is a controversial label that stigmatizes patients and is now being widely discredited by mental health professionals. It has been used as a catch-all for a number of uncategorizeable conditions which are, arguably, natural responses to childhood trauma. Worse still, it implies that the sufferer is the author of his/her own ills. On reflection, I associate my being labelled thus with the negative perceptions others had of me and the resulting harsh treatment I received from some of the staff in Bannockburn Ward. Certainly at that time there was a lot less sympathy and understanding for patients with this label than other so called 'functional' illnesses. If your condition was seen to be attributable to poor treatment in childhood then, ironically, you were further mistreated and stigmatised by services as an adult. There was a perception that your distressed behaviour was simply manipulative and attention-seeking. Most of us were told off in no uncertain terms for 'acting out' although the same behaviours in other mental health patients would be interpreted as genuine symptoms of their illness.

For me the enduring legacy of that diagnosis was the internalisation of blame and shame. That was even more damaging than the punitive treatment by staff. When it is implied that you are personally responsible for your condition then you believe it, particularly when you were also blamed in childhood by your parents.

Because of this, it took years before I could accept that I had an illness which required medical treatment. Every time I stopped taking my medication I became unwell and this resulted in years of revolving door hospital admissions. I was a passionate advocate against the medical model but, looking back over the trajectory of my illness, I realize that a combination of the right medication, along with emotional, psychological and practical support, has been the most effective approach in keeping me well. When I have received one without the others I have always ended up ill.

Much can be said on both sides of the nature/nurture debate on mental health. It seems to me the causes are likely to be multifarious and complex. In my particular case—and with most fellow sufferers I have come across—there was psychological damage in my childhood and a strong prevalence of serious mental illness in my immediate and extended family. Yet I have two sisters who came through the same family circumstances as me but have remained perfectly healthy into adulthood.

It would seem obvious that the best we can do is to accept that everybody is unique, that different things will work for different people and the way we treat each other is hugely important. For me to be told that there was something fundamentally flawed with my personality—the very essence of who I am—was drastically undermining. I am grateful that I have since thrown off the oppressive mantle of such a damning diagnosis and this is reflected in my current treatment.

Back in 1995 however I bought into the label. I thought if I just had enough therapy and challenged myself stringently enough then I could eventually become like the doctors, nurses and other professionals I saw around me—people who weren't dysfunctional and damaged like me.

Because I was sceptical of the medical model I decided to supplement the social work and NHS support I was receiving and started to see an independent psychotherapist, Eleanor Aitken, at Wellspring House Counselling Centre in Leith.

Eleanor and I hit it off immediately. She was extremely warm, kind and accepting of me. I felt an instant bond. At first, owing to my deep-rooted shame, I could not look at her when we were talking. It took a long time for me to feel worthy of being seen and so I would insist she did not look at me either. Eye contact is something I still struggle with when I am not well, though then it is often because I think people can read my mind and can plant subversive thoughts and voices in my head if I look at them.

Eleanor was very patient with me over this, as with many other things I found difficult—for instance maintaining appropriate boundaries! I once bought her a black lacy negligee and suspenders from La Senza (and on another occasion I was to buy a male psychiatrist a leopard skin thong!) Of course she could not accept such a gift and we were able to have a giggle about it in later sessions. We worked together for 18 months—a productive and supportive time for me. I was devastated to lose her to her maternity leave but we kept in touch for a while by letter, which I appreciated very much.

Power dressing for a pizza

Randall House, which I attended three days a week, continued to be my most regular source of support, along with home visits from Kathryn. I became even more overweight around this time—not aided by the habit I had developed of going off on my own for 3 course 'business' lunches to local restaurants during the break between groups. I must have looked quite a sight, increasingly large and sitting on my own—always clad in a suit and tie, with waistcoat and an old battered briefcase. Not a very convincing businesswoman! The suits and ties were part of an ongoing campaign to cultivate an image of the status and respectability I felt I lacked. If I wear them now it is for artistic reasons.

The body politic

I was progressing quickly through the ranks of the Patients' Council, from management committee member to Secretary, and in the following year would be elected Chair. My involvement with the Patients' Council was motivated by a genuine desire to influence improvements in the hospital. My personal experience—both positive and negative—had brought about the realisation that change was not possible if patients (or 'service users'—a term I became acquainted with at this time) were not at its heart.

As one of the first service user groups in the country The Royal Edinburgh Hospital Patients' Council played a pivotal role in the emergence of independent advocacy in Scotland. It was an exciting moment in mental health history and I got a real kick out of being part of it. Although I was not instrumental in laying the foundations, I was able to help shape its development. I found my voice within a diverse social movement.

Indeed the politics and approaches of the different interests within the movement varied widely. One group for which I had much sympathy was the more radical anti-psychiatry faction which advocated a complete end to drug treatment and compulsory detention. Having been detained in hospital for lengthy periods it was hardly surprising. I started reading books such as Peter Breggin's Toxic Psychiatry which exposed the mutually serving co-dependency of drug companies, doctors and the government in maintaining the status quo.

The Royal Edinburgh Hospital was an extreme example of the medical model in practice. The predominant belief in a biological basis for mental illness meant that it was nigh well impossible to gain access to psychological and talking therapies. The few services that did exist, such as Colinton Road Psychotherapy Clinic and the Cullen Centre for Eating Disorders, had lengthy waiting lists. It could scarcely be deemed unreasonable to advocate the need for change.

However, although I was an angry young woman used to bucking the system and often getting in trouble for speaking out against unjust treatment, I allied myself with the more moderate wing of the user movement as a means to achieving my ultimate aim of patient power. At a philosophical level I believed then, as I do now, that the best way to influence change is to work with the people in power and not against them. It sits more comfortably with me to build alliances than to antagonise.

The dialogical nature of the movement meant I could straddle both camps depending on the issues and audiences I was addressing. I found if I managed to stay measured during meetings with service providers they were more likely to listen to what I had to say.

I became used to speaking in public—even adept—although after each session I would agonize over every little faux pas. Everyone has highs and lows but for me the dichotomy between the two is more extreme. I vacillated between over-confidence and cripplingly low self-esteem. Since the onset of my illness in late adolescence, this has created an irreconcilable tension within me and confusion for other people over what they could expect of me. At that stage I was ambitious and passionate. I frequently pushed myself beyond my comfort zone. I became very stressed during the preparation stage and deeply self-critical afterwards—something common enough in the average person, but for me the stakes were rather higher: if the stress tipped me over the edge I would end up in hospital or, worse still, attempting suicide.

Irrational roulette

Suicidal thoughts were still a feature of my everyday existence but because I lacked the resolve for the most part to attempt killing myself, I resorted to the next best thing—deliberately putting myself in the path of danger. I would cross the road without looking left or right, sometimes even with my eyes closed. I ate foods way past their sell-by date which just gave me sickness and diarrhoea and, when I was particularly stressed or troubled, I would go out late at night and wander round deserted parks and graveyards in the hope of being attacked, perhaps even murdered. Sometimes I boozed on Buckfast, swigging from a bottle in the street, or getting drunk in the corner of some pub in a dodgy part of town. I might as well have stuck a plaque on my forehead reading *I am alone, vulnerable and looking for trouble. Please abuse me.*

Onwards and upwards

In my customary way I kept up the appearance of coping admirably by immersing myself as completely as I could in the work of the Patients' Council. This involved taking part in working groups, committee meetings and training seminars; writing and analysing reports; delivering presentations at conferences, and meeting interested stakeholders. When I became Chair in 1996 my duties and time commitment increased markedly. I was now going into the office at the hospital 3—4 days a week, spending a lot of time at home on follow up work, and going out and about to different parts of the country on Patients' Council business.

I came into regular contact with a wide range of voluntary organisations and in time ended up on the board of many. Some of them were user-led such as the Consultation and Advocacy Promotion Service (CAPS) which supported collective advocacy in the community, and Advocard, which provided individual advocacy through volunteers. Others were service providers and allies. Edinburgh Association for Mental Health, or EAMH, was the host agency for the Patients' Council, providing management and staff support.

Owing to a series of grievances between both organisations we broke away from EAMH. This was a major schism at a time when new staff had been hired to support us and many disaffected members left. As Chair of the management committee my opinions held some weight and so I felt internal pressure not to appear weak or disinterested. I struggled to make sense of the complex issues involved and I remember feeling out of my depth when I was interviewed at the independent inquiry launched into the affair. I can't really say I took a strong view on who was culpable. It seemed there were reconcilable flaws on both sides and so, although quite forceful in articulating some observations, I did try to give a balanced view. Sitting on the fence may sometimes appear to be a facet of my personality whereas, in fact, my position usually results from a genuine ability to see both sides.

I had started to widen my sphere of engagement to issues concerning mental health in the community as well as in hospital. I went to Edinburgh Users' Forum (EUF) meetings, which were supported by CAPS. When a post for Development Worker became vacant at CAPS I applied for the position. Allison Alexander at the Patients' Council helped me with the application form because I had no previous experience of applying for a job. I was interviewed by a panel and duly appointed. Nobody was more surprised than me because I felt I had botched the interview through my lack of depth and obvious inexperience.

Nonetheless, the panel saw potential in me and gave me a chance. I am sorry to say that I did not come up to the mark and within two weeks of starting the job I handed in my resignation because of fear and sheer lack of confidence in my ability. The coordinator of CAPS was very patient and understanding with me, going so far as to pay for me to have independent support from a counsellor to help me make the right decision. I came to the conclusion that I just wasn't ready to cope with the demands of such a responsible job. I felt very guilty about having wasted all the time, money and hope vested in me by CAPS. Perhaps unsurprisingly, I ended up in hospital soon afterwards — a short admission but disappointing nonetheless. Although I felt I had disgraced myself publicly, everyone in the mental health community was very sympathetic and understanding about my decision. I was encouraged to shake off the experience and get back on the bandwagon and so, following my discharge from hospital, I fully immersed myself once again in the work of the Patients' Council and the wider user movement.

Bestowing beatitudes

The positive practices of community care and person-centred planning were gaining a widespread hold and I was asked to give public talks about how this affected service users. Among the talks was a speech at a Unison rally on The Mound (my infamous 'sermon on the Mound') where I addressed several thousand people opposing Council cuts.

I also spoke as part of a panel on Channel 5 News and did an interview with broadcaster Ruth Wishart on BBC Radio Scotland.

Having languished in hospital for a number of years, this sudden catapult into notoriety was a major shift in mindset. I struggled a lot with the expectations of my new role but it also felt exciting to be in a position of demand. I liked feeling I had something worthwhile to contribute. Anyone in similar circumstances might do well to become involved in the user movement, or any type of activism. The roles are rich, varied and rewarding and it is possible to find a sense of place and purpose in a ready-made community of like-minded peers.

Looking back on my activist period I can see that I was at times seduced by the power of being in a position of influence. I hope I did a good job and acted with integrity, but I am uncomfortable with the extent to which I was persuaded by other people's flattery, something which meant I probably bit off more than I could chew. Until recently, taking on too much continued to be a problem. I have finally learnt I don't have to accept every piece of work that comes my way. Being swamped by offers to become involved is a common problem for many user activists and learning to discern how much to comfortably take on is a major part of being effective and staying well.

The aspects of the aforementioned work that I enjoyed most were strategic planning and policy development. I learnt at this time to scrutinise, analyse, voice critical opinion and formulate sound arguments on paper. I was offered a place on the boards of a number of voluntary sector organisations, most notably EAMH where I remained a director for 4 years, and Carr-Gomm Scotland where I served for two. Although I enjoyed my involvement on both boards, as the only service user I found it quite isolating at times. Thankfully organisations are much more mindful now of the need to have a number of users and carers on their boards.

'The difference you'll make is priceless'

Besides activism and committee work, I was drawn to other volunteering roles which were more caring or supportive in nature. I can't remember exactly at what point I came into contact with Edinburgh Volunteer Exchange but they were hugely instrumental in helping me to access a range of opportunities and in supporting my engagement with various organisations.

One of these was Penumbra Respite Care, based at Cairdeas House — a guest house in central Edinburgh where people with mental health problems from all over Scotland could come for a short break. For many service users it was their only chance of a holiday. Paid staff not only ran the guest house but provided recreational and emotional support for the guests in order to help them maximise the pleasure and therapeutic benefits of their stay. I became one of a number of volunteers on the team who provided informal befriending by assisting with outings and activities and generally being available to talk if any guests needed company.

The volunteer coordinator did a sterling job of shoring up my confidence and allaying the recurrent fear that I was incompetent and too dangerous to be around vulnerable people. The manager of Cairdeas House also took an active interest in my involvement as with all the volunteers. I remember feeling pleased and proud when I was chosen to have my photo taken alongside the guests for the front cover of their annual report. All the staff and guests at Cairdeas House were a pleasure to work with and they made me feel welcome and appreciated for the 18 months I was there.

The Volunteer Exchange also put me in touch with Edinburgh Community Mediation Service which was recruiting volunteers to be trained as mediators supporting people through conflict situations with their neighbours. This greatly appealed as it was a new and viable skill to apply myself to. I was accepted for the training course following which I worked on several 'shuttle' mediation cases. Our role as mediators was to visit each party separately to ascertain their grievances and what they wanted to achieve from the process. We were then charged with conveying that information to the other party and acting as go-between to help the two sides to meet somewhere in the middle. During my 18 months with the project none of the cases I worked on came to full mediation with both parties sitting around a table. Although I was disappointed not to gain this experience, I was secretly relieved because I felt incompetent and feared I would be more of a liability than a help.

Edinburgh Community Mediation Service was a subsidiary of SACRO (Scottish Association for Care and Rehabilitation of Offenders) and through my involvement I heard about another SACRO project, the Prisoner Befriending Scheme, which was also looking for volunteers. I was recruited on to the training course and spent the next couple of months learning about the criminal justice system and, more importantly, having my attitudes and prejudices challenged. Part of the training course was a visit to Saughton Prison where we were shown round the cells, workshops and recreational facilities and introduced to some of the inmates. I remember feeling anger and intense discomfort when a gung-ho prison warden traipsed us all into a cell where a man was crouching on the floor and announced "this guy's on suicide watch". It was insensitive and an unnecessary breach of his privacy. He must have felt we were voyeurs feeding on his despair.

Following the training I was provisionally matched to a young man in Perth Prison, a convicted arsonist, who like most offenders had had a very difficult upbringing. We had a pleasant chat for half an hour or so in the visiting area. I felt it went well though I worried about being a little too enthusiastic because I was anxious for him to like me. I was really disappointed and embarrassed when the manager called me in the following week to break the news that he didn't want to be matched with me as he had hoped for someone older—'more of a mother figure'. This made complete sense but at the time I was too insecure not to see it as a humiliating rejection and so I withdrew from the project completely.

Move over Sigmund Freud

To supplement my voluntary work I attended Stevenson College to study for a Certificate in Counselling Skills which I hoped would facilitate my own self-awareness and healing as well as giving me the tools to work more effectively with others. The course was for one day a week and ran for three academic terms. It was very intense and emotionally demanding. The tutor had taken a leap of faith in accepting me on to the course as I had been quite open during the interview about the extent of my mental health problems and childhood trauma. I was very grateful because it communicated to me that I was capable of significant growth in my emotional development—to the extent that I could support others.

It often happens in counselling group work that a vulnerable individual assumes the role of 'sick person' almost unconsciously. I found myself conveniently fulfilling this role for everyone else in the group who needed someone to practise on. I was so used to complying with the needs of others that it had become second nature. Our tutor recognised what was going on and he encouraged me to challenge the group dynamic. Although I was made aware of this it is something which I am still learning to deal with because the entrenched remnants of childhood abuse are difficult to expunge.

I also became involved at this time with a consultancy organisation called Scottish Human Services (SHS) which offered capacity building and training to campaign groups and support providers, including the NHS, to help them operate in a more holistic, person-centred way. SHS ran a number of courses I was interested in, the first of which, *Powerful Voices*, was facilitated by tutors who would become personal friends.

Open invitation

While all this was going on I was also supporting my mother in living independently from my father. I was 24 and able to delude myself into interpreting my role as support. It actually consisted of regular visits to her house where she cooked my tea and did my washing!

To mark my rite of passage into my mid twenties I threw a party at a gay cafe in Broughton Street called *Over the Rainbow*. Over thirty people turned up. I was touched and surprised because in those days, given my chaotic behaviour, I found it difficult to attract and hold on to friends. Most of the guests were Patients' Council colleagues and my family. I remember feeling particularly proud to have my old schoolteacher Mr Walls there, and Norman Macrae, the chaplain I met in the Royal Infirmary who had now become a close friend. I had always wanted to introduce them to each other because they had a shared connection. Mr Walls' father and Norman had trained together as Church of Scotland ministers in the 1940's.

My friendship with Norman and his wife, Claire, was an important support and source of joy in my life. Although they were both in their late seventies I could talk to them about anything from spirituality to sexuality. Our conversations would meander for hours. They were extremely open-minded people and interested in others. They loved the company of young people and wore their age and experience lightly. These qualities made them very popular and, with the exception perhaps of the Marchioness, they had more friends than anyone I had ever met. Somehow they still managed to make me feel special and loved.

I often turned to them when I was distressed or in times of crisis. I am ashamed to say I even turned up at their house drunk one night. They took me in without the slightest judgment or reprimand and not only let me stay the night but read and sang me to sleep. Claire sat by my bed and comforted me with words from one of her favourite books, *The Cloud of Unknowing*, which she later gifted to me and which I grew to love. Norman warbled *The Lord Is My Shepherd* from his psalm book which was very touching though quite out of tune. It is a very special memory which I treasure even more now that they are gone, and not least because it was the only time in my life I have ever been read to sleep.

Now that my mother was living on her own without my father's controlling influence, her bipolar behaviour was more giddy and unhinged. It was difficult to spend time with her because she talked at me incessantly. This catapulted me back to childhood memories where I was the receptacle for all her distress. I would sit frozen in a trance-like state as her words flooded over me. Thankfully she didn't require any intelligent response; she just needed a dustbin to offload her baggage.

Roughing it

Back at my flat in C Crescent, the menace of mice crept into my life. I have a phobia about mice which probably originated from seeing them rampage freely round our house as a child. It became so unbearable to spend time in the flat that I desperately wanted to move house. My night time wanderings fuelled with Buckfast became more frequent and I was sleeping rough as much as at home. People always imagine that homelessness is a simple matter of not having a house. A home is so much more than just a house; it is somewhere you feel well, safe and happy—none of which I felt in that flat, particularly after the mice had invaded. I was lonely, frightened and miserable and so the streets were a preferable option. At least there I was connected to a world outside the damning prison of my mind.

In a vain attempt to combat the mouse problem I made the terrible decision to get a cat. She was a shy tortoiseshell called Simba. I say terrible decision because I was not fit to look after her, and, sorry to tell, I neglected her badly. I have always loved cats but Simba was so timid that it was difficult to bond with her. For most of her short stay she hid behind the settee and, as far as I know, never caught any mice. I struggled to feed her and change her litter tray regularly. The flat started to reek of stale urine and faeces and it can't have been pleasant for her living with me. I found it so unbearable to be in the flat I was out for most of the day and wandered round the streets at night. Poor Simba hardly ever had company.

Seeing in the bells

New Year was always a difficult time of year. On Hogmanay 1996 I felt particularly unwell. I had fallen out with the staff at Randall House and so had neglected to go in for my fortnightly 'depot' injection. I had also stopped taking my oral medication. I was psychotic that night and preoccupied with the voices of dead spirits who were summoning me to join them in the underworld. I headed for the local cemetery without a coat or shoes and started digging up tufts of grass and earth around one of the graves with my fingers. I was digging frantically whilst the urgency of the dead voices increased. They were frustrated and angry with me for not digging fast enough. Suddenly a torch beamed down on me. I thought it was Purgatory opening up to receive me. I looked up to see two policemen standing above with looks of perplexed concern on their faces. One of them asked me what I was doing. I got up to run off as the voices were telling me but the policemen grabbed me, one on each arm, and led me hunched out of the cemetery to their vehicle outside. They drove me to the Royal Edinburgh Hospital.

I was assessed by the Psychiatric Emergency Team who ascertained that I was too frightened and psychotic to answer their questions and was admitted to Bannockburn Ward under legal section because I would not go in voluntarily. Over the next few days it felt to me that the staff did their best to make me feel unwelcome. I was threatened with restraint if I ran off the ward or refused to take my injection. The tone of their voices seemed to imply that I was wasting their time and they were just going through the motions with me because they had to.

Once I had had my injection the voices receded somewhat but I felt very distressed at being in a hostile environment. Frightened of being pinned down if I attempted to leave, I clung to my bed for the next few days not daring to go out of the dormitory other than to the toilet. The staff left me to myself. No-one even bothered to notice, or at least enquire, why I wasn't going for meals. By the third day I became dehydrated through lack of fluid and my head was pounding jackboots. Finally, broken and on my knees, I went out into the corridor and fell to the floor sobbing hysterically for someone to help me. The staff walked past me on their rounds completely ignoring me. One of them even stepped over me. When a young student nurse approached tentatively to comfort me, the staff nurse barked "Leave her alone! She's just attention seeking". Because my 72 hour section had lapsed they had no obligation to keep me there any longer. Dr Kelly, whom I never actually saw during the three days I was there, was obviously unconcerned and had given them the all-clear to let me leave. I knew I was not really in a fit state to leave but after their inhumane treatment I felt I had no option but to go if I was not to be driven completely mad.

Whilst I had been in hospital my mother had been looking in on Simba, and she had no trouble persuading me when I got back that it was kinder to let her go. She took her to the Cat Protection League where I hope poor Simba found the love and attention she deserved.

A wolf in sheep's clothing

At Randall House a 3rd year nursing student on his final placement, "Alan", started taking an interest in me. I was flattered that he seemed to like me and hoped that we might strike up a friendship once he had left. I did not find him attractive and hoped that his feelings for me were platonic too. I had been in enough compromising situations with men. Alan had shown an interest in seeing some poems I had written and I resolved to bring them in next day with a discreet note of my contact details in case he wanted to keep in touch. I was concerned however that he should not interpret this as a proposition so I included a short letter explaining categorically that I was not looking for a boyfriend; I just wanted to be friends.

My social world at that time consisted of service users like me — people with no status or perceived value — and also professionals, who seemed to have it all. I was desperate to penetrate their world. I even looked into training as a psychiatric nurse, though, of course, would never have been accepted. My self-esteem was so low and my opportunities so limited by my psychiatric record, that managing to acquire a friend who was 'on the other side' felt like the ultimate endorsement that I was not, after all, a failure. The deep yearning to belong, though it sometimes led me in unhelpful directions, was nonetheless a natural human instinct.

The evening after I had given Alan the letter and poems he telephoned my home. I was delighted initially to get his call though he sounded somewhat wary and I noted a touch of hostility in his voice which surprised me. I wondered if I had done the wrong thing; perhaps he was going to report me to my nursing key worker for making an inappropriate contact. He explained that he was taking a great risk in phoning a patient — which I was aware of but had hoped would soon be of no consequence because shortly he would be finishing his placement and no longer have a role in my care. He demanded that I give him my assurance that I tell no one about our friendship, adding "If you do tell anyone I'm going to completely deny it and say you're making it all up for attention. Then you will get into trouble. I've read your notes and you've got a reputation in the hospital for attention-seeking and lies."

I knew the staff in Bannockburn had no time for me but to hear from him that I was discredited throughout the hospital shocked and distressed me because it was on grounds that were grossly unjust. Insidious voices crept in: "If people are saying it then it must be true". Most of his words washed over me after that but I felt I had no choice but to acquiesce to his conditions. I took a cursory note of the time and place he told me to meet him—2pm on Saturday at the Malt Shovel pub on Cockburn Street. His manipulative behaviour had made me feel uneasy.

By the time Saturday came I contrived every excuse in my head to get out of meeting him but I did not have his number and he had threatened to report me to Randall House with evidence of the letter if I let him down and so I met him as planned.

The atmosphere between us was frosty and strained, not at all what I had imagined being friends would be like. He had always been warm and pleasant to me before the phone call. We exchanged a few shallow details about each other's lives. He went to great lengths to impress upon me that he was a black belt in various martial arts. He was clearly trying to intimidate me.

After an hour or so of terse conversation I asked if I could leave, explaining that I had a birthday party to go to in Leith. Somewhat disgruntled he agreed but said he wanted to see me the next day in Mather's Bar in Broughton Street, and this time I was to keep the rest of the day free.

I left thinking "I'm not going to see you again, you bastard". That night as I turned up outside the restaurant for the party, I inexplicably vomited all over the pavement; I felt disgust at what I had agreed to and dreaded the thought of seeing him again. But like a micro chip programmed to its own obliteration I did turn up to Mather's on the Sunday. Wasn't this the same situation I always got into with men? Hadn't I brought it on myself? It was all I deserved. With a bit of luck he would turn out to be a psychopath and murder me.

I got drunk this time because the conversation was too unbearable to be sober. We clearly did not even like each other but were going through the motions. In spite of my meek resignation to being led to the slaughter, there was a small defiant part of me that hoped the process would reverse. When he told me we were going to his room at the nursing quarters I said "Okay, but please, I don't want anything sexual. I'm not looking for a boyfriend." "Fine" he shrugged, "Come on, get your coat on."

To the unkind observer I was clearly giving mixed messages — saying I didn't want sex but going back with him all the same. We were in a public place, it was broad daylight; I could easily have left on my own. It is true. It's difficult to explain to those who haven't been abused the state of learned helplessness that grips a person in a situation when all the lights are flashing Red for Danger. You lose all natural defence mechanisms — to scream and kick or punch — indeed not to go back to a person's room. You even kid yourself you want it.

So when Alan roughly yanked off my T shirt and jeans I let him. Once again my attacker was oblivious to the fact that I was sobbing, hunched in a posture of distress on the bed, clearly not wanting sex. Perhaps he was aroused by my passive "compliance". Some men are like that. He pushed me back on the bed with his karate fists and lunged furiously into me. This was rape. The scream that escaped from my mouth was caught short by his hand and something in that moment stopped him from ramming, ramming, ramming: Vaginismus — my fortress and my nemesis to intimacy, the stalwart friend that stops ultimate penetration. "You're fucked up!" he spat in my face, then tossed me aside to cry into the wall for what seemed like hours while he turned on the News and guzzled biscuits on the floor.

All I could think was "I wish an angel would take me away from here" just as I used to think as a child when being abused in my parents' bed. I don't remember leaving his room or how I got home. The worst bit was the aftermath, and knowing he wanted to see me again, presumably to finish off the job.

He blackmailed me into meeting him at Ryan's Bar and I had girded up the courage to let him know I wanted it to end. I was beginning to realize that the best way of extricating myself from him was to dangle the threat of telling someone at Randall House myself. I had no real intention of doing this because I felt that I would not be believed. However, it worked and he agreed not to contact me again if I promised to tell no one.

That was a promise I kept faithfully until six months later. Consumed with guilt and the worry he might do something worse to someone else, I told my social worker, Kathryn. I was terrified of getting into trouble or not being believed, but the experience had left me in such distress that I couldn't keep it to myself any longer. Kathryn had suspected all along that I had been keeping something from her. After months of being quizzed by her it was a relief just to get it out. Her reaction surprised me. She did not blame me at all for what happened. She said that he had abused his position and it was a serious matter which she would have to report to the clinical director who also happened to be my psychiatrist, Dr Kelly.

A week or so later Kathryn told me that Dr Kelly wanted to interview me about it and that the nurse manager, who was a man, would be present too. I begged not to have to talk about it in front of a man because I felt so ashamed. Besides I had worked with the nurse manager on a collegiate basis in my role as Chair of the Patients' Council. Kathryn tried her best to ensure that it was a woman who would interview me with Dr Kelly who was also female but Dr Kelly objected saying I had no choice but to meet with her and the male nurse manager.

That response set the tone for her handling of the whole situation. The meeting was very formal. I was grilled by her in such a way that I squirmed and apologised all the way through for having effectively 'led Alan astray'. The nurse manager was clearly very uncomfortable watching me being backed into a corner and I could see that he felt sorry for me but there was nothing he could do because Dr Kelly was so forceful and clearly determined that I should shoulder the blame.

I came out of the meeting feeling that I had been subjected to a disciplinary, more convinced than ever that what I had done was shameful and unforgivable. Alan, it appeared, was exonerated. I know Kathryn felt very badly about the way it was handled and though she had to walk a tight line she did her best to assuage my guilt.

A few months later I ended up in Bannockburn Ward again where I was treated with the same hostile indifference from staff. One newly qualified nurse was kind enough to spend time with me however and when I told him about the incident with Alan which was still preying heavily on my mind, he was visibly shocked. "I can't believe nobody's told you" he said, "that guy was struck off because he did the same to a number of female patients".

I don't really know what to say now in conclusion. It still frightens me to think of Alan and I'm relieved that he won't have access to vulnerable patients anymore. As for Dr Kelly, although I know what she did was wrong, I still can't find it in myself to be angry with her because I cannot bear to think someone I trusted as much as a psychiatrist could have let me down so badly. Inevitably, because of my condition, deep down I will always feel that I was to blame for what happened.

Turning back the clock

My parents were now seeing each other covertly. My father had found out where my mother was living and inveigled his way back into her life by playing on her pity. He was clever enough to make her keep it a secret from us because he knew we would want to protect her (or from his point of view—interfere in their marriage). They had recently, after a 2 year separation, been divorced, but my father, as always, was in denial. He had opposed the divorce in Court on the grounds that they were Catholics and therefore "married for life in the eyes of God". He even went as far as to appeal to the Cardinal to plead his case in

Court. Of course the Church was having none of his nonsense. They are well used to abusive men citing religion as a justification for their controlling behaviour! They had helped my mother in the past and they were not going to help him now.

When the case had reached the Court and the divorce was granted my father had been ordered to give alimony to my mother in the form of half of the proceeds from the sale of their last house. He refused saying that "all the money had gone". When asked to elaborate on this he couldn't. As he was clearly lying he was held in Contempt of Court. He could have faced a custodial sentence but he managed to worm out of this by writing a begging letter to the Sheriff entreating him to have mercy on him on account of his disability and his commitment to his faith—he who had barely set foot in a church since they were married! I saw the letter. It was full of Uriah Heap self-pitying. He got off lightly with a small fine and didn't have to pay any money to my mother.

The case drew quite a stir in the local press. A number of newspapers including The Daily Record and The Evening News gave the story coverage under sensational headlines such as "Bible Thumper's Vow of Silence" over an embittered looking photo of my father.

After all the furore had settled he stole back into her life and my poor mother, who thought she had won her freedom, if not the money she was due, was prisoner once more to his fickle moods. She was too frightened to tell us that she was seeing him again. He had of course sworn her to secrecy and she thought we would be angry with her. I found that they were back together by accident and accepted the situation as inevitable. Many years later my mother disclosed that they then re-married in secret, my father having lied to her that she would be deported back to Italy if she did not marry him. Of course she was forbidden to tell us.

Back to the circus

Reverting to my own intolerable situation, the flat, already overrun with mice, was now also infested with fleas. The pest control department eventually had to fumigate it. I was out sleeping rough much of the time and it became clear once again that I could not manage a tenancy of my own. One of Kathryn's social work colleagues at the Royal Edinburgh Hospital arranged for me to go into emergency homeless accommodation in Cranston Street Women's Hostel off the Royal Mile. I remained there for a few weeks until a place became available back in my old shared supported accommodation house with Q Housing Association.

I moved into my former residence of S Street on a Thursday evening in October 1997. As before, my housemates were people with troubled histories like my own. Some of them had severe and enduring mental health problems. Others had come through the criminal justice system. The senior support worker in charge of the house, Candice Wight, ruled her patch from Q headquarters. The person who had day to day responsibility for the running of the house was Candice's support assistant, Gillian, who worked full time in S Street. I was immediately captivated by Gillian's droll Lancashire wit and apple blossom cheeks and was all fingers and thumbs when she helped me move my bags into my room on the first floor — the biggest room in the house with a bay window view of the garden.

That evening, and throughout my time at S Street, I was somewhat unhinged in my behaviour. Because I was so drawn to Gillian I wanted to make an impression, and at that stage in my life this involved mimicking her accent, cocking my leg to make a fart and telling her I wanted to rifle through her dirty underwear — which certainly made an impression but not the right one! Gillian was shocked. I think I was different from the rest of her charges who, though no older, were frankly more mature and often too concerned with their next methadone fix to take much notice. They seemed faintly amused by my antics because it was fun to see Gillian getting flustered. However they soon tired of the cartoon skit unfolding before their eyes. For Gillian it had become apparent that first night that she was going to have a job on her hands with me. She must have groaned inwardly but managed to contain her exasperation.

Friends along the way

The day after I moved in was the CAPS AGM at the Postal Workers' Union in Brunswick Street. I almost didn't go. Candice Wight felt I should take a few days to settle into the house properly. I decided to buck her advice. I met a fellow service user at the AGM called Justin.

Justin was witty, debonair and handsome. To be honest I would have given in to my infatuation had he not been totally out of my league. It soon became apparent that we were destined to become as complimentary as a pea and a pod (one short and round, the other long and slim). We shared our most vulnerable moments. Also his legendary love of cake made him the perfect companion for languishing away many an afternoon in coffee shops around the city. Whilst we explored the murky terrain of depression and existential angst in our conversations, we could have a laugh about it too. I remember once in the early days of our friendship we sat in the Filmhouse Bar and came up with a list of T-shirt logos with which we were going to make our fortune—the most memorable of which was *At Least I'm Aware of It* which seemed to sum up perfectly our obsession with therapy and self help books at that time.

Living in S Street with five other dysfunctional housemates was not an easy ride and so my friends, Justin, Bruna, Archie, Kate and the Marchioness, were crucial to my survival, as well as two lovely new friends I had met through church—Georgina and Fiona. Marina, whom I had met in Bannockburn Ward, was a huge support to me and a source of unbridled mirth. We sidekicked around on the number 5 bus swapping anecdotes about our dramatic escape attempts. Marina was one of the most charming people you could hope to meet and one of life's characters. I drew a lot of inspiration from her brave struggle with mental distress. We shared an irreverent fuck-the-system attitude and we had a propensity, indeed a necessity, in our natures to form intense attachments to our female care-givers. Marina understood better than anybody the ecstasy and heartache that went along with this. As my attachment to Gillian, my support worker, developed, Marina offered light relief as well as consolation and companionship in weathering the pain.

The patience of two saints

Gillian, by her own admission, really didn't know what to do with me. As the sole worker located in S Street the burden of care for me and my housemates fell on her. Because of my attachment issues, immaturity and ongoing mood swings, I was the highest maintenance of her clients. My arrival in the house must have seemed to her and everybody else like a fish-slap in the face. I have to say she rose to the challenge admirably and proved a natural in dealing with the extremes of my behaviour.

Gillian was no soft touch. She spoke plainly and frankly and we came to blows on many occasions over a cross word or reprimand. She was also kind and generous with her time and had the courage to journey with me to the dark places in my psyche. In many ways she fulfilled the role of a therapist for me. Like many care workers, who disgracefully are only paid a pittance, she did a skilled, vital and difficult job.

The other person who worked over and above the call of duty was my social worker, Kathryn Blythe, who was still supporting me even though I had moved out of her geographical sector. That is what Kathryn did. She stuck with people throughout their journey because she understood they needed time to grow and that commitment in relationships was essential to recovery for people who have had their trust abused.

Red nose days

I was finally discharged from Randall House Day Unit and had a new psychiatrist and GP, and a community psychiatric nurse (CPN) with whom I got on well though only saw briefly once a fortnight for my depot injection.

S Street was a chaotic place to live in. As mentioned, some of the residents had come from prison and were involved in all sorts of dubious stuff to fund their drug addictions. We were on meagre personal allowances and had a shared budget for food and household expenses. Every Friday we would take it in pairs to do the shopping for the whole house. This was part of the therapy to show we could be trusted and responsible. These shopping trips were quite a strain for the other residents who were often stoned and incoherent. To them I was a giggling little chatter-box whom they couldn't relate to. For my part, although I had seen the rough side of life, I was not street-wise and was all out at sea in their company.

Looking back, they were kind to me considering I was so often such an irritation. No one ever lost patience with me for turning up to communal meals dressed as Popeye or Billy the Kid; or, when it was my turn to cook, presenting them with Jelly Babies as a joke. My fantasy dish was to serve up 'plastic turd a-la bourguignon' with a sprig of tarragon when Candice joined us for tea. Thankfully I was never quite able to summon up the courage to go that far.

Sometimes there were 'incidents' in S Street as might be expected in a household of ne'er do wells and misfits. One night when I had taken an overdose and locked myself in my room I was roused from my drug-induced stupor by frantic banging on my door. Eventually I had to open it and was confronted by a bloody scene. Tierney, a newly arrived resident, who appeared loveable and volatile in equal measure, had stabbed her boyfriend with a pair of scissors in a drunken fit. What she wanted was to borrow a carving knife to finish off the job!

Another night I awoke to loud yelling from the landing. Liu, a shy Chinese girl who smiled all the time, had hung herself from the banister. The poor soul to discover her body was Gareth, Alpha male of the house, who had got up in the night. It was a grim sight for everyone as we sat stupefied with horror waiting for the ambulance men to cut her down.

Candice Wight decided that we should go on a house trip to Dunbar the following weekend to recover from the trauma. She cheerfully sent us packing with Gillian and no other support staff. While the others got stoned to oblivion Gillian was left by herself to manage me. I was hysterical and clingy. She did her best to distract me but all I wanted was to talk incessantly about my fear of suicide. It was a real baptism of fire for Gillian who had never had to face a situation like this before. She now uses what she learnt from those experiences to inform the trauma work she does for the NHS through art therapy and counselling.

When we arrived back in Edinburgh we ploughed into our parallel realities as usual with hardly a mention of Liu's suicide—not because we didn't care, but because it was too awful to contemplate. Each of us was battling with our own self-destructive forces.

Opportunities to fly

I was still heavily involved in the work of the Patients' Council. Around this time I got to know Sally Dick, an external consultant. She had been commissioned to work with me and others on developing a quality assurance framework to assess care on the wards from a service-user perspective. This was a piece of work I really enjoyed because it appealed to my analytical side—breaking down the components of care and building them back again into measurable standards. I learnt a lot from Sally about the process of putting together such a framework and from her style of group facilitation. She had a natural way of relating to us which was supportive without being condescending. We were all very proud of the document we put together with Sally's help, especially since it was adopted as a tool in other Health Boards which further validated our hard work.

I decided I would like to do more work with Sally and she was kind enough to engage me in other ongoing projects such as training nursing staff at Hartwoodhill Hospital in Lanarkshire. She assisted many service users like me to go on to work in mental health by mentoring and giving us opportunities for experience.

A year earlier in 1996, I was involved with the Patients' Council in a training video for nursing staff ("This Could Be You") which was conceived by Allison Alexander. At the time of writing it is still used with students at Napier University. It featured a group of service users, including me, talking about their experiences of being in hospital and how helpful or harmful they found the various attitudes and approaches of staff. I found it very empowering to name my experience publicly but I also feared reprisals if I were ever to be re-admitted to hospital, the likelihood of which was strong. I felt it was a risk worth taking, though, since it went straight to the heart of what I had joined the Patients' Council to do—to use my experience to influence better treatment and care for others in my position.

The Patients' Council also did a lot of profile-raising in an effort to reduce the stigma of mental illness and to increase welfare spending on mental health. We had a real ally in our local Labour MP, Nigel Griffiths, who took a keen interest in the hospital and championed our cause over many campaigns. Devolution was to prove a positive development for mental health and indeed for most aspects of public policy in Scotland. We seized the opportunities this offered.

One of the highlights of my personal involvement with the Patients' Council was our national conference on advocacy at the Western General Hospital in Edinburgh in 1998 which I was asked to chair. The conference was attended by a hundred delegates from different parts of the country, all keen to learn more about the success story we had become. The Scottish Minister for Health, Sam Galbraith, accepted our invitation to be a keynote speaker. Of course we were thrilled. Unfortunately, on the day, he was held up and had to send one of his aides. The Chief Executive of NHS Lothian Primary Healthcare Trust also gave an address. He publicly endorsed the Trust's support and was careful to state how much they valued our part in shaping mental health services in Lothian.

I got a real buzz out of chairing the conference. With two years' experience of chairing our monthly Patients' Council meetings in the hospital board room under my belt, I was well accustomed to a packed agenda and expecting the unexpected from the floor. Nonetheless, the conference was a rite of passage and I was delighted that it went down so well with everyone who attended.

As if the above commitments were not enough, I had also recently joined the management committee of Advocard—a user-led organisation which provided individual representation in the community using volunteer advocates. I learnt a lot about independent advocacy in practice through the staff at Advocard and really enjoyed working with them.

All this earned me a place as user representative on the Edinburgh Mental Health Advocacy Strategy Group. Together we set about formulating a 3 year plan for the city. I remember being so fired up by our work that I went off on my own and wrote a lengthy report which outlined several organisational models of how advocacy could be run in the city including an appraisal of the feasibility of each.

Noughts and crosses

The main focus of all my activities about this time was self-improvement. This led me in a number of directions. My friend, Alice, persuaded me to audition for a show called *The Zoo* which was being performed by the Savoy Opera Group for the 1998 Festival Fringe. To my surprise, I was offered a place in the chorus — a considerable step up from a mute cherub and this time I even managed to behave myself on stage. After the Savoy performance there was my unlikely foray into circle dancing where I met my friend, Liz. Dressed in my Levi jeans and Coca-Cola T-shirt, I appeared a clumping and incongruous recruit among all the swaying new age, Tie-dyed and incense-bearing participants as we expressed peace and love through dance.

Another memorable thing I associate with 1998 was my brush with fundamentalism. I had been recruited by two women on the street who were evangelising for the International Church of Christ which I have no hesitation now in calling a cult. In spite of the support I received from friends I was still in many ways a lost soul therefore a vulnerable target for this sort of thing. To be honest, I was more interested in one of the women who picked me up than church doctrine!

Although I still identified myself as a Catholic and went sporadically to Mass, this church seemed vastly more appealing. They offered activities every night of the week. Indeed it soon became apparent that you were expected not to spend leisure time with anyone outwith the church. Naturally I was wary, but the pull of a tight knit community, a so called 'family in God', to ally myself to proved very seductive.

My friend, Alice, was the first to notice the warning signs and she set about collecting information on the church to show me that it was a cult. At first I was resistant to her pleas. It all seemed rather harmless, why shouldn't I hang out with a new bunch of friends? They were really nice people and such good fun—they even had fancy dress parties. But gradually, as they tried to indoctrinate me with their right-wing rhetoric, I came to my senses and realised I could have no part in such an organisation. This church worshipped a God who breathed down fire and brimstone and offered salvation in return for servile obedience, whereas my idea of God was a universal spirit of love, generosity and tolerance.

Encouraged by Alice, I decided to extricate myself from their hold. Since I was in the early stages of initiation it wasn't too difficult. At first I tried to reason with them but they responded by bombarding me with 'corrective' theology. Eventually I wrote down my position in a letter stating my abhorrence for their homophobic values and their practice of trying to brainwash vulnerable people. That seemed to do the trick and they left me alone.

Up the ladder

At the end of 1998 a vacancy had arisen in U Street, one of Q Association's other shared houses. It was less supported and had fewer tenants. This appeared a good option for me since I was feeling more and more alienated from the other residents in my house. I was also struggling to manage on the pittance on which we were expected to live. U Street wasn't a 'registered' property like S Street and so I would be entitled to full benefits there. Also my support worker, Gillian, had recently left to start her art therapy course so I no longer had that particular incentive to keep me in S Street.

U Street was a much calmer environment—four of us in all, each with severe and enduring mental health problems, although the others were more stable than I and had been out of hospital for several years. Nonetheless, it was not without its issues. Throughout my three years there I was the only female in the house which I did not mind too much as I got on well with the guys who were gentle and non-threatening.

We were left to our own devices pretty much, and were responsible for our own shopping, cooking and cleaning. It was a relief not to have to monitor how many biscuits you ate from the tin because everyone else had to have their share, or to have to sit down together in awkward silence at a weekly communal meal. We still received support from Candice at weekly or fortnightly therapy sessions at Q headquarters where we were grilled on what progress we were making in our personal development. While I found these sessions helpful it was clear that the others were not so well served. One of my housemates had serious personal hygiene issues which eventually I had to address with him because no one else would. He was clearly physically as well as mentally ill but no one picked up on this either. I persuaded him to go to the doctor's where he was diagnosed with cancer from which he mercifully recovered. His woes were further compounded because no one had ensured that he was in receipt of the appropriate benefits—something which I had to advocate for him.

Unsavoury acquaintance

One of the key objectives of my therapy was to reduce my risk-taking behaviour. I was still troubled by mood swings, paranoia and psychosis, and still given to night time wanderings fuelled with drink and self-destructive intent. A big part of me still wanted to be picked up by some psychopath and murdered. I came in contact at this time with another one of Candice's clients from a different house, an older man called "Walter" who was charming and kind to me, though somewhere deep down I sensed that his intentions were more sinister.

When Candice found out we were meeting up regularly she went berserk and warned me in no uncertain terms to stay away from him but I felt compelled to spend time with him; it was as if he had a hypnotic effect on me and so I persisted. Eventually, Candice was forced to extreme measures and had to divulge some personal details about him in order to protect me. This must have been a terrible dilemma for her. As a professional, confidentiality was paramount. She told me that Walter was a convicted rapist and paedophile who had recently been released from prison. Furthermore she warned me "If you continue to see him you are likely to end up chopped into pieces in a body bag, he is that dangerous."

That was all I needed to hear. I continued seeing more and more of him behind Candice's back, knowing as she had explained, that he was 'grooming' me. I thought 'it can only be a matter of time before he kills me.'

Even today, when the rest of me is busy getting on with life, somewhere inside is a child so bludgeoned with self-loathing that she wants an abuser to end her hell and give her what she most deserves — a violent death. I suppose you could call this self-annihilating instinct my shadow. In the event Walter did not try to harm me. The association fizzled out but I had the comfort and escape of knowing that a terminal release from my turbulent mental state was possible.

Cracks in the pavement

Ironically, I was still interested in pursuing a career where I could help other vulnerable people. I started volunteering as a detached street worker with a project for the homeless called Streetwork. The work was very challenging for me as I had so little confidence in my ability to provide practical help or emotional support to others. By good fortune the manager of the project was Katie Owen who had met me some years earlier when she was a student psychiatric nurse. She knew a bit about my history and understood my vulnerability. Because I had been open about my circumstances at interview, she took a chance in accepting me as a volunteer.

The job involved going out in pairs around the city centre to engage with clients — many of them rough sleepers — who could be identified as homeless because they were begging on the streets or congregating around well-known locations. We would check that they were warm and safe enough and, if they were rough sleeping and wanted to be indoors, we would help them access a bed in one of the local hostels.

The first point of contact was always to find out more about their situation and to establish trust and confidence for further follow-up work that could be done from our office base. This might involve, for example, liaising with health, social work or criminal justice services on their behalf, helping them access benefits and detox programmes and many other such 'interventions'. A key part of the job was also gathering statistics to build a profile of homelessness trends in the city to inform Council policy and service provision. Thus we were required to take notes and at the end of each shift to input relevant anonymous details into our database.

Katie noticed early on that I was struggling with the challenges of this role, mainly in relation to my confidence and perceived competence. Rather than dismiss me as a drain on the team because I needed such constant reassurance, Katie personally opted to pair up with me for Tuesday night shifts. She became my mentor and showed me how to do a good job. She taught me to believe in myself and she taught me that kindness and commitment are the most important things we could offer to help any person to grow. She demonstrated this in her extraordinary compassion towards her clients, her staff and to me. Katie would never give up on anyone. She stuck with me, investing far more time than she got in return. I think she saw me not just as a volunteer but as a vulnerable person who had been homeless herself and could do with a hand up. As such, the support she gave me extended far beyond the boundaries of her role. She let me talk about my trauma and abuse, and held me through countless distressing memories triggered by the work I was doing with clients, many of whom had similar experiences to mine.

Building on common ground

My volunteering at this time included involvement with Scottish Human Services (SHS). I was accepted as a participant on a leadership development course called 'Allies in Change.' The facilitator, Jo Kennedy, would later become a friend and advocate, supporting me while I was in hospital.

I also took on a research project the aims of which were to find out more about mental health awareness training being delivered across Scotland and to explore perceptions of the relationship between mental health and disability. I enjoyed putting together the research proposal and designed the methodology for consultation with other stakeholders. Owing mainly to my ill health, it took almost 2 years to collect data from different parts of Scotland but at last it was completed. My favourite part of the process was analysing the data and writing up the results in a report called *Building on Common Ground* which I believe can still be accessed online.

Whilst in U Street I was invited to join the Board of Carr-Gomm Scotland, an organization that provided high quality care for people with a range of support needs.

All this voluntary work reflected my political values, fed my creative drive and my interest in working with people. Keith Maloney at CAPS suggested the natural progression was to combine them in studying for a professional qualification in Community Education that would allow me to pursue a career in this field. I applied for a place on Edinburgh University's Postgraduate Certificate course at Moray House. Following an interview with the course director, Liz Elkind, I was accepted to start in October 1999. I was thrilled to be embarking on the next stage of my journey—a route into the world of paid professional work.

The Sky is NOT the Limit!

WORKING LIKE CRAZY | 2000–2005

By the time I started at Moray House I had resigned from the management committee of the Patients' Council. I wanted to move away from the identity of service user and prepare myself for a more facilitative role as a community worker though I did still draw heavily on my experiences as a user activist throughout my studies to relate theory to practice.

I found the course stimulating and relevant. I couldn't get enough of florid debate with lecturers and classmates. We discussed topics such as the meeting point between personal and political spheres of interest in our work and questions about whether we were agents of the State or agitators, whether our role was to instruct or liberate and how we should align process and outcome. Many fascinating arguments were batted like ping pong balls among us. Sometimes our answers fell short of our competence and the tutors would lend a theoretical hand; other times ideas would bounce furiously this way and that, and we'd leave the class buzzing only to finish the conversation off hours later in the canteen.

I was fortunate in having Liz as my personal tutor. We had a good rapport. I respected her for being direct enough to challenge me yet sensitive to, and understanding of, the personal challenges that dogged me—most notably my chronic lack of confidence and self-esteem.

After handing in my first assignment I arrived weeping at her door, distraught. I knew I had failed dismally and was going to be thrown off the course. Liz cautioned me to bide my time and reassured me that nothing was irreparable even if I had failed. She also added that she would be surprised from her knowledge of my contribution in class if I were not to get a good pass.

A few days before the marks were pinned on the student notice board, I got a call from Liz at home with the surprising and delightful news that I had got the highest mark in the class, indeed the highest mark possible: four straight A's with a plus on each! I was tempted to ask if it was a joke but Liz was plain-talking and sincere and there was no arguing with the fact though I found it almost too ridiculous to accept.

My first essay set the bar for future assignments. As far as I recall there was only one assessment during the whole course for which I did not get four A plusses. The tutor who marked the rogue essay evidently disagreed with the consensus on my perceived genius. He gave me an overall mark of B minus which I had the audacity to dispute. I am embarrassed about this now but it was typical of the schism in my self-perception — failure one minute, perfection the next; both set to collapse over the slightest nuance of external opinion.

Pointers in the right direction

I was studying part-time over two years. My first year placement was at Pentland Community Centre in Oxgangs. I had chosen it on the recommendation of my friend Melissa who had worked with the manager, Gary Rose, and felt he would be able to give me good supervision.

Melissa and I had known each other since my student days at Mylne's Court. Now, through mutual contacts in the voluntary sector, we became friends. Aside from work, we shared in common a love of shopping and film, and spent many Saturday afternoons in Top Shop or Next sizing up the latest fashions, followed by a trip to the Filmhouse or Cameo for something altogether more worthy — an art house movie with subtitles. We liked nothing better than a good old gossip over a pot of peppermint tea at the Dominion Cinema café whose photos of Sean Connery and Tilda Swinton on the wall seemed like old friends.

Her recommendation to work with Gary Rose at Pentland Community Centre hit the spot perfectly. He turned out to be a fantastic placement supervisor and I learnt a lot from him. He was challenging, critical, generous and supportive. Lack of confidence was a big issue for me; the converse also applied—a tendency to take on too much—mainly in an effort to please and impress. Gary made it clear he was not impressed with my overstretching myself and taught me that doing a few things well was more useful to the centre and its clients than arriving in a crumpled heap at his door exhausted and upset at the end of each day.

Most of my placement involved assisting with previously established groups. One was the dementia support group which sufferers attended with their carers. They were given access to a range of activities such as bowling, dominoes and reminiscence work. The thing I recall most from this group, apart from the lovely people and the extraordinary commitment of their carers, was the fast paced old time music which was pumped into the room to keep people stimulated. The songs were really catchy and I'd often leave the centre with *"don't sit under the apple tree"* ringing in my head, or a speeded up version of Vera Lynn's *White Cliffs of Dover*.

Another group I enjoyed was the mental health support group for women over 65. There were a number of real characters in this group. They weren't about to be patronised by a young whippersnapper. I was asked to facilitate some of the sessions and the women certainly kept me right. I once designed a quiz and was mortified when I revealed the answers at the end only to be told that half of them were wrong! The lessons learned from this little exercise were: expect the unexpected, and don't delude yourself into thinking that you are the expert.

Twice a week I would help with the lunch club for senior citizens—going out on the mini bus to pick people up, many in wheelchairs, and making sure they were given perhaps their only proper meal of the day and the chance to blether with their neighbours and friends. My least favourite aspect of this job was preparing the sandwiches before they arrived. I have had a life-long revulsion towards margarine. Ironically, having brought us up in poverty and squalor, my father instilled in all his children a snobbish preference for butter.

In addition to working with older people I assisted with two children's groups. The first was for toddlers under the age of five, all of them with additional support needs such as autism and Downs Syndrome. The other, for 8–14 year olds with Attention Deficit Hyperactivity Disorder (ADHD), was exhausting. I was completely out of my depth watching them bouncing off walls or kicking footballs into each other's faces. We once made papier mache models and all the glue was stuck in their hair as they squirted it wildly round the room with squeals of "Take that you dickhead". No doubt the shampoo was abandoned for scissors in many a home that night. Actually they were a nice bunch of kids and gave me a relatively easy time because they could see I wasn't quite up to the job. You often find among kids who are written off for bad behaviour that they can show remarkable sensitivity and insight.

Aside from taking part in groups, much of my time on placement was engaged in reflective practice: filling my journal with what I had learned in relation to course theory and trying to distil the essence of what makes a good community worker. I quickly learnt through my many mistakes that I was not a good community worker! Indeed the excellent marks I got for my course assignments were not matched by any of my placement appraisals. At best these marks showed me to be average.

In search of the perfect mate

While I was on the course and living in U Street my interest in meeting someone to go out with stepped up a notch. For a long time now I had had no libido and was still very frightened at the thought of having sex. I had had a few one night stands over the years—all of which ended in bitter disappointment. I didn't want to have sex but felt I had to please men, though my vaginismus prevented me from 'going all the way'. I think that each of the men I ended up with could probably tell that, much as I was going through the motions of feigning pleasure for them, actually sex and foreplay repulsed and distressed me because I had been so abused in my early years.

I went out with a guy called Russell for a few months but felt lonely when I was with him because he didn't have the depth and sensitivity I craved. Besides, he was in love with a female friend of his and I was always going to play second fiddle to her. I think he hoped at least the sex with me would get better if he chugged along but it didn't happen. Eventually he split up with me over the phone. My pride was hurt that he didn't respect me enough to tell me to my face, and much as I didn't love him either, it was a humiliating rejection. I wrote him an angry letter which I have regretted since. There is no point in being angry with someone who doesn't love you—especially when you don't love him! It shows considerable lack of grace.

After this relationship I decided to try my luck on the gay scene. Perhaps men were not for me. My deepest yearnings, though unfulfilled, were for women; I had considered exploring this aspect of my sexuality in the past but had been too frightened. But the break-up with Russell motivated me to think outside the straight box in which I'd packaged myself; if I couldn't connect spiritually and sexually with a man, then why not a woman?

I went along to 'Icebreakers'—a group run by the Lesbian and Gay Switchboard—to meet other LGBT men and women in the process of coming out. We met in a bar called CC Blooms. As always I felt the least cool person there and totally out of place among the foppish quiffs with boxers peeking out of jeans. Of course there was the odd 'femme' in lipstick with Joni Mitchell flowing hair. None of them gave me a second glance. It was as if their gaydar was pointing "fraud, freak" in my direction. In retrospect, I think my crude stereotyping was a way of projecting on to others my fear of not being worthy of a girlfriend. I never went back.

Nothing daunted, I stepped up my search for a suitable man. My quest was as much to herald to the world that I'd 'arrived' as it was for a relationship. I cut to the chase and consulted the classifieds in The Herald & Post because it was free to put in an advert. I described myself as a 4'10" postgraduate student who liked films and concerts. In fact I had only ever been to one concert. I wrapped it up in the euphemistic caption "Cuddly and Curvaceous". If I'd written "Grossly Overweight" I might not have bagged my man. As it was I received 16 notes of interest which was very good for my confidence—even though no visual assessments had yet taken place.

I whittled my choice down to three and gave them a call, hardly daring to believe that this might actually work. The first two I dated only once and decided by the end of each evening that they weren't for me. I smiled gracefully and said "Thank you for a lovely evening but I don't think I want to take it any further". This was gratifyingly assertive, so much so that I could hardly believe the words had come from my own mouth.

Somebody loves me!

The third choice was special. His name was Simon. I think he was attracted to my ad because he himself was only 5'2" and he really was into concerts. His voice was so sweet and gentle that I was smitten there and then.

We arranged to meet on the morning of Friday 28th July which happened to be the day he was moving house and so he invited me to be his first visitor. I decided to take a risk and wear a navy pin stripe trouser suit and purple tie—not the most feminine look—but it turned out to be a good choice because Simon liked quirky women. I completed the effect with a bunch of matching irises to give him as a housewarming present. I had never given flowers to a man before and found that it really worked. At least it did with an unconventional guy like Simon. By unconventional I mean unusually sensitive and thoughtful; a man who doesn't pander to gender stereotypes; a man who respects women. Maybe it's not so unusual to find this type of man but, given my past, I felt I had found a real treasure. I knew that here was a quality guy who would treat me well.

Our first few dates were so romantic it felt like a film score was playing in the background. The third time we met he arranged to pick me up in his car ("Just an old banger" he said) and take me out for a run. Of course I couldn't let him come to the door and see where I lived. Although the house was respectable enough from the outside, if he asked to come in he would be met with the full horror of institutional living: strip lighting, fire exit signs on the doors, social work inspectorate certificate on the wall, industrial carpets, and the smell of schizophrenia. It was not an aphrodisiac for the uninitiated and here was a guy—as far as I knew—with all his faculties intact, clean and shiny as a bright new penny and earning more money in a respectable profession (he was an IT consultant) than my benefits would stretch to in a lifetime. No, I couldn't give the game away just yet. I don't know at what point I planned to tell him about my situation. I hoped if he got to know me well enough, if I could perform sexually to please him (there was always a first) then maybe he'd be able to look past my mental illness, to see the butterfly trapped in the jar and set her free.

It was a modern fairy tale waiting to happen. My prince charming arrived as promised, up the street in a car but not a beat-up old banger as he'd led me to believe. It was a gloriously hot August day and he pulled up in a stunning bright yellow sports car with the roof down and a smile as wide as the bonnet was long. I was astounded. Was this really happening to me? He whisked me off down the coast to Gullane with a light breeze sassying my hair and The Drifters playing on the radio. When we got to the beach he opened the boot and took out two glasses in a cooler, some champagne and a packet of Cadbury's Mini Rolls—strawberries would have been far too obvious! We ate our little picnic on a tartan rug. He got up and drew a massive love heart in the sand with our initials in it and sat back down beside me with tears in his eyes and told me he had a good feeling about us; I was special and he wanted this to work. I think we even got as far as planning to take our grandchildren here to the spot where we first declared our love.

You know that feeling when something is so good you're floating above yourself and you can't take it in? That's how I felt; disconnected from my body. I could have cried inside because I knew it wouldn't last. Fairytales don't happen to a girl like me. I told him enough to watch the smile drain from his face. He put a stoic arm around me and said it didn't matter. He was here to help me now, all of that was in the past. The journey back was heavier, as though an invisible hand had placed an elephant between us. We didn't talk about it but traded chit chat instead, adjusting to the role of the 'just good friends' we knew we would become.

The summer of 2000 when Simon and I met gave way, as all things must, to autumn and winter. For my birthday in October he delighted me with gifts so thoughtful it seemed he held a mirror to my soul: compilation tapes with tender music he'd introduced me to, the lyrics always perfectly aligned to us; a silk kimono he had brought back from a recent trip to Vietnam; a velvet scarf in midnight blue and pairs and pairs of pretty earrings scattered like the stars. He baked me a cake with his pet name for me, 'Cherub', and he took me to "The Witchery" by the Castle—Edinburgh's most romantic place to dine. He knew to book The Secret Garden in particular and wept at my reaction. His consummate desire was to please me.

Sex was difficult—the spectre in the room. We tried and tried but vaginismus drove a wedge between us. Simon was patient and didn't blame me, but how long could I realistically expect him to wait? I was referred by my GP to a sex therapist, Dr M, at the Royal Infirmary. She was a medical doctor whose role it was to 'fix the plumbing', not to psychoanalyse me. The prescribed treatment for vaginismus was to insert ever expanding test tubes whilst in the bath to relax the muscles and stretch them to the point where a penis could enter. All the work was done at home with my monthly sessions with Dr M dedicated to monitoring my progress.

She insisted that Simon come with me to some of these sessions, encouraging us to see it as a problem for us as a couple rather than something personal to me. Simon found the sessions particularly difficult, not just the intimate nature of the discussions, but knowing where the origins of the problem lay — in childhood abuse. Because he loved me it was unbearable for him to be reminded of this. Eventually after a year of trying we were able to have penetrative sex but it was still painful for me and unpleasant for us both, tainted as it was with the association of abuse.

Simon tried as hard as any human being could to reconcile my shadow with the woman that he loved. We remained a couple for three years. He would ask me to marry him twice in that time then change his mind. My heart was a bird in his hands. Worse for him; he knew he had the power to crush the thing he wanted to protect.

Juggling on the edge

During the winter of 2000 I had applied for and was waiting to hear from the Mental Welfare Commission about a part time public appointment as a service user commissioner. I wanted this post more than anything I had ever applied for and became more and more fixated on the fantasy of having a direct role to play in improving conditions in psychiatric hospitals throughout Scotland.

Meanwhile I was in my second year at Moray House and due, after the Christmas holiday, to start my second placement. I was still volunteering at Streetwork and still on the boards of EAMH, Carr-Gomm, and Advocard. I was also still writing up my research findings for SHS.

Simon delighted and terrified me in equal measure with the news of a surprise five day trip he had arranged for us to New York in December. Because he knew I didn't have a current passport he had to tell me about New York sooner than he would have liked. Although I was excited about the trip and loved announcing to everybody that my boyfriend was taking me to New York, I was also nervous. I worried about being so far from home in a strange city with a man whom I had only been seeing for a few months even though I felt I loved him. There were also tensions between us because of his concerns about going out with me. He desperately wanted to make me happy but the ongoing cracks in my mental health, my mood swings and psychosis, were unsettling for him.

Around this time I had also applied for a Winston Churchill travelling fellowship to take my research findings to New Zealand the following year with a view to sharing them and learning from their progressive mental health system. Thus I was juggling with a number of high octane balls which was stressful as well as exciting. I had been seeing a Gestalt therapist, Mimi, for about a year and she was helping me make sense of all the changes and to ground myself as far as possible to the reality of the limitations my mental illness placed on me. Mimi challenged me about the volatility of my fragile ego—how I was seduced by the fantasy of success and its ensuing status, yet didn't have the maturity or experience to achieve the things I wanted. Such confrontations were highly charged and I resented her for bursting my bubble. Everyone else was telling me how wonderful I was. My mood had soared and I was ripe for an imminent crash.

New York, New York

Simon and I went to New York in December as planned and, far from helping our relationship, the trip served to highlight how incompatible we were. In terms of travel, he was adventurous and daring, wanting to seek out new experiences and constantly challenging himself whereas I was a 'nervous Nelly' without the spirit or courage to try anything new. As such New York was the last place in the world I should have been, especially since I was becoming unwell.

When we first arrived I was disturbed by the assault of lights and noise on my senses, by the frenetic pace of life and the volume of people on the streets with their seeming indifference to one another. More than once I was left with my mouth agape at a bar or restaurant because I hadn't ordered my drink or meal swiftly enough. People seemed exceedingly rude and I took their behaviour as a sign of hostility towards me. Rather than defending me in these situations, Simon seemed embarrassed and ashamed of me. He became irritable to the point where we fell out more than once during the trip. I felt so insecure and so over-stimulated that I was hallucinating and having terrible nightmares. One night in bed, I let out a bloodcurdling scream that shocked Simon. He tried to comfort me but I could see how disturbed he was at my instability. I think we both knew that scream was a death knell for our relationship.

By the time we headed to the airport we were both frazzled and worn. Of course there had been lots of lovely things too: breakfasting on waffles and maple syrup every morning at the Tick Tock diner and eating hot dogs on the Staten Island ferry. We visited MOMA and the Natural History Museum and saw the musical *Rent* on Broadway. We strolled through Central Park, hailed a cab on 5th Avenue and did our Christmas shopping in Macy's, and of course there was our iconic trip up the Empire State Building. Lots of special memories were captured by Simon's SLR in black and white.

Tension was beginning to outweigh the good times however. Like tightrope acrobats we balanced the wire with flimsy poles. On the way to the airport we stopped off at a bookshop to kill some time. I headed straight for the self-help section in a defiant statement of "I know I'm fucked up. Deal with it!" I bought a book about Borderline Personality Disorder called *I Hate You, Don't Leave Me!* then proceeded to tell him on the plane that I didn't love him, that I wasn't into men anyway. At the prospect of our splitting up Simon burst into tears and blurted the defining words of our relationship: "You're like no one I've ever met before. I don't understand you and I don't want to love you but I do, and I can't bear to be without you".

By the time we touched down in Edinburgh we were snuggled up once more in each other's arms, planning our next trip to Amsterdam. The following night we saw Suzanne Vega play at the Liquid Rooms. When she sang *The Soldier and The Queen* the hairs on my neck stood on end. I imagined I was that haughty queen closing like a fan to the possibility of love. Though we were holding hands Simon was a million miles away from me now. I felt utterly alone in the enormity of my self-loathing.

Moment of truth

Christmas had bad tidings in store. Having been shortlisted I was turned down for the Mental Welfare Commission job. I also got a letter of rejection from the Winston Churchill Fellowship. This double blow was a huge knock to my self-esteem. What more evidence was needed to know that I was a total failure? I felt unloveable and pathetic for even thinking I could rise above my situation. I would be better off dead and everybody else would be better off without me.

On Hogmanay 2000, after having neglected to take my medication for several days, the stress and misery of my situation finally drove me to the edge. There were whispering voices in my head, malevolent and growing in intensity. Although I couldn't yet decipher the words through the volume and swell of the voices, I felt a gravitational pull towards the cliff of Salisbury Crags—which I knew to be the final drop for countless before me who had taken their lives. I was terrified at the prospect and, being still rational enough to know I needed help, I called my therapist, Mimi. Although providing crisis support was outwith her remit, I was too frightened to approach the emergency team at the hospital because they had been dismissive and judgemental when I had called for help in the past. It seemed I was still living in the shadow of my damning Borderline Personality Disorder diagnosis. It was hard enough to pick up the phone in such a state of being overwhelmed, but to be made to feel like a 'time-waster' because I couldn't put my distress into words was a humiliation too far. So when Mimi told me to phone the hospital immediately because she couldn't help me, I knew the coffin of my fate was sealed. Her voice drifted off the line and I replaced the receiver with a sudden cold detachment. The whispering in my head ceased, giving way to a clear authoritative voice which said "You know what you have to do".

I gulped down a can of cider I had been hoarding for Dutch courage and took a knife from the kitchen with which to slit my throat in case I didn't have the guts to jump. My movements were mechanical and swift, the icy determination and precision of an executioner at work. I marched through the pristine snow of Holyrood Park and up the path to Salisbury Crags. There were tears streaming down my face which seemed to belong to someone else. A woman walking her dog saw me crying and approached to see if she could help. I couldn't look her in the eye. She knew what I was going to do. "I'm fine thanks" I said, "just out for a walk in the dark". I insisted that she leave me. Knowing that she would probably head off to fetch help I was aware I had to act quickly. I sat on the edge and screamed my heart out to the darkness; "Why?"—a cry ringing down the centuries of every tortured soul who had ever lived.

I swung my hips off the edge and hurtled down the cliff face crashing against the rocks all the way down and landed with an almighty thud on my stomach in the snow. I was so shocked and winded at first I thought I was dead. Then I felt intense pain in my left ankle and realised that I had survived. Because I couldn't move from the neck down I thought I was paralysed—even more reason to be dead I thought bitterly and cursed God. So I buried my head in the snow and waited for the falling flakes to cover me like a shroud.

Next there was a high-pitched yell as a group of students throwing snowballs almost trampled over me. "Oh my God, she's still alive" I heard one of them say. I did not know I was bloodied and bruised head to toe. One with a mobile phone had rushed away to get a signal and she called for an ambulance. The students tried to comfort me as they waited for help. "It's never as bad as you think" one of them said and though I didn't believe her then, now I realise those gentle words were uttered with prophetic wisdom; only a god could have saved me that night.

When the ambulance arrived it could not drive up the hill and so the Fire Brigade was brought in to assist. I was immobilised and placed on a stretcher then lowered down the mountain path to the ambulance. I heard one of the firemen say "Christ that must be a hundred feet she fell, how unlikely to survive that!"

They took me like a miracle wrapped in blankets to the Royal Infirmary where I was x-rayed and prodded to determine the damage. "You've only broken an ankle" the doctor beamed at me triumphantly.

By now even I was beginning to feel lucky. After the plaster cast was fixed I was wheeled on a trolley up to the ward and because I was still a suicide risk I was placed on constant observation. Visiting psychiatric nurses from the Royal Edinburgh Hospital came to sit with me all night. When I looked in the mirror I saw the full horror of what battering down the rocks had done to me. I was so bruised that not an inch of me remained flesh coloured.

My sisters and various friends came to visit me. A mixture of shock and relief registered on their faces. When Simon turned up he was so tearful he couldn't speak. "I'm sorry" I kept whispering, "I fell, it wasn't deliberate". But he and everyone else knew I was lying. I had plunged into the dreadful abyss and here I was, alive to tell the tale.

You may think you want to die but the love reflected in the faces of your family and friends will tell you all you need to know about how precious the gift of life is. It is by universal grace that you are blessed enough to live another day. But not everybody gets a second chance.

Grin & Tonic

After a few days in the Infirmary I was transferred once again to the Royal Edinburgh Hospital, this time to Flanders Ward. My consultant was Dr Sutton, a shy gentle man, not much older than me, who saw me many times over my admission and listened intently enough to get to know and understand me well. Initially I was on constant observation. This was reduced to nurses checking me every five minutes; then gradually to general confinement to the ward with hourly checks. I often tried to run away only to be brought back each time by the police or exasperated nurses who were detailed to find me in Morningside before I made it on to the number 5 bus.

Dr Sutton was patient yet persistent. He understood the tension between my wanting to feel safe and not being able to stand the awful white noise in my head, something which I associated with the Here and Now. I thought it would stop if I could only get away. Simon made a joke of my escape bids by giving me a recording of the old American classic *Don't Fence Me In*. In spite of my distressed state I was able to laugh. Simon and my friends seemed to be able to diffuse the macabre nature of my situation with humour. He helped me keep a sense of perspective even in the darkest moments. Looking back it must have been incredibly difficult for him to cope this way. My mental health was so precarious that he worried constantly about another suicide attempt but he knew I needed him to stay strong for me and his humour was powerful ballast for us both.

Kathryn Blythe, my social worker, liaised with Dr Sutton lending her intimate knowledge of me to help gauge each milestone of recovery. Both were cautious as was required at such a critical time and, whilst I didn't always appreciate this, I understood deep down that they were trying to keep me safe. In my lucid moments I was grateful for their intervention.

Candice Wight had left Q Housing Association and my new support worker was a woman called Trish with whom I got on well. Trish visited me in hospital and I think she was shocked at the deterioration in my mental health. One day she was chatting to me and I was distracted by visual and olfactory hallucinations. I thought I could smell death all around me—the rotting flesh of children whom I'd raped and murdered. Suddenly a blood-curdling scream from the devil in my head startled me and I imagined I saw a meteor smashing through the window. Terrified, I fled the room and ran full pelt to the edge of the ward where I was restrained so I could not escape.

I was detained on the ward for several months, receiving many visitors, cards and flowers. Well-wishers cannot know how vital their support was to my recovery. Even the smallest gestures can give you something to hold on to when you are in the grip of despair.

Simon did the sweetest things. He made compilations for me to listen to, each song chosen so carefully and with love; they brought tears to my eyes. I felt cherished. One song in particular that touched me was Sinead O'Connor's *This is to Mother You*. It was Simon's way of holding me and still means a lot to this day.

The mortar board has its day

As the time for my discharge approached I became increasingly elated and anxious to get on my feet. As during my first degree, I had been asking classmates to bring in lecture notes. I was determined that I was going back to finish my course. I even negotiated my way officially out of the ward one evening to attend a Board meeting at EAMH — plaster cast and all!

My course tutor urged me to think seriously about the implications of my decision. It was a requirement of the certificate that I would have to do a final placement. This was sure to be stressful and tiring. Was I resilient enough not to become overwhelmed? Was I resourceful enough to ask for help if I was struggling? In the end what made it possible for me to continue was Katie Owen's offer to take me on placement at Streetwork with which I was already familiar having previously been as a volunteer. The staff team was supportive and generous in welcoming me back. Katie herself, who knew my strengths and weaknesses well, was the perfect supervisor to see me through.

Whilst I was a student on the team, Katie assigned me to an action research project. It was to facilitate user involvement within the organization — in particular sourcing opportunities for young people we worked with. I approached my task with the usual combination of gung-ho ambition and crippling self-doubt. Part of my role was to pave the way for a new worker to be recruited to co-ordinate user involvement in the longer term. I drew up a job description and person specification in consultation with the young people. I also supported them in interviewing the candidates on their way to making their final decision.

It was part of Katie's vision that I would feel strong enough to apply for this post myself when it was first mooted. In all honesty we both knew that I wasn't ready to take on a paid job. Indeed, whilst I loved working with the young people and they knew I cared about them, I wasn't confident or proficient enough at youth work to do the job well.

Katie and her team helped me through the placement with support from my tutor, Liz. I was proud to stand beside her in our graduation photo outside the McEwan Hall. It was a lovely sunny day. Simon, my sister Lena, and my friend Justin came to the graduation as my guests. This time when my name was called from the podium I felt I had earned my scroll which sadly, because of the head space I was in, I had not been able to feel about my first degree.

Joining the literati

Following graduation I was delighted when one of my favourite tutors, Mae Shaw, invited me to write an article for the professional journal, CONCEPT, which she edited. My article was called *Paying Attention to Process: a Lesson from the Mental Health User Movement.* In it I shared my insights from the Patients' Council on the many opportunities in our work to use campaigning to politicise activists, and to encourage critical analysis of power structures. I cited examples such as gender discrimination and the disproportionate number of black people detained in psychiatric hospitals to show how oppression intersects and self-perpetuates. My article went down well and I was invited to give a talk to her new intake of students which I enjoyed very much.

Round the block enough times to know

Whilst all this was going on, I had several relatively short admissions to hospital mainly precipitated by stress. My tendency to push myself to breaking point was self-imposed. I still felt I had something to prove — that I could manage without a safety harness. I saw being a service user as limiting my opportunities and keeping me in my place. If people kept treating me with kid gloves I would never learn to grow. Given that my own mistakes were responsible for holding me back, one might be forgiven for pointing out my faulty logic. I think a big part of me was trying to run away from my mental health issues. All of us are vulnerable and needy in different aspects of our lives. Admitting to that is a strength — not a weakness. I have learnt to reconcile my strengths and achievements with my need for support to keep me well and I no longer feel ashamed of it.

Viva Espana!

Holidays were one of the joys of my relationship with Simon in spite of the trauma they elicited. After New York, and shortly before my graduation in the summer of 2001, we took a ten day trip to Spain, five days in Barcelona and five in Madrid. I had never been to Spain in spite of all the years I'd invested in learning the language at school and university. It was quite a shortfall in my education.

Simon delighted in watching my imperfect attempts at conversation with the locals. Of course to him the conversation seemed fluent as I nodded furiously to register a semblance of comprehension. I thought one way to make up for poor linguistic skills was to talk with my hands and so I resembled a wriggling octopus by the end of the holiday.

The Barcelona/Madrid trip was the favourite of all the places I went to with Simon. I love city breaks more than any other type of holiday — chilling in cafes, visiting art galleries and museums, taking in the architecture and, in particular, popping into churches and cathedrals for a quiet prayer. It never fails to delight me that faith alone can inspire such great works of art. In an age when architects and builders could not see the completion of their efforts in their own lifetime, all they had to inspire them was the glory it would give to God and the generations who would come to praise Him through their work. Gaudi's gothic 'Sagrada Familia' in Barcelona was particularly impressive and I felt that in his legacy throughout the city you could see the hand of God.

Barcelona is more contemporary than Madrid. While I loved the catwalk style of its youth, a highlight for Simon was our visit to the famous Neu Camp — one of European football's most celebrated stadiums. We sat in one of the uppermost terraces high above the ground and watched Barcelona play Liverpool United in a match where neither side scored. It was exciting to us nonetheless. I still don't know what Simon paid for the tickets but it was a lot.

In Madrid we bought a day ticket which gave us entry to the three prominent galleries. The Prado was the most famous and impressive however we preferred the more modern artwork of the other two. We also went to the Palacio Real and made a tour of the city on an open top bus by night, viewing the majestic buildings which were floodlit for full effect. In a gourmet steak restaurant we ate one of the most delicious burgers I have ever tasted. Rather gruesomely, it sourced its produce from the local bullring. And the ice-cream was divine. There was the famous 'tres bolas grandes/dos cucharas' (three large scoops/two spoons) incident where I was too ashamed to tell the ice-cream vendor that the whole tub was for me. When he asked if I wanted two spoons I just blushed and said "Si por favor!" All in all it was a wonderful trip.

Minus the ring

After I graduated Simon took me to stay for a week in the West of Scotland in a cottage on the Ardnamurchan Peninsula. We went for long drives round the coast in 'Oscar', Simon's yellow Mazda MX5. My friends said it was a hairdresser's car and it certainly looked incongruous in such a rural setting but we loved it.

Towards the end of our stay at the cottage Simon took me for a long walk through forest and farm to an isolated beach called the Singing Sands. He turned to me and with a grave expression said "Jo I've got something to ask you". My stomach knotted because the look on his face suggested he was going to say something critical of me. Because we were standing facing each other I thought he was going to ask me if I had brushed my teeth (which of course I had). "Yes" I replied tentatively. He stammered in a small boy's voice "Jo will you marry me?" I was staggered. There had been no forewarning of this — only the same ambivalence in our relationship as over the past year. "Yes!" I squealed and flung my arms around him. He looked as though he would cry. We walked back to the cottage in virtual silence; I knew he needed to be alone with his thoughts as was often the case when we confronted some milestone in our relationship.

Later in bed, the atmosphere was so heavy that I thought we would suffocate while he tossed and twisted all night. "Simon" I said, softly turning him into me "It's okay, we don't have to get married". And he cried I think with a mixture of relief and the terrible burden of wanting so much to do the right thing by me but not having the heart to go through with it. It was not a question of love. Simon loved me more than anyone before or up to now has loved me. That was what pained him so much. When I was unwell, which was often, he seemed to feel it too. He was so finely attuned to me that he got no respite from my helter-skelter mood swings and the psychosis that preyed upon me. He could not escape the awful life events that clogged my arteries and veins and then ran like a river of grief through us both. So many times we would just hold each other and cry ourselves to sleep because the situation seemed unresolvable. Simon had said it all on the plane back from New York: he didn't want to love me but couldn't bear to be without me. He was a slave to his own sensitivity and a prisoner in our relationship. I wasn't strong enough at that point to let him go and so I clung on hoping in vain that I could somehow magic myself better for him. Ours was an impossible love and its chances of survival doomed.

When we returned from Ardnamurchan we settled into a routine of sorts though it was tinged with sadness all the same. We were not an insular couple: that would have been a disaster. We both had many friends and some in common. Two very special friends Simon introduced me to were his colleague Greg, and Abigail, Greg's partner. They were kind and patient and had a stabilising influence on us. We spent many weekends at their flat in East Kilbride where, with their friends, Gary and Scott, they would entertain us with live music. Simon always seemed a little embarrassed at these impromptu sessions, not quite knowing where to put himself but I know he enjoyed them too and appreciated their talents.

An honest shilling

Towards the end of 2001 an opportunity arose to work for eight weeks with the Mental Health Foundation in Glasgow as a research coordinator. My role was to provide support and guidance to five teams of user-researchers in Scotland and Northern Ireland, each working on different projects.

The job was only one day a week and I was employed on a freelance basis. The nights before work I would stay over at Simon's so that he could get me up in time next morning. He would make me a packed lunch to take through on the train. Salmon and cream cheese bagel was my favourite in his ever-changing repertoire. I found the work interesting and challenging. I received early positive feedback but I couldn't see what difference I had really made to the researchers. Nevertheless I did realize that I was able to provide a point of contact for them and a sounding board to test out their ideas. I also contributed to their training in data analysis. In addition to my duties as research coordinator, I was asked to provide a policy response to a Scottish Executive consultation on suicide and self-harm on behalf of the Mental Health Foundation. The real significance of this temporary job for me was that it marked my initiation into the world of paid professional work and the fact that I managed to stay the course for the duration of my contract was a great boost to my self-esteem.

Dublin's fair city

Simon and I spent that Christmas in Dublin where we hired an apartment for five days in the trendy Temple Bar district. It was a lovely trip, our first Christmas together as a couple on our own. I went to Midnight Mass on Christmas Eve and despite being late was fortunate to be ushered to the front pew where I had a perfect view of the altar. The full theatrical splendour of an Irish Catholic Midnight Mass is something to behold. The next day we cooked a Marks & Spencer turkey dinner and went for a walk round St Stephen's Green which was utterly charming. It was beautiful crisp weather and the bare branches seemed like old friends bending down to greet us.

All grown up

When we got back to Edinburgh I had the sudden reassuring sense that I had finally grown up. Having recently celebrated my 30th birthday it was a somewhat delayed coming of age but my life so far had been somewhat unconventional. Anyway, I felt it was time for a change and I decided to take the bold step of moving out of the supported accommodation where I had lived for four years and into my own tenancy. I was offered a Housing Association flat in L Square—a vibrant exciting place to live although I did not appreciate the dog mess, or being accosted by drunk men spilling out of pubs on every corner. I had recently made a decision to abstain completely from alcohol—perhaps the best decision I ever made. Having used it for many years as a crutch or to anaesthetise myself it was time to say goodbye to the fiendish old friend which had so regularly fuelled my self-destructive impulses.

Living in L Square meant I had to change my psychiatrist because I was in a different geographical sector. I was sad to lose Dr Sutton whom I had found sensitive and insightful but I seized on the opportunity to break away from psychiatry completely and branch out on my own. I had a willing accomplice in my new consultant, Dr Ross. I only saw him once on which occasion I announced I would like to come off my depot injection and be discharged from his care. Having so recently had a major suicide attempt, a string of hospital admissions and just moved from supported accommodation, this was perhaps not the wisest course of action for someone in my position. However, having only met me once and having apparently given scant attention to my notes, Dr Ross cheerfully agreed. He arranged for me to transfer to oral anti-psychotic medication, again somewhat careless of him given that I had a long history of non-compliance over medication. Therefore it was only a matter of time before I would once again stop taking my tablets and end up in hospital.

Professional pride

Meanwhile I was still doing voluntary work and studying in the evenings for a part-time Higher National Certificate (HNC) in Training Practice. I decided to look for a full time job and applied for two positions simultaneously. Both were with national charities; one was as a coordinator of user involvement within a mental health service; and the other as a development worker with the Advocacy

Safeguards Agency (ASA). I was offered both jobs and chose the latter as I felt it was more versatile, embracing as it did wider issues than just mental health.

ASA was funded by the Scottish Executive "to develop, promote, safeguard and evaluate independent advocacy" for all vulnerable client groups across Scotland. We worked with stakeholders in a variety of fields including mental health, learning disability, physical disability, older people including dementia sufferers, children and young people, black and minority ethnic communities, LGBT (lesbian, gay, bisexual and transgender) communities and mentally disordered offenders — all in all quite a range!

Independent advocacy is a process whereby vulnerable people are supported to have a direct say in their care by someone independent of their care provision. My specific role was to assist with the strategic planning of independent advocacy in local areas by providing advice and guidance to local authority and Health Board commissioners. I also had a role in assessing their performance and funding levels and giving regular feedback to the Scottish Executive. I covered eight out of the 16 Health Board areas which comprised roughly 65 advocacy organisations in hospital and community settings. I also had responsibility for supporting advocacy provision in the State Hospital at Carstairs. The other main part of my remit was national development work including some policy and research. One instance was the contribution made to the Mental Health (Scotland) Act 2003 and another was conducting, along with a colleague, a national action research project into independent advocacy for children and young people.

Describing my job was quite a mouthful and I didn't have the sophistication to dismiss inquiries with a quip. Thus any poor soul who approached me at parties was treated to the whole speil. So besotted was I with my job that I remained insensitive to the glazed responses and carried on unaware. I was even crass enough to slip my business card into one taxi driver's hand along with his fare!

Burning the midnight oil

As the saying goes, pride comes before a fall... and so it was with me. In addition to working self-imposed crazy hours and dotting about by train all over the country, I was still on the Boards of several organizations. Furthermore, I was studying part time for both my HNC and an MSc in Equality and Discrimination at Strathclyde University. As though all that were not enough, I had taken on two new voluntary jobs in the evenings and at weekends. The first was with the Scottish Prostitutes' Education Project (Scotpep) which was an organisation to support women on routes out of prostitution. While they were still working in the sex industry Scotpep also helped to keep them safe with condom and needle exchange services, offered emotional support and provided a point of contact with the police. I was part of a team which provided these services through outreach support from a mobile unit. The other organisation was Linknet, an ethnic minority project run by Edinburgh University Settlement, the role of which was to provide vocational and educational mentoring to refugees and asylum seekers. Not content with such a manic programme, I also applied, and was accepted, for the Children's Panel. Inevitably my mental health collapsed before I could do any more damage with my one-woman mission to save the world.

Over the course of six months I lost four and a half stone because I was eating so little and burning up so much energy. I even became enamored of physical exercise, something which had hitherto been anathema. There was hardly any time for sleep, and Simon was way down the pecking order in terms of my priorities even though he had proposed for a second time. Of course, planning the wedding was yet another project to relish. Simon, who desperately wanted to save me from myself, was also getting cold feet and who could blame him?

I had now moved out of L Square and was living with Simon in his flat in Bruntsfield. This meant he was more exposed than ever to my erratic, often bizarre behaviour. I became obsessive about planning. My rate of speech increased to exhausting levels and after only a few hours sleep I would be up doing star jumps at 5am. I didn't have a psychiatrist anymore and, for obvious reasons, had fallen out with my social worker,

Kathryn. I had been off my medication for several months but didn't tell anybody and so the only professional support I had any access to was my GP, Dr McCall Smith. Fortunately, she was an excellent doctor: thorough, sensitive and caring. Indeed she cared enough to insist that I be seen by Professor Garnet, the consultant psychiatrist for that area. Still I refused and, because I had not yet attempted to harm myself or anyone else and was not on a Compulsory Treatment Order, there was nothing she or the hospital could do.

Some people put my manic energy down to high-spirits. I was still going into work and firing out an endless and often unwanted supply of guidance papers and protocols. Although it was difficult for me to concentrate when speaking to people because my mind was buzzing, I managed not to say or do anything too inappropriate to cause alarm. My colleagues were beginning to notice that I was on an elevated plane and Jonathan, with whom I worked most closely, found my behaviour irritating and disruptive. Our egos clashed at the best of times but this caused tension between us and eventually I cracked under the strain and went off sick. There were also major disruptions at this time throughout the wider organisation which, in any event, created a highly stressful situation for me and indeed for all of my colleagues.

Meanwhile, Simon, who had borne the brunt of my mania and was filled with anxiety at my impending crash, was so distressed that he retreated into himself. I would even say he became unwell. The writing was on the wall. It was time to call it a day. We split up and I moved in with my sister, Paula, until I could buy a flat of my own. I was still clinging on to my job at this point and so I was able to negotiate a mortgage relatively easily. Although we were no longer a couple Simon stuck by me and supported me practically and emotionally through this transition. To meet the deposit he lent me £8,000. He also came with me to view the little flat and we both fell in love with it.

Almost making a splash

A month after we split up and I had now moved into my new flat, the walls came crashing down around me. I had been running on empty for some weeks. My mood had plummeted and the conflict at work was causing me so much stress that I started to feel suicidal. Ever since starting the job, a year prior, I had had recurring hallucinations, both visual and aural—hallucinations which had been a feature of my illness since I was a teenager. You never grow accustomed to such horrors but rather consign them to a corner of your mind. They wait till your defences are down then suddenly, like ghosts, they jump out and attack you. The period that follows is a gruesome haunting, a macabre feast in which you let yourself be picked apart by forces you cannot control. There are things you can do to assuage the appetite of your demons but I did not know that then and it is difficult even now not to let myself be devoured when I feel overwhelmed by madness.

I was now signed off work and Dr McCall Smith was monitoring me closely. She had fast-tracked another referral to Professor Garnet at the Royal Edinburgh Hospital. Lying on my bed one afternoon I experienced the sensation of my head being strapped back while I was forced to watch a video of me as I raped and tortured children. The children were screaming as I garroted them one by one. Seagulls then circled ominously outside the window. All at once they seemed to enter the room and the sinister noise of their cries overpowered me. I felt myself elevated from the bed at the will of the seagulls. They were shrieking "Jump! Jump! Jump!" and an image formed in my head of the Forth Road Bridge. I had been fighting the instinct to go there for some days now. Earlier that day I had tried to get help from Bruntsfield Medical Practice but Dr McCall Smith was on annual leave and I couldn't communicate to the doctor who saw me what was going on in my head.

Eventually I could take no more. As if powered by the seagulls shrieking in my ears I left the house and got on a bus to the Forth Road Bridge. I had to take a taxi for the last mile or so because the bus stopped further inland. It was dark but there were cars on the bridge whizzing to and fro. The noise became deafening and I had to cover my head and ears to try to keep it out. I made my way on to the pedestrian path on the bridge and stood at the edge terrified staring down into the black water. There would be no parachute this time. The fence was very low. All it would have taken for an average sized person was to swing their legs over and jump. But at 4'10" the fence came up to my chest and I had to climb it. It was that which saved me.

As I clumsily tried to mount the fence I was grabbed without warning by a policeman from behind. Two cars had pulled up with their lights and engines off. Because I had been so preoccupied with the shrieking seagulls in my head and the barrage of noise from the road, I had been totally oblivious to their presence. I screamed and tried to wrest myself from the policeman's hold but his colleague supported him. They pinned me down and handcuffed me. They then charged me with Breach of the Peace, explaining all the while that they had to do so to get me to safety. The charges were later dropped. I was taken to a police station in Fife and put in a cell for several hours till a psychiatrist came to assess me. She arranged for me to be taken by Lothian & Borders Police back to Edinburgh and to be admitted to the psychiatric hospital there. I was so confused and frightened I wet myself on the way back. I was now in my new sector ward, "Richmond".

In safe hands

The next day I met my new psychiatrist, Professor Garnet. At 6'6" and as broad as a billboard, he towered above me but his voice and manner were gentle and I felt safe in his presence. He explained that I had been admitted under Section 24 of the Mental Health Act and would be kept on the ward initially for three days although he expected I would stay longer. In the end I spent two months in hospital—under an extended section because I did not want to be there. It's hard to explain how unsafe I felt. Even though this was the safest place for me to be I couldn't bear it and I had to try to escape. The nurses were patient on the whole but they had to restrain and forcibly inject me many times because I kept flaring up and trying to run away. Professor Garnet was well used to this behaviour and he didn't judge or reprimand me for it.

Towards the end of the second month my mood was much more stable and the intensity of voices and intrusive thoughts had lessened.

I felt I had to return to work in case I defaulted on my mortgage payments. I was now established once again on an antipsychotic depot injection, mood stabilisers and an antidepressant. My frame of mind was positive and the grandiose delusions had subsided. Professor Garnet agreed, with certain checks in place, that I could return to work from the ward for three half days a week.

Immediately I was back, I found work very stressful. My colleagues were very supportive but Jonathan told me that he had enjoyed the job much more when I wasn't there. His comment confirmed to me my anxiety that I was a toxic, damaging person to be around. He didn't say it to be cruel but it was insensitive nonetheless. In any case it fed my deep-rooted fear of causing harm to people around me and was the catalyst for my being off sick again. My colleagues, Nadia, Stephanie, and Shaben from our sister organisation SIAA, kept in contact with me though, and have been loyal friends eversince.

I had started re-attending Mass. I went to my childhood parish, St Mary's Cathedral. I chose the evening Mass which was attended by many foreigners — people whom I felt comfortable with because they were in some way displaced like me. There was a strong ethos of caring and support. This was a great comfort to me and some of these parishioners became close friends, among them Gosia and Belen. The priest in charge at the cathedral was Monsignor Gemmell, 'Father David' to us. I was very fond of him and had known him most of my life. Fr David was extremely popular with all the parishioners and we were devastated to lose him when he died prematurely of a heart attack. His sidekick was Fr Hugh and they were great fun. Both, however, took their duties seriously and, for me, created a spiritual atmosphere in which I could thrive. Everything was perfect: the pace of the Mass, the choice of music and the well thought out sermons. After Fr David died and Fr Hugh left for a new parish I missed the intimacy they had created and stopped attending Mass.

Butter and bile

I tried several more times in 2004 to return to work but just wasn't strong enough to stick it. One night, after having been psychotic for days, I was taken by Kathryn Blythe to be assessed by the Psychiatric Emergency Team (PET) because she felt I needed to be in hospital. I was reluctant to go with her because I had had some very negative experiences when I had previously approached PET for help, finding them to be cold and judgmental. I was feeling paranoid around other people anyway and didn't need anything to tip me over the edge but Kathryn insisted that I go with her for my own safety. When we got down to the hospital I couldn't look at the doctor and nurse who were assessing me because I believed they were trying to plant thoughts in my head. I sat hunched in a posture of self defence. Eventually one of them became exasperated and was sharp in his tone which instantly confirmed to me that they planned to do me harm. I bolted for the door and ran full pelt along the road, crashing into several cars on the way back to my flat because I was so frightened and desperate to get away from them.

Kathryn's judgment that I should be sectioned and admitted that night was overturned by the people who had assessed me. I was so paranoid I thought Kathryn had hidden cameras in my flat, that they were all watching and laughing at my distress, that they could hear what the voices were saying to me and were using them to drive me to suicide. I felt I had to get away from the Royal Edinburgh as far as possible and I boarded a night bus for London. The journey was hell because of my mental state. When I arrived next morning at Victoria Station I felt vulnerable and exposed. I imagined that I had been followed. I could hear cameras clicking all around me. London was busy and frenetic. It seemed everybody was deliberately banging into me and trying to put messages from the hospital to kill myself into my pocket. I had to get out of there. I boarded the next available bus which was leaving for Oxford.

When I arrived I was exhausted and resigned to the will of the voices. I bought 6 large boxes of Anadin Extra, each with 16 tablets. They were all from different shops so nobody would suspect I planned to take an overdose. I bought some mineral water and six croissants to keep the pills down, a pad and pen for suicide notes and a tie from a charity shop in case the overdose didn't work and I needed to hang myself. I needed a hotel and so I withdrew all the money I had from a cash-point to pay. I didn't want to pay by card in case I could be traced. I then checked myself into the first one I could afford under a false name. The booking was for two nights in case the pills took a long time to work. I went up to my room, placed a Do Not Disturb sign on the door, then I swallowed the pills, box by box, between croissants so that I wouldn't throw up the tablets. It took almost an hour because I was becoming so nauseous. I then lay curled in a ball on the bed and began counting cracks on the wall.

I lay in that detached state for a while until suddenly I heard angels singing to me and I felt elevated from the bed. My eyes flooded with tears of longing and tenderness for the world. I imagined that I was the Messiah come to liberate every living being through my death. I can only describe the feeling as one of combined intense joy and grief. There was a Gideon's Bible on the dresser which I opened. I started writing passages from it in letters to my family and friends. I wrote to Kathryn asking her to move in with Simon, as though they were mother and son. I asked my family and friends to forgive me for the terrible things I had done in my life but said that now I was going to redeem them all and that they should rejoice. Everything would now be okay.

Then the vomiting started. I retched so much that there was no more bile left to eject from my stomach. My insides felt as if they had been turned out and skewered on a rack. Eventually I could take no more and staggered towards the bathroom to hang myself from the shower head with my tie. I slipped on the vomit and crashed to the floor with an almighty thud. I yelled out in pain, "Fuck! Fuck! Fuck!" There was a loud knock on the door. Someone must have called reception to report the noises from my room. All I wanted was for the vomiting to end and I begged them to call an ambulance.

I was taken to John Radcliffe General Hospital where I remained in the poisons unit for 72 hours not knowing whether I was going to live or die. I had taken a massive overdose and the tablets had been in my system long enough to enter my bloodstream and the doctors did not know if I would pull through. I suspected they were worried as no one could look me in the eye. Simon was called and he flew down immediately, sobbing his heart out on arrival to see me in such a sorry state. "It's so sad" he kept saying over and over. Kathryn called, and my two sisters—all were very emotional. "Is it going to be painful?" I asked one of the nurses. Averting her gaze she said "we'll help with the pain. If the antidote doesn't work... you'll be comfortable".

I started convulsing with panic so that they had to hold me down and give me tranquilisers. It was a long wait. The drips were changed, bag after bag, and each time people seemed a little more hopeful. Eventually on the third day a male nurse who had just come on shift beamed at me "You're going to be okay". Simon held me tight and cried out "Thank you God, thank you God". "I thought you didn't believe in God" I quipped feebly but inside I was thanking God myself.

A salutary lesson

One thing my failed suicide attempts have taught me is that however much you want to die or feel compelled by voices or paranoia to kill yourself, once you realise you've survived, the natural impulse is to feel relieved and thankful. Madness isn't logical; opposing forces pull you in every direction. People have romantic notions about the right to take your own life. When you are mentally ill your reason is so impaired that you can't make the sensible decisions you might otherwise have made. Having been ripped from the clutches of death several times I know that the natural instinct is to want to live. Any instinct compelling you otherwise is not to be trusted. It is humane therefore to intervene and I am deeply grateful that people have done that for me.

Another Penny Drops

After the overdose, I was transferred to Warneford Psychiatric Hospital where I was detained under the English legal system for two weeks until I was well enough to be brought back to Edinburgh. There I was admitted once again to Richmond Ward under Professor Garnet's care. I realised then, for the first time, that I did have a mental illness which required treatment and had to be taken seriously. "Professor Garnet, do I have a borderline personality disorder?" I asked. "That's rubbish" he laughed, knowing that I already knew the answer. He considered the term borderline personality disorder "lazy and ignorant". I know from my time on the wards that it is most often applied to young women who have suffered childhood abuse. I found it stigmatizing and unhelpful. My official diagnosis, it turned out from my notes, was schizoaffective disorder. Professor Garnet, however, was wise enough to see beyond the label. It did nonetheless account for my severe mood swings—often rapidly occurring—and symptoms of psychosis, even when my mood was within a normal range.

Although Professor Garnet helped me develop insight into my mental health difficulties, it was difficult to describe my symptoms at the time of their occurrence. This was due to a combination of being overwhelmed, not trusting people and not wanting to be a burden. So sometimes I would claim to be fine when I wasn't. I could, however, describe my experiences retrospectively because I had the objectivity not to be immersed in them.

Making baskets not an option

I was discharged—this time with the support of a community psychiatric nurse as well as my social worker, Kathryn. I was also referred to the Occupational Therapy Rehabilitation Unit (OTRU) where I started attending three mornings a week to do clerical work for the NHS. Some new friends came into my life around this time. Along with the 'Old Guard' these friends gave me many moments to treasure and reasons to feel blessed.

I still hadn't learnt the vital lesson about pacing myself. I tried again to go back to my job and this time it was confirmed beyond a shadow of doubt that I couldn't cope with the stress and demands of paid employment. To be fair to myself, personal ambition aside, there was huge financial pressure for me to go back to work. The threat of repossession was hanging over my beautiful little flat—the first place I'd ever felt was truly home. If I didn't go back to work how could I keep up my mortgage payments? My sick pay had run out and I wasn't eligible for housing benefit other than on the interest. Once again Simon tried to help me but I couldn't keep relying on him to support me. It just wouldn't be fair to bind him further to our degenerating relationship just because of his uncommon kindness.

Fortunately a new scheme saved the day: Mortgage to Rent allowed public funding for Manor Estates Housing Association to buy the flat and provide me with a secure tenancy. I also had just enough money from the sale to pay Simon back everything that I owed him.

I've heard Newcastle's nice this time of year

Shortly after the Oxford 'trip' was a subsequent admission to hospital in the summer of 2004 from where I escaped and ran off to Newcastle. Once there, I ended up with a group of homeless people and was picked up by a criminal who had plans to involve me in the world of prostitution and drugs. Back in Edinburgh the hospital authorities had informed the police I was missing. After a few days sniffer dogs had been brought in to search the grounds and the local newspaper had taken up my story.

Meanwhile in Newcastle my situation was becoming increasingly precarious. I had missed my depot injection and was in the throes of psychosis. The man who had picked me up, "Trevor", could see that I was vulnerable and this seemed to make me an attractive prospect. His eyes appraised me like a blood hound would a juicy steak but his approach was tender: "You look a bit lost. Can I help you? Have you run away from home?" He told me later he had presumed I was about 15 or 16 years old. In actual fact I was 32, though in a baseball cap and bomber jacket looked much younger. "I've been homeless for years" I lied, trying to project an image of streetwise cool. He looked unconvinced. "That's a Scottish accent, isn't it?" he persisted. "Edinburgh?" "No, Glasgow" I replied quickly, averting my gaze. I was terrified that I would be traced back to the hospital and so decided to lie about my true identity. I couldn't trust anyone. My pseudonym was Jill McGregor. Beyond that and the fact I was homeless and came from Glasgow I did not have the wits about me to fabricate. Over the few days we spent together my mental health deteriorated to the point that anyone could guess I had escaped from a psychiatric hospital. Trevor never let on till the end that he had guessed all along.

He persuaded me to hang out with him and a friend whom he was going to meet. I say 'persuaded', actually the firm proprietorial grip on my arm told me I did not have a choice. First I was taken to a greasy spoon café. Banging his fist on the counter he ordered us a couple of cheap coffees. The waitress seemed to know him. Her tone was friendly, though deferential. "Coming up" she said brightly, her hand betraying a slight tremor as she carried them to our table. While he slurped his coffee Trevor tried to engage me in conversation but I was monosyllabic. He didn't ask me any more questions about where I had come from. It suited him not to know. The chatter soon ran out. "Not drinking that?" he pointed to my untouched cup and without waiting for an answer drank it up himself. "Coming?" he stood up and ushered me out of the door without paying for the coffees. His stride was so much wider than mine that I had to trot like a little dog to keep up. All the while he kept a vice-like grip on my arm. "Here's what we're going to do" he said, "my mate Vinny is going to meet us with some tobacco. I want you to take it into a pub I'll show you and you hand it to the guy behind the bar. No big deal, just hand it over. We've been barred so that's why I need you to do it. Fair exchange for looking after you, eh?" he added with a wolfish grin. Vinny arrived looking edgy and bedraggled with the small brown parcel of 'tobacco' in his inside pocket. He took it out and handed it furtively to Trevor who glared right through him. Trevor bent down to my level, grabbed me by the shoulders and looked me squarely in the eye. "All you have to do is hand this to the ginger bloke behind the bar, tell him Trev sent you. Don't speak to anyone else. Come straight back out and we'll be waiting across here for you. Don't let me down now." Although I was far from convinced it was tobacco I'd be delivering I went along with it.

I was far too frightened to say no. The job was done in under a minute. There were no questions asked by the barman and I exited the smoky den as unobtrusively as I'd entered.

Trevor seemed pleased. "Good girl!" he beamed, patting me on the back and promising me a cheese toastie before we settled for the night. We walked with Vinny for half an hour or so to a night shelter under a bridge. Outside there were prostitutes hanging around and thick-necked men with tattoos on their arms dragged on cigarettes. Trevor pressed past them grunting acknowledgement, his grip on me tighter than ever. The warm air from an overhead ventilator hit us as we walked through the door and it reminded me of the stifling heat of hospital wards in summer. Men stared vacantly into a TV screen, their bulbous noses like tomatoes absorbing sunlight through glass. A female shelter assistant registered our arrival. Her demeanour suggested it was an uncommon occurrence and she glanced hesitantly at me as though unsure of my right to be there. "This is Jill" said Trevor in a slow deliberate voice, "She's with me okay. We're just here for a cuppa and a bite to eat before we look for somewhere to kip." The assistant started to say something then checked herself before asking me "Would you like a toastie love? You must be hungry?". "She's fine" interjected Trevor, "Just bring us the toasties will you" Trevor ended up with them both as I was too anxious to eat. Shortly afterwards, we headed off leaving the trail of unanswered questions which nobody had dared to ask. As we strode into the darkness I was revisited by the old familiar sense of having been prematurely ejected from the nest.

We walked for what seemed to my aching feet like miles. I longed to lie down and for the voices in my head to go to sleep. Our destination was a derelict van out of town concealed in a wood. I was horrified that this was to be my home for the night. A gale was howling through the broken windows and the van rocked precariously as we climbed into the back. Trevor and Vinny wasted no time in lighting up a joint and I could feel the musky whiff of hash pull me into sleep. Trevor saw his opportunity to nestle in but I froze at his touch and he did not pursue it. A wash of gruesome dreams spun round my semi-conscious brain and made me start several times. I imagined the van was going up in flames with us in it. As though tossed from the belly of a fitful whale, I woke to the dawn and the loud swell of voices.

Trevor took me to a different shelter for breakfast. He informed me I'd like it as they served porridge. I didn't think it wise to tell him that I'd avoided eating porridge all my life. Perhaps because I looked so young or so unwell I was met with worried looks from the people running the shelter. I could hardly look anyone in the eye because my paranoia was so bad. My cap was pulled over my eyes to avoid being seen. Of course this had the opposite effect. Sensing the attention I was attracting from the shelter workers and clients, Trevor put his arm around me as though to claim his property. The fear he seemed to elicit from everyone we met indicated he was on familiar turf. When he went to relieve himself he left me under the charge of Vinny and a homeless man took the opportunity to tell me to get as far away from Trevor as possible. I was warned in no uncertain terms: "He's dangerous. He's hurt lots of young girls like you." But Trevor had no intention of letting me go anywhere.

He exited the shelter like a gangster with his moll, his menacing glare spraying bullets into everyone we met. By now I was so desperate to escape I tried to run in front of a car but Trevor grabbed me back and gripped me tighter than ever. Vinny seemed very perturbed but, frightened of Trevor, he carried on a few paces behind. Eventually we reached a run-down flat in a block of local authority housing. We climbed the steps to the third landing, the stench hitting us before we even entered: a nauseous blend of excrement and body odour.

Trevor gave four loud thuds on the door. A shadow emerged from inside, a sickly-looking character, pale and drawn. He bared his rotting teeth. "In you come Trev, my man" he said with false joviality whilst surveying me with curiosity and lascivious delight. We followed him into the dark and stinking interior. I was shocked and frightened to see him bolt the door behind us with a crow bar. There were more men inside, glassy-eyed with drink and drugs. I saw a dirty needle on the floor and empty cans of lager crushed and discarded. The only furniture was a threadbare sofa and some wooden boxes to sit on. The brown scrapings on the wall betrayed the origins of the disgusting smell. I was too exhausted to retch.

I asked Trevor if I could lie down somewhere. He gestured to the bedroom. I was relieved to get away from the company of men and I climbed into bed wrapping the dirty blankets round me. I shivered in the draught from a broken window. Soon, however I fell asleep and the voices gave way to vivid dreams.

I was rudely jolted awake. Trevor was standing inside the door. Banging the wall with his fists he seethed "You little fucking bitch! After all I've done for you…" His eyes were flaming. I thought he was going to attack me but could see he was struggling to restrain himself. A man had climbed into the bed while I was sleeping and was trying to conceal his nakedness. "Trevor, it's not what you think, man. I didn't fucking touch her" he quivered. That was when I realized for sure I was regarded as Trevor's property. Despite my terror I knew instinctively that I had to go over and appease him. "It's okay" I whispered, "I haven't done anything. I was sleeping." He was sobbing now, this hard man with Love and Hate tattooed across his knuckles. I reached out to comfort him. He wilted in my arms, somehow oblivious to the sound of the other man frantically dressing.

We walked through to the empty lounge and he drew me on to the sofa, hugging me as though he would never let go. "I don't understand what's happening" he said. "This isn't supposed to happen". Then he launched into a bumbling speech about how he had fallen in love with me and knew I had been sent to him so he could protect me. All his life he had been bad news but that was going to change now. He told me that he was on the run from the police in Ireland. He had served 9 years for armed robbery and was wanted for having assaulted and crippled a man. Suddenly taken over by the imperative to confess his sins, he recited a litany of the crimes he had committed. I was stunned and didn't know how to respond. Why was he telling me all this? The 'love' he was professing had not been apparent over the few days we had spent together. Yet he had been protective in his way; he hadn't taken advantage of me sexually as was clearly his intention at the outset. He had told me over and over that he had been good to me and had provided me with food and shelter but I had assumed all along that this was the prelude to something sinister. Now he was telling me he wanted us to run away together, make a life on the road. I explained to him that I wasn't well; that I had run away from a psychiatric hospital and needed to go back. "I know" he said, "But I can protect you. You don't need to go back. The police won't find you if you stick with me". The prospect of this jolted me out of my detached state and I started to cry. "Please, let me go home. I don't feel well. I need my medication".

Trevor looked devastated. "But I need you and you need me" he pleaded, "We're meant to be together". I kept sobbing uncontrollably. It felt like I was in a horror movie with some psychopath about to chop me into pieces. Eventually he was moved by pity at my distress and told me he would let me go. I asked him to let me call my social worker and we walked together to a telephone box around the corner. Kathryn sounded relieved to get my call. I told her I was safe and was being looked after. The sound of her voice made me tearful. She asked me to put Trevor on the phone and must have given him a series of instructions because he just responded "Yes" several times then put the phone on the hook. His face was white and he could hardly find the words: "I've to take you to the local hospital and they're going to send a nurse from Edinburgh to bring you back". "Thank you" I sobbed, for once in my life relieved at the prospect of captivity. We walked hand in hand in silence to the hospital and before we entered the grounds he said "I have to leave you here. It's not safe for me. Promise you will hand yourself in. Please tell them I didn't hurt you. I love you. I would never hurt you". Then he took out of his pocket a lucky shamrock pin and stuck it to my lapel. "Look after yourself, Jill" and he hung like a shadow in the distance as he watched me walk away.

I handed myself in and was told they were expecting me. They took me to a holding ward and let me call my sister and a friend both of whom were relieved and emotional to hear my voice. A few hours later two nurses from the Royal Edinburgh Hospital arrived in a car and drove me back. I was shocked to hear the extent of the manhunt my disappearance had unleashed. The experience was a valuable reminder to me of how loved I was by my family and friends. It also taught me that kindness comes in unexpected forms, sometimes when you least deserve it.

Where there's a will...

After the Newcastle episode things were stable for a while. I had been on sick leave for over a year. Then, along with everyone else in the organization, I was made redundant. This was a huge relief because I could see no way of becoming well enough to return to work. At around the same time I was diagnosed with a rare form of dyslexia. This had never been picked up before because writing was not a problem for me, it was reading which caused the trouble. I got through my university courses by opening books from the reading lists at random pages. I would scroll down with my finger to quotes and add a selection of these to my own understanding of lectures. An essay would emerge every time. I gained my degrees more by listening and writing than reading books. Although challenged in this, as with many aspects of my life, I was infinitely more resourceful than I had given myself credit for.

Winging It

FAITH, LOVE AND CREATIVITY | 2005–2011

2005 marked the point on my compass where the prevailing wind began to change direction and I was blown into a new affair: my love of poetry. As the law of synchronicity dictated, my recent diagnosis of dyslexia turned out to be a timely blessing because it led to a referral to a creative writing group led by Dorothy Baird at the community mental health team base where I had recently started receiving treatment.

I was reluctant to attend the writing group at first because my life-long mantra had been "I'm not creative!"—a somewhat self-fulfilling prophecy. I have always enjoyed writing essays, reports and articles—anything analytical—but when asked to use my imagination the shutters came down. Now I was at a point in my life, with a failed career and relationship behind me, where my pride couldn't face another blow. Did I really want to try my hand at something new?

It took some persuading to get me along to that first group but I couldn't have been more pleasantly surprised. Far from having to prove myself, the whole objective was to have fun. Our tutor, Dorothy, seemed to free me from the fear of failure just by saying "let the pen take you where it will". I'm still not very good at following a stream of consciousness on the page. It comes as second nature that I must censor everything I write. Somehow I managed to suspend sufficiently with inhibition to surprise myself. Here is the first poem I wrote:

What Is The Moon?

Comfort of the frosty night
A dollop of hope in the darkness of my soul
A syrupy sweet in Daddy's grubby hand
Infinite wisdom winking her curious assent
A pristine polka dot in the galaxy's sharp silk cravat
Whatever you want her to be

I was extremely blessed in having such a fantastic teacher as Dorothy to get me started. Not only did she support and encourage me to have fun; she tapped into my love of the English language and the latent desire in me to create new forms and rhythms. I naturally fell into poetry for a number of reasons: its musicality—I have always loved music; its accessibility on the page—visually it is much easier for me to read something short and shapely than a densely packed piece of prose. Poetry speaks directly to my soul, whereas prose trundles along tripping me up with its cumbersome load. To my mind prose which flies is really poetry.

My first foray into poetry had actually been in 1991 when I had written my collection for Julie called "The Little Book of Secrets." It was a rather primitive effort which had taken a week to complete and sat at the bottom of my drawer all these years waiting for an editor to breathe some magic into its stagnant lungs. It was only now in 2005 that I felt the impetus, through Dorothy's class, to create another poem.

Mayan treasure

One of the people who had encouraged me to go to Dorothy's writing class was my community psychiatric nurse (CPN), Maya. I had been seeing her since the beginning of 2005 and had grown very attached to her. She was kind, gentle and skilled at her job. The relationship was not without its problems though. Maya had a habit of turning up late, or missing appointments altogether. She would also fail to return my calls sometimes after I had left her a message. This made me feel unsafe as I did not trust she would be there for me in a crisis. If I am honest I also felt hurt and rejected. I took it as evidence that she did not care about me. However I took my time in broaching the issue because I was concerned about hurting her feelings and did not want to be perceived again as a 'difficult' patient. I felt rather cowardly because I addressed my concerns with my social worker rather than with Maya herself.

Kathryn insisted that the three of us meet to discuss matters to find a way forward. I think she felt the problem was compounded by my attachment to Maya and my unrealistic expectations of what the service could offer me. My friend, Jo, offered to come with me to the meeting to help me have my say. I had recently written an advance statement to be included with my medical notes which gave my preferences with regard to treatment if I were to become acutely ill. I had included in it that I wanted Jo to act as my independent advocate.

We met Kathryn and Maya at the hospital. I was quite cowed during the meeting but Jo raised all the points which I felt unable to make myself. She put them across so reasonably that we were able to resolve the matter in a satisfactory way. Maya explained that each of the times I felt she had let me down were because of crises she had had to respond to. She needed to be flexible in her response to situations which arose out of the blue and this sometimes meant having to re-arrange appointments at short notice. She did acknowledge that I had a right to expect her to call me. She then agreed to respond in future if I left a message. We also discussed a crisis plan that would involve the Psychiatric Emergency Team in situations where Kathryn and Maya were not available. Kathryn knew that I was wary of the PET team because of past negative experiences and so she spoke to Merrick Pope, one of the nurses there, to pave the way for a better relationship. Merrick had not worked with me before but she immediately understood where I was coming from and was very helpful. We all left the meeting feeling that it had been positive and productive. I was impressed by how open Maya had been in listening and responding. Thereafter things improved. I started to feel safe and to trust that I would be taken seriously if I called for help when I was suicidal.

Not long afterwards, however, I went through another meltdown. Far from being there for me, Maya's contact had become less reliable. I had been attending the Occupational Therapy Rehabilitation Unit and felt that my erratic mood swings were causing disturbance and irritation to the staff and other service users there. I became paranoid that they were plotting to get rid of me and so I stopped turning up. I got back in touch with Marion Findlay at the Volunteer Centre to source an opportunity for voluntary work.

But Marion was concerned about my safety because I was distressed and confided in her that I was feeling suicidal. She called the community mental health team. Because Maya wasn't there she spoke to a substitute colleague. It was arranged that the substitute would visit me that evening. When she arrived she was not taking me seriously and merely going through the motions because she had had to respond to Marion's concerns. It is a characteristic of my behaviour that I tend to play down how bad I am feeling if I perceive that someone doesn't want to hear. The substitute asked me a few brief questions about what I had been up to that day. Because I was able to tell her I had been to the cinema with a friend before seeing Marion, she satisfied herself that I must not be doing too badly. In fact I had found it very difficult to be with my friend because I was so distracted by suicidal thoughts. The substitute left and said she would ask Maya to call me the next day. But Maya did not call. Having been up all night fighting the urge to jump out of my third storey window, I phoned Kathryn and told her I did not feel safe. By the time she called round to take me to hospital to be assessed it was late evening and I had deteriorated markedly. I was hearing voices and rocking backwards and forwards in repetitive motion with my hands over my ears. Merrick was on duty that night at the PET team and she admitted me straight away.

Keep taking the tablets

I was kept in hospital for a couple of months during which time Professor Garnet took the opportunity to do a radical review of my medication. I had been on Olanzapine for several months and it didn't seem to be working for me. It is prescribed as a mood stabilizer and anti-psychotic. My weight had soared during that time because the drug has a stimulating effect on the appetite. Professor Garnet introduced a new antipsychotic called Risperidone to be taken in fortnightly depot injections. He continued with my antidepressant, Fluoxetine, which had the least side effects and also introduced a mood stabiliser called Lamotrigine. This is the drug combination with which I am still prescribed. It has worked best for me in terms of alleviating my symptoms and reducing crisis admissions to hospital.

Whilst undergoing changes to my drug regime, my mood fluctuated dramatically. Professor Garnet had to assess me on an almost daily basis and adjust my observation level according to how safe he felt I was to spend time away from the ward. He did not have an easy job. He was very patient as I followed him round the ward like a terrier at his heels threatening to bite his ankles if he didn't let me out. I even tried to follow him into the toilet one day and he hid in there till I had gone.

At Easter time he granted me special dispensation to go to Mass at St Mary's Cathedral. I went wearing a crimson cloak set off with a lurid pink headdress. My hat was huge and fussy and nearly as wide as I was tall. In my manic state I thought I was the bee's knees. Along with my clashing outfit my shrieking voice drew attention from the congregation. After Mass we were milling around the porch with cheese and wine, chatting. From time to time I would let off a prolonged and piercing laugh at some comment no-one else was finding funny. People around me were wincing and quickly found excuses to leave, some leaving unfinished glasses of wine because it was too uncomfortable to remain. The Cardinal then became my target. He was standing at the door shaking hands with the last of the stragglers when I marched up to him and yanked him down to my level, kissing him with my painted lips. "Happy Easter, Your Eminence." I was slurring even though I was quite sober. Startled, he backed away. He then regained his composure and gave me a warm smile before making his excuses and also leaving.

During this manic period I would "entertain" the other patients by dressing up in a crown and robe and pretending I was the Queen or would transform into a dashing cavalier with a Cossack hat and scimitar—all items I had foraged from home on passes off the ward. The nurses would roll their eyes as I bestowed courteous little bows on one and all. I began to feel I needed a handlebar moustache to complete the Cossack persona and so I slipped off the ward and bought a pack of moustaches from a joke shop. My monthly benefits had just come through and in the space of half an hour I had blown the whole lot on tacky presents for the staff: a banana shaped ashtray, a diamonte cowboy hat, a T-shirt with *Dip Me in Chocolate and Throw me to the Lesbians* emblazoned on the front, a singing nun savings bank; the notorious leopard skin thong for Professor Garnet who, of course, made me take the whole lot back.

A week or so later, when my mood had settled, I was allowed to go to a friend's party in Viewforth. I met a man there who was a friend of hers. We immediately hit it off. Iain was handsome with a warm smile and lovely manner. He wasn't at all fazed when I told him I was in hospital. He just squeezed my hand in a gesture of empathy and support. Once I was discharged we went on a couple of dates. I really liked him but I told him all I wanted was friendship. I was frightened of sexual intimacy and couldn't see myself ever being in a relationship again. Iain was gallant enough to accept the situation and has remained a friend to this day.

Attachment is another name for loss

I was discharged and started going back two mornings a week to the Occupational Therapy Rehabilitation Unit where I received good support from the staff but I never really took to the work offered so my attendance gradually became sporadic. Maya continued to visit me once a week. I saw Kathryn at the hospital for fortnightly appointments and Professor Garnet monthly at his outpatient clinic. In spite of the issues I had over Maya's unreliability, I grew more and more fond of her to the point where my attachment became obsessional. The same old pattern was repeating itself. I could tell she was uneasy about this and it made me feel that she didn't like me. As a result I became clingy and insecure and sought to win her favour with presents or by telling her funny stories. She did find me amusing at times but was wary and tried to keep her distance; it was a difficult time for us both.

As Christmas 2005 approached I started to buy cards and presents for my family, friends and care workers. My tiny flat was cluttered with parcels and there were so many that I was up night after night wrapping gifts and writing cards. I had stopped taking my tablets so I wouldn't need to sleep. My mood became more manic. One night my friend Justin and I went to a candlelit carol concert at the Usher Hall. I was so elated that I felt I was swelling to the size of the auditorium and bursting beyond. The music was like a carousel of mad horses spinning round my head and I found it difficult to stay in my chair. When the concert ended I leapt to my feet in whooping rapturous applause. I was the only person in the audience standing. I practically waltzed to the bus stop, chatting at such speed that Justin couldn't keep up and was desperate to get away. In my mood I became entangled with my surroundings as though my very being were folding into the wind and swirling high above the city lights. It was both exhilarating and scary.

I didn't get a wink of sleep all night, nor for several after, because the music in my head was an endless crescendo. I had an appointment next morning with my GP and dressed up for it as a soldier in a khaki jacket, tartan trews and a Glengarry. I marched to the florist's on the way and bought several bunches of flowers which I proceeded to hand out to strangers in the street. I even forced one on the bus driver. When I arrived at the surgery I greeted everybody in the waiting room as though they were my friends. Dr McCall Smith seemed alarmed by my dramatic entry to her room. I then proceeded to insult her with a barrage of grotesque observations about the pictures on her wall. She said "You seem quite manic. Do I need to call the hospital?" — more a statement than a question.

"Noooooo!" I replied, "Just give me the candy" as I gestured to her prescription pad.

"I'm going to call your CPN" she concluded, "You may feel high now but your mood usually plummets." She stood up and ushered me out because it was obvious that I had greatly exceeded my appointment time and was too uninhibited to leave.

When I got home I put on *Songs that Won the War* at full volume and marched up and down the room to the triumphant words of Winston Churchill set against a sweeping score. I noticed the curtains twitching in a flat across the road, so marched up to the window, halted and gave a salute to the mortified neighbour who closed her curtain and scuttled off. Next I heard banging at the door and went to answer it. Maya was standing red-faced in front of me. "Turn down that music" she ordered. "In fact, turn it off!" I did so and she made me sit down. "You need to calm down and get some sleep" she said. "You can't go on like this. Look at all these presents!" I promised her I would not buy any more and would go to bed as soon as she left.

She arranged to meet me in a cafe the next day to see if I had settled. I turned up dragging a sack of presents to her table and she lifted her hand to her mouth in horror.

"Dear Lord" she said, "Please don't tell me all of those are for me."

"No" I giggled nervously, "One of them is for your cat and another one is for your friend's little boy—the one you babysit for."

She took the presents reluctantly. We chatted for a while over a coffee, or rather, she listened as I buzzed at a thousand words a minute. Then I helped her carry the presents to her office in the hospital grounds. We parted company with a promise from her that she would call me next day. Instead she called later the same day and insisted that I take back all the presents.

I did not hear from her till a week later when my depot injection was due. By this time Christmas had come and gone and my mood had nosedived to suicidal paranoia. I also contracted the worst case of flu I have ever had. I was inevitably run down through lack of sleep but what I didn't realise then was that I was immuno-suppressed. I had coeliac disease which was not diagnosed until later. I lay in my bed doubled over with chest pain and headaches, having vomited for several days. Because I couldn't move my neck or look into the light I assumed I had meningitis. I seriously thought I was going to die. I was also reeling from the terrible news that I was to be assigned a new psychiatrist because Professor Garnet was soon to be leaving. I felt abandoned. Of course I wasn't alone. Bruna, my sister, Paula, and my ex-boyfriend, Simon, had been checking in on me regularly. I had spent Christmas at Justin's house and he too was trying to get through on my mobile phone because I wouldn't answer the landline.

As the flu symptoms dissipated and I started feeling physically stronger I became angry with Maya for having "abandoned me" and with Professor Garnet who had not told me himself that he was soon to be leaving. Along with all his other patients I had been issued a letter from the new consultant with the news that he was taking over. Professor Garnet tried to explain to me later that this was the only fair way the news could have been communicated to all his patients so that we would find out simultaneously from an official source and not through hearsay. I totally understand and agree with that now but at the time I was too overtaken with the grief of losing him to concede the point. I responded with an angry letter of complaint towards him and Maya which I addressed to the Chief Executive of NHS Lothian. Ever since I have wished with all my heart I could take that letter back. It was pompous, self-righteous and cruel to both of them. Each had cared for me well and neither deserved the wrath I unleashed on them in that letter.

Nil by mouth

On the day that my injection was due I showed the letter to Kathryn and she was able to warn Professor Garnet and Maya that it was coming. Maya arrived that evening with a colleague which immediately put me on my guard because usually she visited me on her own. She then told me it had been decided she was going to be replaced as my CPN because it was clearly not working out between us. I was devastated. Although I was angry with her I did not want to lose her and this felt like the ultimate rejection from someone whose affections I had battled hard to win all year. I refused to take my injection and ordered Maya and her colleague out of my house. They had no choice but to leave though they were worried about what I might do. They could see how hurt and angry I was. I double-locked my door, took to bed for 3 days and didn't eat or drink a thing. I took my phone off the hook and switched off my mobile so no one could contact me. I waited for dehydration to take me or for the voices to drive me over the edge. Eventually my sister turned up with a key and entered the flat, dreading what she might find. She was relieved initially to see that I was lying in bed with the duvet pulled over my head and breathing. But I wouldn't open my eyes or answer her questions. Quite apart from the voices, my head was being hammered by migraine because I was so dehydrated. Paula called the community mental health team and I was taken by two nurses to hospital to be admitted once again to Richmond Ward.

It was evening and the duty doctor was a Senior Registrar. His name was Dr Townsend. He approached me gently with a lovely Northern Irish lilt and coaxed me to drink some water saying that they would have to put me on a drip if I continued to refuse. I would have done anything for Dr Townsend. He was the kindest, sweetest man imaginable. He was also incredibly handsome, though I didn't find that out till days later when I was finally able to look at him. Dr Townsend played Good Cop as I continued to project my anger on to Professor Garnet. One day I even lunged at him and Dr Townsend had to pull me back. I was put on constant observation for the weekend because I was so unhinged. When Professor Garnet saw me on the Monday I had calmed down enough for him to tell me that he thought it best if Dr Townsend work with me in the interim till I was appointed with a new consultant. This was because I was clearly very angry with him and anyway he would soon be leaving. I had mixed feelings about this. On the one hand I saw it as rejection but on the other I was happy to work with Dr Townsend. He had already built a good rapport with me and I trusted him. The next thing was to persuade me to work with a new CPN to provide ongoing support so that I could be discharged safely. However, I refused to have anything to do with the community mental health team as I felt they had let me down so badly and I didn't want a new CPN. I wanted Maya. Refusing support was more an angry and punitive gesture than a genuine wish to go it alone. My pride had been lacerated and I had to make a stand. Quite aside from that, I felt I couldn't trust the community mental health team to respond when I was in crisis and this made me feel unsafe. Dr Townsend understood this and set about resolving the situation by establishing a relationship with me himself so I would trust him to mediate on my behalf.

Moved by my plight, and fearful for my safety, my sister, Paula, and four friends (Justin, Sally, Katie and Jo) decided to form what they called a 'circle of support' around me. We met three times in my flat and discussed ways they could best help me to stay safe and well and to negotiate with the hospital. The meetings were informal and fun. I think the others saw them as much as an opportunity to show me how much I was loved as well as a think tank for practical solutions.

Meanwhile Dr Townsend saw me as an outpatient twice a week which was more than generous. My sister joined us for some of these meetings to provide him with feedback, information and ideas from my circle of support. A few months in and I was ready to discuss the possibility of accepting a new CPN. It was suggested that it would be easier all round for me to work with two people together so that I didn't become too intensely attached and they could support each other in shouldering the emotional load. At first I was dismayed to hear that the CPNs they had in mind were the two charge nurses. I had worked with one of them before and liked her but took the fact that I was being offered two 'big guns' as evidence of my being viewed as a difficult patient. Dr McCall Smith, my GP, persuaded me to see it as a positive thing, saying "You will be getting the two most experienced nurses on the team".

I took her point and agreed to attend a case conference with my new CPNs, Dr Townsend, Paula, and the man who was to be my new consultant—Dr Fowler. A complaints' officer from NHS Lothian also attended in the role of mediator and she proved very helpful.

The meeting was a success because the community mental health team accepted that there had been failings on their part and apologised. This immediately gave me an opening and I, in turn, was able to acknowledge my difficult behaviour at times and to apologise for the way I had dealt with my grievances by refusing to negotiate up till now and by writing such a heavy-handed letter. Far from admonishing me they all agreed that whilst the process had been difficult it was a good thing for me to be honest about what I needed and for them to hear that. The meeting was concluded with a positive result. My sister, Paula, as always, was assertive and diplomatic in building an alliance with the professionals without compromising my needs. I have always had tremendous respect and admiration for her ability to be so level-headed and fair because this is something I find difficult. In any case, it worked. I had two new CPNs. I was sorry that my time with Dr Townsend had to come to an end though. He had been a huge help to me and I missed our regular chats. I also missed, and still miss, Professor Garnet who by this time had moved to Oxford. He was a brilliant psychiatrist who understood me so well and treated me with great kindness.

Physician heal thyself

Whilst I was still in hospital Dr Townsend had applied to the Mental Health Tribunal to place me on a Compulsory Community Treatment Order. My solicitor from the Legal Services Agency advised me not to oppose it. She felt that status as a 'formal' patient would afford me greater rights because of the Health Board's reciprocal duties to me under the Mental Health Act. I was not disputing that I needed treatment; my conflict with the hospital was about the terms of my treatment. The advice proved to be excellent because the new consultant and I clashed immediately. I found him lacking in interpersonal skills. Perhaps it was just a provocative device but his style was confrontational and he often introduced sensitive issues in to alien contexts which left me feeling powerless, vulnerable and bemused. During my first appointment he suddenly interrupted me:

"So you jumped off Salisbury Crags, what was that like then?"

"Er, it was sore..." I flushed, not knowing how to continue. His questioning became more provocative:

"And you attacked nursing staff in Bannockburn ward, didn't you? Why did you do that?" He seemed to be goading me into an angry response. I was too confounded to be angry. "Yes, I did lash out at staff" I admitted "and I'm not proud of that. But it was a long time ago and I was very ill. I was also treated badly and felt powerless to change anything." I left the meeting feeling disconcerted and badly shaken.

I felt so terrified at the prospect of another meeting that I boarded the first bus leaving Edinburgh—to Inverness—and resolved not to return. The stress had set off the usual symptoms, voices and paranoia, and as I wandered round the town I became increasingly influenced by bludgeoning thoughts that my only escape was suicide. Once again my mind was spiraling out of control and this had all happened in the space of a few hours in response to a difficult meeting. I stood by the banks of Loch Ness and stared hard into the gushing black water. Should I jump? Should I jump? I was frightened for my soul. When I'm rational I don't believe that God would send Her beloved children to hell, but certain states of mind catapult me to a morbid fear of damnation. In the past the imperative to suicide has overridden this fear, but on this occasion I was too terrified to take my own life. I headed for the nearest police station and collapsed in a tearful heap at the door. When I explained the situation they were sensitive enough not to send me back to Edinburgh.

I was taken to the local psychiatric hospital, New Craigs, and admitted to a locked ward because I was deemed to be a suicide risk. I remained there for a week while the consultant tried to negotiate the best way forward with my Edinburgh psychiatrist. The staff at New Craigs treated me well. I was impressed by the facilities and the conditions on the ward. I was allowed to talk at length about my fears and was never given the impression of being a burden. Because I felt listened to and rested I was more amenable to the awful news that, in spite of my requests, a new psychiatrist would not be appointed.

I was escorted back to Edinburgh by two nurses in a car and admitted to Richmond Ward. Dr Townsend dealt with the immediate fallout. Apparently Dr Fowler had perceived that our meeting had gone very well and was shocked that I had become upset and run away. This made me wonder if he genuinely did struggle with interpersonal skills. Over the course of the following year I veered more towards this conclusion. I began to see he was trying his hardest to be nice, however clumsy his approach.

Three heads are better than one

The Mental Health Tribunal hearing for my Compulsory Treatment Order came shortly after my return from Inverness. I had worked with an independent advocate, Tina Hannan, in hospital and with Helen McGinty, my solicitor, to prepare my case. They represented me admirably. I even managed to speak with calmness and clarity about the points which I wanted the panel to include in their 'recorded matters.' On the whole the hearing was a positive experience and I felt that I was listened to even though not all my points were included. What a far cry from 1991 at the Sheriff Court when I was patronisingly lectured about honouring my father and my mother. The CTO was granted and I remained a formal patient in the community for the next year.

Perfection comes in a pair

I briefly worked with my new CPNs but both left to do other jobs. After a bumpy start, where I failed to turn up for my first appointment, my experience with my next two key workers, CPN Jenifer Neilson and OT Marlyn Rafferty, was to prove a success. They soon allayed my fears and suspicions and provided me with effective coping strategies as each difficult situation arose. Together they set about drumming me into shape! The first session consisted of a verbal contract over some new ground rules. I had to agree to work hard between sessions at applying and reflecting on what I had learnt. I had to concede that there were many areas of my life which required attention. Of course there were some issues over compliance with treatment but those were overcome because they were able to establish a basis of trust and mutual respect on which we could work cooperatively. Whilst firm and demanding in their expectations of me, Jenifer and Marlyn were kind, warm and fair. They challenged me appropriately about recurring features of my behaviour whilst being non-judgemental and accepting of me as a person.

My usual destructive pattern was either to become complacent and stop taking medication, or to push myself to the point of stress and exhaustion where I would end up in hospital after having gone missing or attempted suicide. I not only over-loaded my system at work, but also, mirrored the same pattern in my social life by taking on too many commitments. Therefore, what would begin as pleasure would rapidly nose-dive into pressure. Friends had to book appointments in my diary weeks or months ahead. Indeed I was busier than most of them and they all had full time jobs! Something had to give and it was always my health. Thus a big part of the work Jenifer and Marlyn did with me was around time management and negotiating boundaries with other people in my life. The simple but effective strategy they recommended was to leave my diary at home. Ditching my diary took a lot of re-learning and it is still a conscious act of discipline not to succumb.

Jenifer and Marlyn taught me many useful strategies but it was the therapeutic bond between us which made the biggest difference. Much of the progress I have made to date I attribute directly to the work they did with me.

Soul-searching

In the summer of 2006, after I had started working with them, something else happened which was to revolutionise my thinking. I had been groping for a direction and purpose in my life. I still assumed this would come from paid employment. I was now redundant from my job and my involvement with the Occupational Therapy Rehabilitation Unit was on the wane because it had become clear I wasn't suited to clerical work. I was not engaged in voluntary work any longer because of the sharp decline in my health and confidence. I couldn't imagine being good enough at anything to give it a go or indeed well enough to sustain it. But pressure from an over-zealous work ethic spurred me to explore over and over what I could do to find a career. Every job I contemplated led me to an insurmountable wall and the threat of its collapsing over me. Having had so many brushes with suicide I was terrified of being driven to it and finally succeeding. I needed to stay well and to lead a decent and purposeful life.

One Sunday evening after Mass my friends and I were having our usual meeting at Mather's Bar. We had just decimated all opposition in the pub quiz and won a crate of Stella Artois. Following our victory anthem I got chatting to a visiting Jesuit priest who was part of our group. We struck an immediate rapport and I felt able to confide to him the vocational dilemma that was troubling me. He suggested I read a book by a fellow Jesuit and psychologist John Monbourquette, called *How to Discover Your Personal Mission*. Because of my dyslexia when someone recommends a book I usually smile politely and inwardly dismiss the recommendation but there was something about this man that compelled me to follow his suggestion.

I went to Waterstone's and bought the book thinking it might guide me to a suitable job. The author referred to mission as "an orientation towards some societal action that is ascribed in each person's soul. In other words...our need to find fulfilment in an activity that corresponds to our identity and serves the community". There were exercises throughout to help readers to explore what this might mean for them. Something which stood out for me was an invitation to identify with one or more of the classic 'archetypes' (societal roles defined since the beginning of civilisation) outlined by the author. Two archetypes which leapt out at me were the Lover, 'whose priority in life is to preserve love and friendship', and the Artist, 'who is fascinated by all that is beautiful'.

At first I was surprised to identify with these archetypes, perhaps because I imagined a lover to be someone successful in romance and lovemaking—which I most certainly was not; and I thought an artist had to be someone who created beauty rather than perceiving it. My life-long mantra had been "I'm not creative!" but, as for delighting in beauty, that was something I could certainly claim. All my life people have remarked on how I am able to see the beauty in others and my legendary love of the Arts certainly qualified me too—once in a moment of unbridled ecstasy as the curtain came down on *Madama Butterfly* I turned weeping to Simon and exclaimed without a trace of irony *"I live for the Arts!"* Of course he has never let me forget it since!

Revelatory though it was, the list of archetypes got me no closer to discovering what career path I should be following. How could I survive by simply loving and being fascinated by beauty?

Towards the end of the book the author confidently asserted that the reader should now feel ready to write a mission statement for herself starting with the words My mission is to... He recommended this be encapsulated in four lines or fewer. Brevity was never my strong point and, still having no clue what my mission was to be, I felt exasperated with myself and the author. However, when I picked up my pen the most miraculous thing happened. I was suddenly filled with what can only be described as the most complete feeling of harmony and joy I have ever experienced. My eyes flooded with grateful tears and I started writing as though the pen were moving of its own accord:

My mission, the purpose of my life, is to know You in all things, to love and worship You with every fibre of my being, and to radiate Your love to the world.

There, I had done it in two lines!

In that moment my whole life suddenly made sense, and I knew with absolute clarity that I was having a spiritual experience. It was very different from the pseudo spiritual experiences of my manic psychosis where angels would sing to me or I would levitate from the bed whilst a voice told me I was the Saviour of the world. This feeling was grounded in reality yet clearly divinely inspired. The fact that I addressed the mission statement to "You" (understanding this to be God)—which the author had not asked us to do—meant the words came from within me as though they were the deepest yearning of my soul.

My life's journey so far and the path to come were converging now in this moment of indescribable joy and fulfilment. I understood all at once that by loving those around me I was loving God; by perceiving beauty I was experiencing God; and that by feeling the extremes of ecstasy and suffering through my illness I was called in a very intimate way to understand and know the love of God. This wasn't just a textbook understanding of scripture; it was a total affirmation from within.

It is difficult to describe such an experience without sounding like an evangelical fruitcake. As someone deeply uncomfortable with having religion rammed down her throat, I worry about alienating people with the mere mention of God. But this wasn't about religion. It was a spiritual awakening in the purest sense; something which can and does happen to anyone regardless of belief. It was a manifestation of grace. For me it made sense with reference to Christianity. Others might apply it in another context. It was a moment in which the purpose of my life became clear and it changed everything.

Blast from the past

As if in synchronicity, an old school friend came back into my life at the same time. She introduced me to a book called *The Artist's Way* by Julia Cameron which outlined a spiritual path to higher creativity through exercises and reflections. Naomi was also a poet and we started meeting in one another's flats to generate new writing. We had more in common than poetry and school: we were both bipolar. We enjoyed the rough and tumble that came with hysterical laughter, depression and angst—the gift of shared affliction. We remained friends for five years. I think of her now as an image from one of her own poems: a much loved cat who came into my life for a privileged time then slipped away when she had other hearts to heal.

Love comes when you least expect it

Around this time, September 16th 2006 to be precise, I met the man who was to sweep me off my feet and make his home in my heart for the next four years. Justin was throwing a birthday dinner party for his flatmate. There were eight of us altogether, one of whom I had not met before. He was the last to arrive and was clearly inebriated. His rich baritone laugh, which could be heard half way along the street, was like a barrel of delicious thunder. When he walked into the room I turned to acknowledge the source of the laughter and was immediately left floundering in his Titanic eyes. It would have needed a lifeboat to keep me afloat and it seemed the attraction was mutual. He set about wooing me and I lapped up the attention all night. We were so caught up in each other that Justin had to reprimand us for neglecting the others. Of course I was mortified but Fraser laughed delightedly. "She's gorgeous!" he said, flashing his seductive eyes in my direction.

The infatuation took us both by surprise. Fraser, like me, was a confirmed singleton though for very different reasons. I learnt enough about him that evening to ascertain it wasn't just his laugh or his dishevelled appearance that were unconventional. With the first stirrings of self-consciousness he began to tell me his circumstances. I listened, intrigued. He was the youngest of a large family and had come from a privileged background. He had been educated at a top boarding school. That I had never heard of it said more about me than it did about him.

His father had a high profile career and I listened with interest as he regaled me with happy tales of school holidays spent with his family in the Middle East, South America or wherever they happened to be posted that year. Fraser had always been gregarious and popular and so boarding school was a happy place for him. He thrived despite the beatings he occasionally elicited for smoking or eating magic mushrooms in the surrounding woodland. Like most of his peers he was very bright and had secured a place at university.

In his first year of studying Business and Economics he was knocked down by a speeding drunk driver. He bounced off the bonnet and was thrown thirty feet along the road. His injuries were so significant that he "died" four times on the operating table. The only reason he pulled through was because the accident happened two minutes away from the Royal Infirmary and the only surgeon in Scotland who could perform the necessary operation happened to be in Edinburgh at the time. He spent several months convalescing where he gradually learned to walk and talk again. However, his memory, amongst other things, was impaired. He had devoted the last twenty years of his life to rehabilitating himself. Yoga and Tai Chi had aided his recovery and he was passionate about the benefits of both but cognitive changes still precluded him from working. He had looked after his mother until her death from heart disease and dementia two years before. Clearly he had been close to her and missed her terribly. I felt emotional myself after hearing his story, all the more so because there wasn't a trace of self-pity in his demeanour. He considered himself lucky to have survived the accident. Not only that but he felt fortunate to have had the course of his life altered because it had opened his eyes and given him perspective. He felt he would otherwise have been a cynical and materialistic person.

As I later came to learn, he was extravagantly generous with what he had and refreshingly positive and hopeful. That first night, however, the prevailing concern was that he was extremely drunk! He offered to take me home in his taxi and, because his flat was closer than mine, I insisted that he be dropped off first. Besides I wasn't quite ready for him to know where I lived. He knew I spoke a little bit of Spanish and so he asked me for 'un beso' (a kiss) as we pulled up outside his flat. Rather primly I turned my cheek to refuse him and said in a school ma'am voice "Goodnight Fraser." This seemed to delight him all the more and he fell out of the cab laughing.

The next day he called me. He had asked Justin for my number and I was delighted to hear from him. He was much less assured when sober. In fact he was positively gibbering and could barely finish his sentences. When I realised he was nervous it made my heart leap because it meant he was interested. We arranged to meet for coffee two days later. Tuesday arrived—it was glorious and sunny. The Fringe Festival was on and the streets were crowded. I had just been to see Jenifer and Marlyn and they were almost as excited as I was at the prospect of my new romance. "Don't do anything we wouldn't" quipped Jenifer. Marlyn chuckled: "As if!"

Fraser was seated by the window when I arrived at the cafe. He was chatting with the proprietor whom he seemed to know well—it turned out that he knew almost every cafe owner in the city. He welcomed me with wide smiles and pulled up a chair. His manners were impeccable which I found very attractive. The proprietor took my order with a bow and winked at Fraser before coming back with the most marshmallow-laden hot chocolate I had ever seen. Whipped cream dribbled down the sides and, projecting from the mound of marshmallows, was not just one Flake but two. This was promising: a man who liked to spoil me. We chatted for a while and it was friendly though not with the raucous energy of Saturday night. I could sense that Fraser was holding something back but wasn't sure if it was just nerves. We took a walk down The Royal Mile and it was there in another café I asked if he had ever been married or had children. He was 41 years old when I met him and so it seemed natural to expect that he might have some history. Looking back, given what he had told me about his circumstances, it was insensitive of me to ask. He flushed uncomfortably, "No, I've not been very successful in that department" and abruptly changed the subject. He clearly didn't want to stray into this territory and I interpreted his reaction as a sign that he didn't fancy me. I visibly withdrew. My pride was hurt and I wanted to protect myself. "I have to go" I said. "I'm going to a friend's house for dinner". "Can I walk you to the bus stop?" he asked. In spite of the urge to cry, I agreed. A bus pulled up to the stop. He tried to hug me as I lunged for the platform. I did not even wave as the bus sped off taking me in completely the wrong direction.

I had told quite a few friends I was going on a date and Jo, whom I was visiting that evening, asked me excitedly for the details. I shrugged off her questions with "It didn't really work out. I don't think I'm his type". She looked sad. "Oh well, there'll be another one that's right for you" she consoled. The next day Justin phoned and asked how the date had gone. I felt embarrassed telling him that Fraser hadn't seemed interested after all. He interrupted me "Jo, I think you've got the wrong end of the stick. Fraser does really like you. He's just not experienced. He hasn't had a girlfriend before. You're going to have to be patient with him." My excitement renewed. "Really" I said, hardly daring to believe it. This could not have been more perfect for me. I didn't want someone worldly who was going to pressurise me into sex. I needed someone gentle and unassuming so that we could explore slowly and help each other. For once it seemed my sexual dysfunction might turn out to be an asset rather than a hindrance.

Fraser called to arrange another date. This time we went for a meal and then to a play at the Lyceum. When I arrived at the restaurant I was touched to see him dressed in an old fashioned navy blazer with gold buttons and a brown tie—quite uncoordinated but not a stain in sight. He had clearly made a big effort to look his best. He was pacing the corridor anxiously and looking at his watch. When I walked over to him he almost picked me off the floor he was so pleased to see me. During the meal the same impeccable manners were in place, very old school and all the more endearing for that. He told me that his mother had schooled him well in how to be a gentleman. She would reprimand him if he ever let a lady walk on the outside of the pavement, forgot to offer his seat or to take her coat. This took me back to my Savoy Opera days when Michael, also raised to be a gentleman, would make a wide sweep behind me to the outside of the pavement whenever we turned a right corner.

The evening was a great success and we arranged to meet again in a few days. Fraser wanted to meet the next day but my schedule was somewhat busier than his and I didn't want to start cancelling appointments. Neither did I want to see less of friends just because I now had a boyfriend—a pitfall which I have always tried to avoid. Although a little disappointed, Fraser understood since friends played a significant role in his life too.

Despite my valiant attempts at restraint I did want to see more and more of him. After our fourth date I had the bold idea of inviting him to Pitlochry that weekend. We felt like naughty teenagers as we boarded the bus to make the two and a half hour trip and we snogged and groped all the way there. This was the closest we would ever come to sex. Besides my fear of it, neither of us had much libido to speak of — I think in both cases this was due to medication. Still we enjoyed sexual intimacy, playing with the idea of sex. In truth I would have liked in time to take the relationship to a new level. It seemed a natural next step in a loving relationship, fraught with problems though it might be. Fraser, however, kept putting me off whenever I broached the subject. He clearly didn't want sex and somewhere underneath, it was convenient for me also because it meant I didn't have to face my demons in the bedroom.

Over the weekend we discovered just how much we had in common in spite of our different backgrounds. We were both quirky. We had both been thwarted in young adulthood because of illness, and had remained in a child-like state ever since; Fraser in the constant company of his mother, me with my dependence on the hospital. We understood how much these ties meant to each other although, in time, Fraser would come to be critical of my relationship with the hospital. We each shared a sense of gratitude for our respective lots and a positive attitude towards the circumstances life had thrown at us. We both felt that illness had helped to shape our identities and direction. It had enriched our lives as much as it had visited suffering. In this sense we were kindred spirits.

Although we did not share religion and Fraser had no particular respect for Christianity, in typical open-mindedness he would join me at Mass on Sunday evenings. Perhaps it was the chance to belt out the hymns. He could never get the words or even the tune quite right but he was at his happiest when singing. I loved to watch him sing. He had no inhibitions and was oblivious to the distorting effect he had on melodies. But he was beautiful when he was in his element and others found it charming too.

Fraser alternated between Hinduism and Buddhism His spirituality could be summed up in one word: "Om" — the glorious freedom of being at one with himself, his surroundings and whatever he happened to be doing. Fraser was tender, supportive, and a joy to spend time with.

He made me laugh with his sharp, irreverent wit. I was overwhelmed by wonder at his beauty and with gratitude for his love.

One of the great joys for me in having a boyfriend was the opportunity to dress up my own life-size Action Man like a catwalk model. I was addicted to charity shopping and poor Fraser became the focus of most of my impromptu purchases. Sometimes he would put his foot down and say "No! I am not dressing up" but usually he went along with it and would try on the tailored suits and trendy jeans I bought him, smiling enthusiastically in the mirror as was required of him. There was an unspoken understanding that this earned him the right to smoke his last roll-up of the night without my disapproval.

One of the enduring things Fraser did for me was to nurture my development as a writer. He took a generous interest in my poetry and it was he who persuaded me to self-publish my first and subsequent collections. Seeing the poems in print was a huge boost to my self-esteem and it spurred me on to a new level. Fraser also encouraged me to take an evening class where I could receive critical feedback from other poets and learn new techniques. I only attended the class for a term. I thought the teacher was arrogant and rude and could not for the life of me understand why the others deferred to him so much. Instead, on my own initiative and, with Fraser's encouragement, I started attending two other writing groups. The 'Diggers' and the 'South Bridge Scribblers' were not only more instructive but more democratic in style.

'Stormin Norman' and other reasons to celebrate

As a result of this, the following year, for my friend Norman's 90th birthday I wrote a book of poems dedicated to him. Norman, modest as ever, was embarrassed by the gesture. He didn't like to draw attention to himself but I think he was secretly pleased. When I had a short admission to hospital in the spring of that year he came to visit me with my book in his hand. "You really do go over the top you know" he squirmed after reading a particularly gushy poem and I thought "that might be a suitable epitaph for my gravestone!"

My friend, Naomi, suggested we put on a poetry gig in aid of St Columba's Hospice. We chose our venue, organized live music and invited two other poets to perform with us. Fraser was very proud of our efforts and, keen as ever to help, sprang into action. He looked and took in the empty tables and disappeared. Within half an hour he had returned and every table was adorned with its own pint glass full of straggling coriander—a somewhat unconventional flower but pretty nonetheless!

That same month, October, my friends Belen and Carlos got married in Santiago de Compostela in Spain. Fraser and I were invited to the wedding. It was a beautiful ceremony and I was honoured to have been asked to do a reading from St Paul's letter to the Corinthians in Spanish. I had rehearsed in front of Belen several times so that I wouldn't fluff it up. In the event, I sounded quite fluent to the extent that there were some embarrassing incidents when other guests initiated conversations with me in Spanish only to be surprised by my impoverished response. Miss Dugan would have been ashamed of me!

In the garden of contentment

For the third year in a row Fraser and I were invited for Christmas to his friends' house. Twenty or so of us gathered each year to stuff ourselves on turkey and kilted sausages, swap party hats and fight over Trivial Pursuits. Christmas was great but fissures had been appearing in our relationship for some time. Fraser found my anxiety states frustrating and difficult to understand even though he himself could sometimes become anxious and paranoid. But this was never a part of his make-up that he wanted to own. He seemed to regard mental turmoil as character weakness which didn't sit with the perfect yogi aura he had wrapped around himself. He always tried to instruct me on the right way to live as though he had solved this conundrum for himself. It used to infuriate me. When I started to become unwell he would try to snap me out of it. He mistakenly thought it was a simple matter of mindset and I felt judged as a failure in his eyes.

One of his coping strategies when we first met was drink. Like me he did not have a chemical dependence on alcohol but he did abuse it nonetheless. I was concerned about the extent of his drinking because he was diabetic—a condition often resulting from physiological changes related to head injury. I both cosseted and reprimanded him over this and gradually he changed to much healthier patterns—but it was to take nearly a year. I saw the situation as a battle of wills between me and the friends with whom he went bingeing; the issue was more than just the drink. I found it difficult to accept the way some of his friends let him pay for all the drinks on a night out. I felt they were taking advantage of his generosity. There were two in particular whose social lives he subsidized and they had no qualms in letting him. They even came to expect me to pay for their drinks—not just that but meals and tickets too. It infuriated me. There was no gratitude, just expectation, and never reciprocity. Like Fraser, I was too unassertive to challenge them and so the anger festered inside. I took it out on him by constantly nagging him to stand up to them. Needless to say this caused conflict within him and increasingly between us. Like me, he felt a desperate need to please others and it was not easy to stand by and watch him being leeched.

Money was an enduring source of tension between us. Although Fraser was over generous with his friends he did not contribute his fair share to our living expenses as a couple. I don't think this was to do with meanness on his part. He genuinely didn't see the discrepancy in our contributions however many times I provided him with concrete evidence of it. I actually enjoyed spending money on him and took pride in providing for his meals, clothes and bills but the way he splashed so much of his income on a select few of his friends rather than contributing to our life together made me feel taken for granted. I began to interpret this as a lack of commitment on his part.

My weakness was bingeing on sweets and chocolate. Over the course of our time together I put on several stone in weight. This distressed me and, naturally, bothered Fraser. He could see my eating was out of control and assumed it reflected my mental state, which it often did. My insecurity within our relationship did not help. In fact it was that which was feeding my compulsion. I became more and more anxious that he would leave me for being overweight and this would spiral into ever-increasing circles of fat round my middle. After a while Fraser stopped commenting which was a relief but it also made me think he had given up on ever finding me attractive again.

The vast majority of Fraser's friends were women. He was charming, gregarious, affectionate and fun; women enjoyed being around him. I could understand his appeal better than anybody and had no interest in keeping him all to myself. He loved the company of other women and I trusted him not to betray me. Besides, I too had a number of friends of the opposite sex whom I saw regularly. But there was one friendship of Fraser's which did bother me. He had known Prunella for a few years and they had been meeting up several times a week. They also went on Buddhist retreats a couple of times a year. Because these excursions were directly connected to their spiritual interests neither her husband nor I attached any ulterior motives to them. However, Fraser was clearly under her influence and she seemed to exploit this. I believe she enjoyed having charismatic power over him. He was devoted to her. I began to feel that their relationship was becoming more important to him than being with me. What made it worse was that she was rude, patronising and disdainful toward me. Other people, even Fraser himself, admitted to observing this. I perceived his reluctance to address her behaviour towards me as a betrayal. Because the situation had accrued incrementally it was very difficult to set boundaries around it.

We skirted around the issue for much of our time as a couple; it was our main source of conflict and eventually the thing that split us up. I would never have asked Fraser to stop seeing her but I did ask him to arrange a 3 way meeting in which we could all speak honestly about our feelings. I wanted her to start giving me my due as Fraser's partner and for their friendship to take account of that. I knew that she was fuelling his intolerance towards my ongoing health problems and wanted her to put a stop to it. Like many people with mental health problems, this is something I often had to put up with. I had picked up enough psychology along the way to realize that Prunella had her own inadequacies which she was projecting on to me. She reverted to form when Fraser communicated to her that I would like the three of us to meet. She refused to meet with a "madwoman" and threw him out of her house for even daring to ask.

There were other of Fraser's friends whom we used to visit regularly—people he'd known since school and who were a great support because they understood how his head injury had affected him. His best friend's wife was an art therapist. Her caseload consisted of clients who had had similar childhood experiences to mine and needed therapy for the ongoing effects of the trauma. She understood my situation well and she tried to help Fraser understand me better too. I think she and her husband could see how much I loved him and they wanted it to work for both our sakes. However Fraser was not always able to take their advice, particularly in relation to Prunella with whom he was so besotted.

Although Fraser and I still had many good times it was becoming clear towards the end of 2010 that these were being outweighed by the bad. At times I blamed myself for this and, as in many relationships, thought I could redress the balance by subjugating my needs to his and being over-reasonable. I had always made allowances for the difficulties Fraser's head injury caused him—all the more so because of my own health issues and the fact I relied on others to do the same for me. Slowly, however, the realization dawned that our relationship had become destructive for me and that things would never change. With a heavy heart I finally asked him to leave. This was a major milestone for my self-esteem as I had finally been able to take ownership of the situation. By this time Prunella had abandoned him as punishment for daring to request a 3-way meeting.

Around two months later Fraser got back in touch and said he wanted to give things another go and so he moved back in. After a few weeks it became apparent that he was still besotted with Prunella and that he blamed me for the demise of their relationship. Enough was enough. I confronted him over this and then sent him packing. It was Christmas day but I didn't care. I even enlisted Simon's help to move his stuff out of the flat.

It took nearly two years to get Fraser out of my system. When I see him now it is always on friendly terms. All in all, our relationship was a positive experience which left me open to the possibility of future love.

Perfect harmony

My next partner, Ralph, whom I met through our mutual interest in mental health and the Arts, turned out to be an extra-special choice: a gifted musician and an incredibly lovely man. Though we only remained a couple for five months, he is still a treasured soul mate and companion to this day.

If there's a microphone, I'm game

Going back to the spring of 2009, I had been invited by the Lothian Recovery Network (an alliance of professionals, service users and carers interested in mental health recovery) to recite my poems at their annual conference. I was delighted to be asked though understandably nervous at the thought of sharing my poetry in such a public arena. Fraser had helped me prepare a few poems. It was a short slot, which was ideal to start with. On the day I was so anxious waiting to go up to the stage that I thought I wouldn't be able to remember my lines. Of course in my activist days I had done lots of public speaking but this felt very different. I was sharing my soul with the audience in these poems. I felt vulnerable and exposed. Fortunately the mood of the hundred or so people in the audience had been buoyed up by the excellent previous speakers and workshops and so my job was only to leave them on a celebratory note. I took a huge risk in replacing one of my poems at the last minute with a rude one because I thought it would make people laugh. I had done a recital for a charity AGM a few months prior which had gone well but I had stuck rigidly to the script and read from the page. This was my first experience of actually performing a poem without the words in front of me, and one which

I hadn't prepared to do. I was winging it. Adrenalin got me safely to the end of my poem. I stepped off the podium to loud applause. It was a great feeling and it was what made me realise I wanted to be a performance poet. I would swap the precipice for a stage and jump into the joy of being alive from now on.

Goodbye seems the hardest word

Later that year my social worker, Kathryn, retired. I knew I was really going to miss her. She had kept me on her caseload all these years out of kindness, often seeing me in her own time, and she had been my rock through many crises. I didn't deal with the ending well at first but gradually came round to facing facts. I was pleased that she had been able to see how far I had progressed through her support over the years. She had taken more of a back seat in my care since Jenifer and Marlyn had started to work with me but she had still been there to lend a hand. Our shared history over 17 years—all the scrapes she'd seen me through—meant that she would always have a special place in my heart. Sadly Kathryn died of cancer in 2012 at the age of 63 having only enjoyed two and a half years of her retirement. She was an institution in herself and her passing has left a gaping hole in the hospital community.

I was glad that before she died Kathryn was able to attend the Fringe show I performed with Naomi in 2010. She was one of many "celebrities" in my life who attended the performance—among them Miss Dugan, Ms McGhee, Mr Walls, Dr Lomax, Jill, Jenifer, Marlyn, my GPs, Dr Calvert and Dr Boyd; even Richard Holloway. That my former teachers and care workers still felt enough loyalty and affection to show up was very touching and it was affirming for me to have justified their efforts by putting on a performance where they could see for themselves how they had helped me to grow.

Although Fraser and I had split up a couple of months after the show we stayed in each other's lives for a year or so and he continued to support me through a number of recitals including the 3 biggies in 2011: The Scottish Recovery Network Conference at which there were

300 people in the audience and several hundred more watching online, the Scottish Government Mental Health Nursing Review Conference, and the Mental Welfare Commission Principles into Practice Awards.

The above are just a few of the many conferences and events I've recited my poems at over the last few years. Each recital I deliver is bespoke, often with newly commissioned poems, and each event is unique and memorable for me because I am always made to feel welcome.

2010 was turning out to be a year of departures. My beloved key worker, Marlyn, retired but I am delighted that we still keep in touch through phone calls, cards and the occasional lunch date.

Perhaps the saddest departure was Maya's premature death at the age of 29. I had not known that she had had her own struggle with mental health. This knowledge put past misunderstandings into perspective and it confirmed the innate empathy I always felt she had for my plight which could not hitherto be articulated.

I took it very badly when Maya passed away and had a relapse in my mental health. I managed to avoid a lengthy hospital admission by accepting treatment from an alternative NHS service, The South Edinburgh Intensive Home Treatment Team. My experience was positive. I found them flexible, proactive, competent and caring. It has given me hope that if in the future I have significant relapses, the IHTT might be able to keep me out of hospital.

The best medicine

A welcome new addition to my 'entourage' has been my current GP, Dr Caroline Calvert. Of course I was devastated when I heard Dr McCall Smith was retiring, but she was kind and gracious in responding to my ongoing collections of poetry forwarded to her by her colleagues. With one of her lovely letters I was delighted to receive a signed limited edition copy of a beautiful short story written by a very famous author with whom she is acquainted!

I couldn't have been better compensated for her departure than by the arrival of Dr Calvert. She is a diamond of a GP whose immense warmth, kindness and skilled interventions have averted many a crisis and kept me on the straight and narrow. We have built a strong rapport and I trust her with my safety, wellbeing and ongoing recovery.

Feet on the Ground

THE POET IS PRESENT | 2011…

Just as 2010 was a year of endings so 2011 was a year of beginnings. Nowhere was that more evident than at my 40th birthday party in October 2011. Bruna organized the party for me. She had insisted on it. I, however, was too preoccupied with being fat. "That's the next thing we're going to work on", she said. I am so glad I let her spoil me that night. The party was such a fun, joyful and affirming experience. Well over a hundred people were there—all in celebration of me. I found it hard to take in. Even some of my schoolteachers from St Thomas' turned up.

Among the evening's highlights were several performances given by my friends. The Marchioness sang *To All The Girls I've Loved Before* and a composition she had specially written for me, *The Girl From Edinburgh*. If you had asked me would this be happening after all I put her through twenty years earlier the answer would have been an emphatic *No*! But there she was, and all my other loyal friends too. Simon and his new girlfriend had choreographed a dance routine. My writer friends, Rosie and Steve, performed a hilarious and very affectionate poem about me. The 'East Kilbride posse'—Abigail, Greg, Gary and Scott—then entertained us with some of my favourite songs. Justin gave a beautiful speech and I was ordered to sit on a 'throne' in the middle of the room while my "subjects" delighted me with their offerings. After all these years of dressing up as a queen I finally got to be one!

One of the funniest moments of the evening was when my innocent little mother landed the final prize in pass the parcel and almost wet herself laughing when she found a plastic jobby nestling in the heart of its tissue wrapper. What can I say? Like mother, like daughter!

Three days later, on my actual birthday, Tuesday 11th October, I was taken out for tea by my beloved CPN, Jenifer. As we sat in Ocean Terminal looking out across the bay I finally began to sense that my ship was coming in.

Although still difficult to allow myself to celebrate my strengths and achievements, the "lover and the artist" in me knows that doing this will also have a positive impact on people around me. To paraphrase Nelson Mandela: if we shine our light to the world it invites others to do the same. That, without wanting to sound too precious, is what I have decided I want my life to be: an invitation to others, through encouragement and example, to embrace their talents with pride and joy. To me it is the sacred work in which I become more fully who I am called to be.

These days I am often asked to volunteer my skills. When I'm performing my poems at an event I dress up in a suit, tie and hat—my signature attire. By this I invite others to wear whatever they want and take pride in their unique identities. It is an opportunity to play and have fun. The subtext, however, is more serious—it's about mutual respect and valuing diversity.

As for my poetry, I write and perform at times to make people laugh but also to make them think. Sometimes I use my poems to provoke. Last year I performed for the first time at the Scottish Parliament for the launch of Disability History Month. It provided a platform to challenge the politicians as well as to celebrate the progress we've made as a community.

Simon Bradstreet, the Director of the Scottish Recovery Network, referred to me in public recently as "Scotland's poet laureate of recovery." I felt both thrilled and validated. If I can move people with my poems or inspire hope and a sense of mutual responsibility then I have achieved my purpose in a way that the conventional working route, which has so eluded me, could never have allowed. By sharing personal experience of therapeutic relationships, both positive and negative, I try to influence professionals in the audience to reflect on their own practice. Nurses, doctors and care workers can make a huge difference. For that reason I was thrilled to see my CPN, Jenifer Neilson, voted Scottish Nurse of the Year 2012. Her work with me played no small part in the award. I always refer to her as an ambassador to recovery for the nursing profession and I was proud to feature in her nomination. Jenifer's warmth, sensitivity and kindness to me have made the biggest impact of all.

Two ladies leaping

The most exciting development is that I have recently met the partner of my dreams, and — she's a woman! Up till now I could not identify with any of the main sexual orientations (straight, bisexual or gay). When I was younger, teenage hormones did come into play but, as an adult 'asexual' has seemed more appropriate to describe my lack of libido and aversion to sex. I have always dated men, but looking back, my most intense feelings of being 'in love' have always been with women. Because my emotional investment in women was so much stronger it was always too scary to make the leap from 'schoolgirl crush' to sexual relationship. Besides, it had been impressed upon me by some professionals that my attraction to women was a default position in response to childhood sexual trauma rather than a genuine preference. This compounded my sense of hoplessness at ever being able to enjoy sexual intimacy as part of a loving relationship. In retrospect I could have done with support to explore my sexuality rather than being pathologised as a damaged straight person. I've been in love with both men and women but the deepest calling of my heart has always been for women.

It may have taken me a mere 42 years to come to terms with my sexual orientation but I'm certainly making up for lost time. Coming out has been possible through the encouragement of family and friends, the support of LGBT Health & Wellbeing and of my CPN, Jenifer; and not the least because the woman I love is so adorable that I couldn't possibly resist! I met Sally through a film screening where she heard me speak publicly about how I jumped off Salisbury Crags and was immensely grateful to have survived. We connected immediately, not least because Sally has had her own share of dark cliffs to overcome. The grace, beauty and wisdom with which she has done so are profound and inspiring. I have never experienced such joy and fulfilment with another human being. I know she is the person I want to spend the rest of my life with. Together we are taking a leap of faith into the magnificent unknown.

Truth and Reconciliation

In addition to the skydiving quote, I have two cards on my bathroom door. They read: "Friends are the sunshine of life" and "If I know what love is, it is because of my friends". Intimate friendships have saved my life, shaped its direction and given it meaning. Some of them have cropped up in the story so far but there are other equally special friends whose names are not mentioned yet who play a significant part in my life today. They enrich my life beyond words.

If friends are my sunshine, the soil from which I grew and nourishes me still is my family. A big part of my healing has been coming to terms with my troubled childhood. Although it was unhappy I always knew I was loved and that is what gave me the security and confidence to achieve what I have.

Both my sisters have provided inspiration, support and companionship all my life. It is perhaps a rare thing for a sibling to admit, but I do not recall ever once having fallen out with either of them. Their children — my nieces and nephews — are a constant source of pride and joy to me too. They are all such lovely people — sensitive, thoughtful and kind.

My mother and my brother have had perhaps the most difficult lives of all—yet both have retained their childlike innocence and trust. Their tenderness of feeling is a gift to us all and I am thankful for their love in my life. My mother, in particular, is a truly inspirational woman to have come through what she has with no bitterness. She was, and still is, my greatest teacher in the art of selfless love.

As for my father, without wanting to excuse his behaviour, his response to the unkind hand that fate dealt him made him the most damaged of us all. His behaviour was not all bad. Every one of us, I believe, has untold beauty in our hearts and an infinite capacity to grow towards the light. For all the violence in his soul my father raised children who turned out to be decent, caring and just. That is part of his legacy too. On balance I am thankful for my father's many lovely qualities and I forgive him for the harm he did me.

Along with "roots and sunshine" are the blessings showered from above in the form of guidance and support from teachers and caregivers. I have had a lot of professional intervention in my life—most of it positive and helpful. There are many people who have had much harder lives than mine yet without the support I have been given.

In particular, the Royal Edinburgh Hospital has been a surrogate family when I've needed it, providing safety, nurturing and hope. Whilst I have not had a perfect track record of care I consider myself lucky to have ended up on their doorstep because most staff treated me with kindness. Many people who looked after me on the wards and in the community will remember a patient who was demanding and disruptive, and perhaps unpleasant to work with. But, in so much as they stuck with me and believed in me, they helped me grow to be the person I am today.

When I look at where I am now I realize that the intervals between my suicidal episodes are longer and my recovery times commensurately shorter. Although unable to hold down a regular job I feel I am able to make a genuine contribution through my recitals. In turn they give me direction and self-esteem. I still have a mental illness but I consider myself to be 'in recovery' because I lead a rich, satisfying and purposeful life. I still experience psychosis and despair. Sometimes I have to call the Samaritans to make it through the night. My recurring fear is that one day I will succeed at a suicide attempt. I do not want my life to be defined by tragedy. More importantly, I would hate to hurt my partner, family and friends.

I don't take the good days for granted and consciously focus on enjoying them. This is one of the secrets of my approach to recovery: to relish the miracle of being alive. On the days I can't do that I surround myself with people who can remind me how good life is. My friend, Norman, who passed away last year at the age of 93, was a great example of someone who went "skydiving" every day of his life and was eternally grateful for the experience.

As for keeping well, I have a toolkit of strategies which is accumulating day by day. I've reached a point in my life where I can recognise the signs of stress and try to avoid situations which I know I will find overwhelming. A certain amount of challenge is a good thing. It keeps me open to new experience. By trial and error I have found which situations tend to make me ill.

Unfortunately there are still things I consistently ignore though I know they would be good for me. Exercise and healthy eating come to mind. My body's not so much a temple as a trash can. This is one of the last bastions of resistance but, just as I managed to give up my chronic habit of binge drinking and sleeping rough some years ago, I need to trust that it is in my power to change my eating patterns too.

I now trust that the universe will take care of me, come what may. Providence and effort have both played their part in my story; their companions have been love, laughter and poetry. Now I have so much to look forward to. I am able to keep the bad days in perspective and I'm not too proud to ask for help when I need it. Above all, I am trying to be kind and gentle with myself and getting better at it every day. As for regrets, I still dwell on the mistakes of the past. However, I am able to acknowledge that many of them were governed by my circumstances. Now I am stronger, wiser, more resourceful. The little girl who couldn't fly is now a woman who has soared beyond her wildest dreams; yet her feet are—for the most part—firmly on the ground!

I hope my story will provide comfort and a point of identification for those who have shared similar experiences. I also hope that it will generate awareness and empathy in those who have not. Above all, I hope it shows that recovery is possible. There is profound truth and wisdom to be found in the dark tunnels of the mind. Mental illness offers a privileged insight and is a process through which we can grow.

Invitation

Let my life be an invitation,
my heart an open prayer

Let my story be justification
that hope triumphs over despair

Let the weeping I've done
walk with you in your pain

Let the joy that I feel
serve to touch, serve to heal

Let the goodness I've known
flow out through my being

Let me live the life I'm called to live,
share with others what I have to give

Let me love, let me laugh,
let me go when it's time

When I'm gone
let my light shine on in this rhyme...

Acknowledgements

Many people have helped me get to where I am today and this book has been an opportunity to reflect on, and be thankful for that.

I am deeply grateful to Claire Lamza for bringing unexpected joy into my life; to my beloved partner Sally Fox for making me complete; to my family, friends and all the people who support me: in particular, my inspirational sister, Paula McGee, whose devotion as my carer is nothing short of saintly; my lovely GP, Dr Caroline Calvert, for always going that extra mile; the excellent staff of Bruntsfield Medical Practice and South West Community Mental Health Team, especially Dr Jude Boyd, Dr Chiara Focone, Dr Lorna Donnelly, Dr Meg Davies, Jane Sutherland, Julie Bagbakan, Pam McDonald and my CPN and 'soul mother' Jenifer Neilson. It was she who gave birth to the poet in me when she said, "Jo, you are an artist, your job is to write".

For their exceptional care in the past I would like to thank: Marlyn Rafferty, Heather Millar, Cathy Maxwell, Gael Norton, Linda Douglas, Marjorie Irvine, Julie Hendry, Donald Morris, Martin Gaughan, Caroline Hickson, Dr Fiona Forbes, Dr Rob Wrate and all the staff of the YPU (1989–92); Merrick Pope, Edinburgh South IHTT and Meadows Ward, especially Colin McMahon; Professor Klaus Ebmeier, Dr Elizabeth McCall Smith, Dr Andrew Stanfield, Dr Katy Johnson, Dr Brian Venters, Tina Hannan; and Helen McGinty from the Legal Services Agency. To name but a few.

Grateful thanks also to the wonderful chaplains of the REH (Fr Tony Quinlan, Lynne McMurchie, Maxwell Reay, and Sr Rosemary Bayne); Murray Chalmers, Norman and Claire Macrae, Mgr David Gemmell, Fr Norman Cooper, Fr Alex Davie and Valerie Gillies, all of whom for much needed spiritual care; to all the therapists and counsellors who have helped me to grow; to Marion Findlay, Sarah Cleary, Harriet Eadie, Cam and Elaine at the Volunteer Centre for believing in me; to everyone in the advocacy & recovery movements for generous opportunities to contribute; to Dorothy Baird, Nancy Somerville, Billy Cornwall, Laura Marney, Colette Paul, Ian Brotherhood, Artlink, the 'South Bridge Scribblers' and the 'Diggers' for supporting my development as a writer; to my teachers at St Thomas of Aquin's High School, Stevenson College and Edinburgh University for shaping the values I still hold dear; to the Samaritans for offering comfort and hope in the desolation, to all my colleagues and friends in the voluntary sector, mental health user movement, Government, Mental Welfare Commission, Mental Health Tribunals, Law Society, Education, Police and NHS.

Among the friends I would like to thank are: Lindsay Brown, Ben Stollery, Ralph Turner, Neville Lawther, Rosemary Harris, Steve Tasane, Nadia Lazazi, Melissa O'Riordan, Alice Wilkinson, Shaben Begum, Rod Dalrymple, Arthur Allen, Paul de Havilland, Sally Dick, Gosia Kubiak, Belen Rodriguez, Sandra Rodriguez, Agnieszka Govenlock, Lesley Smith, Georgina Rosair, Marina Russell, Anne Fleming, Emma Fitzpatrick, Stuart and Vivienne Mackenzie, Abigail Farrow, Gregor Frame, Olga and Wallace Frame, Gary Kelly, Scott Kelly, Cathy Maxwell, John and Kate McCormack, Maxwell and Lewis Reay, Robin Parkinson, Lisa Barcan, Trish Burnet, Belinda Burch, Sarah Barron, Allan and Margaret Beveridge, Anne-Marie Comber, Asia Zalewska, Neville Blaszk, Mairi McCafferty, Ian McCafferty, Mary Dugan, David Walls, Shelagh McGhee, John & Mary Dames, Mary Walker, Jo Arksey, Sabine Goldhausen, Michelle Howieson, Kate Cochrane, Nancy Somerville, Lou Peterkin, Mike Dillon, John McCaughie, Mae Shaw, Ian Martin, Alasdair Niven, George Lamb, Sasha Callaghan, Tom and Jane Fairnie, Jim Brown, Rachel and Ronnie MacKenzie, Liz Elkind, Chris Vickerman, Barbara Hurst, David Christie, Elaine Wilson, Jo Kennedy, Katie Owen, Elspeth Anderson, Chris Mahoney, Ken Bridges, Kris and Rex, Mike Ford, Fiona Farrell, Montana MacKenzie, Margaret Brebner, Ruth Rooney, Jane Rubens, Karen Anderson, Kirsten Maclean, Mary Weir, Keith Moloney, Chris Mackie, Simon Bradstreet, Steve Tilley, Rachel King, Kirstin Leath, Linda Irvine, Dick Fitzpatrick, Hilary Patrick, Hilary and Phil Whitfield Macrae, Rory and Catherine Macrae, Callum and Alex Macrae, Laura Kerr, Nicky Hill, Jennie Renton, Chris O'Sullivan, Archie Munro, Michelle Lloyd, Lesley Boyd, Sylvia Wilson,

ACKNOWLEDGEMENTS | 259

Linda Keys, Liz Cooker, Allison Alexander, Liz Melville, Maggie McIvor, Dave Budd, Katie James, Sarah Collins, Sam Waylen, Scott Watson, Stephanie Taylor, Tina Hannan, Tim Randall, Eileen Ingram, Elspeth Morrison, Lili Fullerton, PLUS Perth, Lucy Wren, Chris Taylor, Alex Conway, Celia Donoghue, Rona Fleming, Rhona McCall, Marie Small, Susan Moody, Katie Bayne, Rebecca Braby, Paula McKee, Freddie Mazzei, Kevin O'Donnell, Julie Cochrane, Grace Allen, Irene Allen, Amanda Steven and ALL my old school chums.

Finally, I would like to thank all the people who have helped bring this book to fruition in whatever way—by encouragement, practical support or commenting on drafts. In particular, my best friend, Lindsay Brown, who provided the impetus for me to write it and who has tirelessly promoted it; my sister and the rock of our family, Paula McGee, who let it breathe with her blessing; Rosemary Harris, Jenifer Neilson and Sally Fox who nurtured it; Dr Allan Beveridge for his generous introduction; Dr Richard Holloway and Liz Lochhead for their beautiful endorsements, Tony Marsh for allowing me to use his photo on the cover; Alison Wren at LGBT Health & Wellbeing for helpful advice; Debbie McPhail at BBC Radio Scotland for feedback and coverage; Sandra Falconer at the Scottish Government who provided funding; Shaben Begum, Muriel Mowat and all the staff and Board of The Scottish Independent Advocacy Alliance who, along with designers Luminous Creative, facilitated its publication and launch; and, most importantly, my former schoolteacher, Shelagh McGhee, who played the biggest part of all in significantly editing the book over many months and guiding its direction. It's been quite a journey and I couldn't have done it without her.

Special thanks to all the unsung heroes whose names slipped off the page!